INSTRUCTION MANUAL No. 17

FOR

Motorcycles

THUNDERBIRD
TIGER 110
TROPHY TR6
BONNEVILLE 120
SPEED TWIN (5T)
TIGER 100
TROPHY TR5

FROM

Engine No. 0945 (1957)
and D101 (1960) onwards

SEPTEMBER, 1956 Up to AUGUST 1962.

TRIUMPH ENGINEERING CO LTD

MERIDEN WORKS · ALLESLEY · COVENTRY · ENGLAND

TELEPHONE MERIDEN 331   **TELEGRAMS "TRUSTY COVENTRY"**

Ref. 800-62   Published November 1962

A Floyd Clymer Publication
This edition published in 2024 by
www.VelocePress.com

All rights reserved. This work may not be reproduced
or transmitted in any form without the express written
consent of the publisher

INTRODUCTION

Welcome to the world of digital publishing ~ the book you now hold in your hand was printed using the latest state of the art digital technology. The advent of print-on-demand has forever changed the publishing process, never has information been so accessible and it is our hope that this book serves your informational needs for years to come. If this is your first exposure to digital publishing, we hope that you are pleased with the results. Many more titles of interest to the classic automobile and motorcycle enthusiast, collector and restorer are available via our website at www.VelocePress.com. We hope that you find this title as interesting as we do.

NOTE FROM THE PUBLISHER

The information presented is true and complete to the best of our knowledge. All recommendations are made without any guarantees on the part of the author or the publisher, who also disclaim all liability incurred with the use of this information.

TRADEMARKS

We recognize that some words, model names and designations, for example, mentioned herein are the property of the trademark holder. We use them for identification purposes only. This is not an official publication.

INFORMATION ON THE USE OF THIS PUBLICATION

This manual is an invaluable resource for those interested in performing their own maintenance. However, in today's information age we are constantly subject to changes in common practice, new technology, availability of improved materials and increased awareness of chemical toxicity. As such, it is advised that the user consult with an experienced professional prior to undertaking any procedure described herein. While every care has been taken to ensure correctness of information, it is obviously not possible to guarantee complete freedom from errors or omissions or to accept liability arising from such errors or omissions. Therefore, any individual that uses the information contained within, or elects to perform or participate in do-it-yourself repairs or modifications acknowledges that there is a risk factor involved and that the publisher or its associates cannot be held responsible for personal injury or property damage resulting from the use of the information or the outcome of such procedures.

WARNING!

One final word of advice, this publication is intended to be used as a reference guide, and when in doubt the reader should consult with a qualified technician.

INTRODUCTION

This Maintenance Manual has been compiled to enable the owner to service his motorcycle and thoroughly to understand its mechanism. The book is written on a practical basis and no attempt has been made to introduce the theoretical side.

Although the book is comprehensive in its instruction regarding major overhauls, we strongly advise the uninitiated to entrust such work as the repair of engines, telescopic forks and gearboxes, to a recognised Triumph Dealer who will have the necessary facilities and special workshop tools available. Remember that the purchase of special tools can be very expensive when only required for limited use.

Each section of the book is headed by a general description. It is then followed by a complete account of the dismantling, inspection and re-assembly of units and final assembly. This has been compiled in the most simple form to obviate any difficulties on the part of the operator, who may be a newcomer to motorcycling or not fully conversant with repair procedure. Each chapter deals with a specific operation (i.e. Dismantling the Engine) which is then broken down into sub-paragraphs. The sequence in which they are broken down is the correct dismantling and assembly procedure. To avoid confusing the operator during this procedure, the sub-assemblies (i.e. Cylinder Head or Crankshaft Assembly) are dealt with as separate units under the heading "Dismantling, Preparation and Assembly of Units".

The book is well illustrated with exploded and assembled illustrations of the main units, which will give the operator a comprehensive view of the internal parts before commencing an operation and will also assist during assembly.

Finally, remember that if the essential adjustments are neglected and only casual attention is paid to the lubrication and periodical maintenance, reliability will be affected and in time the servicing costs will be very high.

If additional information is required, please consult a Triumph Distributor or Dealer who will always be pleased to assist. Should any difficulty then arise, write to the Triumph Service Department **quoting the model and full engine number.** The latter is stamped on the left hand crankcase just below the cylinder base flange as shown in the example below.

EXAMPLE — 6T-019727

SERVICE ARRANGEMENTS

CORRESPONDENCE

Technical Advice, Guarantee Claims and Repairs

Communications dealing with any of these subjects should be addressed to the **SERVICE DEPARTMENT.**

> In all communications the full engine number complete with all prefix letters and figures should be stated. This number will be found on the L.H. side of the crankcase just below the cylinder flange.

TECHNICAL ADVICE

Owners will appreciate how very difficult it is to diagnose trouble by correspondence and this is made impossible in many cases because the information sent to us is so scanty. Every possible point which may have some bearing on the matter should be stated so that we can send a useful and detailed reply.

REPLACEMENT PARTS

Please obtain your requirements from your nearest Triumph spares stockist. We can no longer supply direct to private owners.

There is a nation-wide network of stockists, a list of which is available from the factory on request.

REPAIRS

Before a motorcycle is sent to our Works an appointment must be made. This can be done by letter or telephone. When an owner wishes to return his machine for guarantee repairs, he should first consult his Dealer as we do not normally accept machines in our Repair Shop until the Dealer has inspected them. Frequently the Dealer can overcome the trouble without the delay and expense of sending the machine to the Works. This avoids the machine being out of use for some days when it could be on the road. Where parts such as cylinders, petrol tanks, etc., are forwarded for repair, they should be packed securely so as to avoid damage in transit. The owner's name and address should be enclosed together with full instructions. In the case of complete motorcycles, a label showing the owner's name and address should always be attached and all accessories such as tools, inflator, handlebar mirrors and other parts removed.

PROPRIETARY FITTINGS

Ancillary equipment which is fitted to our motorcycles is of the highest quality and is guaranteed by the manufacturers and not by ourselves. Any repairs or claims should be sent to the actual maker, or one of their accredited agents who will always give owners every possible assistance. The following are the addresses of the various manufacturers.

Carburetters ... ... Amal Ltd.,
Holdford Road, Witton,
Birmingham, 6.

S.U. Carburetter Co. Ltd.,
Wood Lane, Erdington,
Birmingham, 24.

Chains ... ... Renold Chains Ltd.,
Wythenshawe, Manchester.

Electrical Equipment ... ... J. Lucas Ltd.,
Great Hampton Street,
Birmingham, 18.

Rear Suspension ... ... Girling Ltd.,
King's Road, Tyseley,
Birmingham, 11.

Sparking Plugs ... ... Champion Sparking Plugs Co. Ltd.,
Feltham, Middlesex.

K.L.G. Sparking Plugs Ltd.,
Cricklewood Works,
London, N.W.2.

Lodge Plugs Ltd.,
Rugby,
Warwickshire.

Speedometers ... ... Smith's Motor Accessories Ltd.,
Cricklewood Works,
London, N.W.2.

Tyres ... ... Dunlop Rubber Company Ltd.,
Fort Dunlop,
Birmingham, 24.

Technical Data

THUNDERBIRD (6T) TECHNICAL DATA

ENGINE
Type	O.H.V. Twin
B.H.P. at R.P.M.	34 at 6300
Bore	2.79 in. (71 mm.)
Stroke	3.23 in. (82 mm.)
Capacity	40 cu. in. (649 c.c.)
Compression Ratio	7.5 : 1
Valve Clearance (Cold)	0.010 in. (0.25 mm.)

Valve Timing:—(with .020 in. (0.50 mm.) tappet clearance for checking)

Inlet Valve opens B.T.C.	35° ⎫
Inlet Valve closes A.B.C.	85° ⎬ —0°
Exhaust Valve opens B.B.C.	73° ⎬ +5°
Exhaust Valve closes A.T.C.	50° ⎭

IGNITION
Distributor Contact Point Gap	0.014 in. - 0.016 in. (0.36-0.40 mm.)
Distributor Range	12½°
Sparking Plugs	Champion N4
	K.L.G. FE100 (3 point) or Lodge HLN
Sparking Plug Gap	0.020 in. (0.50 mm.)

Ignition Timing (Fully Retarded):

Crankshaft position	6° B.T.C.
Piston position	$\frac{1}{32}$" (0.8 mm.) B.T.C.

CARBURETTER
Type	Amal Monobloc
Main Jet	220
Needle Jet	.1065
Needle Position	3
Throttle Valve	376/4
Pilot Jet	25

See Page 145 for S.U. Carburetter.

Technical Data

TRANSMISSION

Gearbox—Type	Positive Selection (Foot operated)	
Speeds	Four	
Gear Ratios	Solo	Sidecar
4th—Top	4.67	5.12
3rd—Third	5.55	6.1
2nd—Second	7.88	8.65
1st—Bottom	11.4	12.5
R.P.M./10 m.p.h. Top Gear	625	685

CLUTCH

Type ... Langite in Oil

SPROCKETS

	Solo	Sidecar
Engine	22 teeth	20 teeth
Gearbox	18 teeth	18 teeth
Clutch	43 teeth	43 teeth
Rear Wheel	43 teeth	43 teeth

CHAIN

Primary-Front-Pitch	$\frac{1}{2}'' \times .335'' \times \frac{5}{16}''$
Links	70
Secondary-Rear-Pitch	$\frac{5}{8}'' \times .400'' \times \frac{3}{8}''$
Links	98 Solo

CAPACITIES

Fuel Tank	4 galls.	(18 litres)
Oil Tank	5 pints	(3 litres)
Gearbox	$\frac{2}{3}$ pint	(400 c.c.)
Primary Chaincase	$\frac{1}{4}$ pint	(150 c.c.)
Front Forks (each leg)	$\frac{1}{4}$ pint	(150 c.c.)

TYRE SIZES

Front	3.25 × 18 in.
Rear	3.50 × 18 in.

SUSPENSION

Front	Telescopic
Rear	Swinging Fork

BRAKES

Type	Internal Expanding	
Front Diameter	8 in.	(20.32 cm.)
Rear Diameter	7 in.	(17.78 cm.)

OVERALL DIMENSIONS

Seat Height	30 in.	(76.2 cm.)
Wheel Base	54.75 in.	(139 cm.)
Length	83.25 in.	(212 cm.)
Width	28.5 in.	(72 cm.)
Ground Clearance	5 in.	(12.7 cm.)

WEIGHT

Unladen	392 lbs.	(177 kilos)

Technical Data

TIGER 110 (T110) TECHNICAL DATA

ENGINE
Type	O.H.V. Twin
B.H.P. at R.P.M.	40 at 6500
Bore	2.79 in. (71 mm.)
Stroke	3.23 in. (82 mm.)
Capacity	40 cu. in. (649 c.c.)
Compression Ratio	8.5 : 1
Valve Clearance (Cold)	0.010 in. (0.25 mm.)

Valve Timing:—(with .020 in. (0.50 mm.) tappet clearance for checking)

Inlet Valve opens B.T.C.	35°	
Inlet Valve closes A.B.C.	85°	—0°
Exhaust Valve opens B.B.C.	73°	+5°
Exhaust Valve closes A.T.C.	50°	

IGNITION
Magneto Contact Point Gap	.012 in. (.3 mm.)
Sparking Plugs	Champion N4, K.L.G. FE100 (3 point) or Lodge HLN
Sparking Plug Gap	0.020 in. (0.50 mm.)

Timing (Fully Advanced):—

Crankshaft position	35° B.T.C.
Piston position	$\frac{23}{64}''$ (9.2 mm.) B.T.C.

CARBURETTER
Type	Amal Monobloc
Main Jet	220
Needle Jet	.1065
Needle Position	3
Throttle Valve	376/4
Pilot Jet	25

Technical Data

TRANSMISSION

	Solo	Sidecar
Gearbox—Type	Positive Selection (Foot operated)	
Speeds	Four	
Gear Ratios:—		
4th—Top	4.67	5.12
3rd—Third	5.55	6.1
2nd—Second	7.88	8.65
1st—Bottom	11.4	12.5
R.P.M./10 m.p.h. Top Gear	625	685

CLUTCH
Type ... Langite in Oil

SPROCKETS

	Solo	Sidecar
Engine	22 teeth	20 teeth
Gearbox	18 teeth	18 teeth
Clutch	43 teeth	43 teeth
Rear Wheel	43 teeth	43 teeth

CHAIN
Primary-Front-Pitch ... $\frac{1}{2}'' \times .335'' \times \frac{5}{16}''$
Links ... 70
Secondary-Rear-Pitch ... $\frac{5}{8}'' \times .400'' \times \frac{3}{8}''$
Links ... 98 Solo

CAPACITIES
Fuel Tank ... 4 galls. (18 litres)
Oil Tank ... 5 pints (3 litres)
Gearbox ... $\frac{2}{3}$ pint (400 c.c.)
Primary Chaincase ... $\frac{1}{4}$ pint (150 c.c.)
Front Forks (each leg) ... $\frac{1}{4}$ pint (150 c.c.)

TYRE SIZES
Front ... 3.25 × 18 in.
Rear ... 3.50 × 18 in.

SUSPENSION
Front ... Telescopic
Rear ... Swinging Fork

BRAKES
Type ... Internal Expanding
Front Diameter ... 8 in. (20.32 cm.)
Rear Diameter ... 7 in. (17.78 cm.)

OVERALL DIMENSIONS
Seat Height ... 30 in. (76.2 cm.)
Wheel Base ... 54.75 in. (139 cm.)
Length ... 83.25 in. (212 cm.)
Width ... 28.5 in. (72 cm.)
Ground Clearance ... 5 in. (12.7 cm.)

WEIGHT
Unladen ... 390 lbs. (176 kilos)

Technical Data

TROPHY (TR6) TECHNICAL DATA

ENGINE
Type	O.H.V. Twin
B.H.P. at R.P.M.	40 at 6500
Bore	2.79 in. (71 mm.)
Stroke	3.23 in. (82 mm.)
Capacity	40 cu. in. (649 c.c.)
Compression Ratio	8.5 : 1
Valve Clearance (Cold):—	
Inlet	0.002 in. (.05 mm.)
Exhaust	0.004 in. (.10 mm.)
Valve Timing (with .020 in. (0.50 mm.) tappet clearance for checking):—	
Inlet Valve opens B.T.C.	34°
Inlet Valve closes A.B.C.	55°
Exhaust Valve opens B.B.C.	48°
Exhaust Valve closes A.T.C.	27°

IGNITION
Magneto Contact Point Gap	.012 in. (.3 mm.)
Sparking Plugs	Champion N4, K.L.G. FE100 (3 point) or Lodge HLN
Sparking Plug Gap	0.020 in. (0.50 mm.)
Timing (Fully Advanced):—	
Crankshaft position	35° B.T.C.
Piston position	$\frac{23}{64}''$ (9.2 mm.) B.T.C.

CARBURETTER
Type	Amal Monobloc
Main Jet	250
Needle Jet	.1065
Needle Position	3
Throttle Valve	376/3½
Pilot Jet	25

Technical Data

TRANSMISSION
Gearbox—Type ... Positive Selection (Foot operated)

Gear Ratios:—
- 4th—Top ... 4.88
- 3rd—Third ... 5.81
- 2nd—Second ... 8.25
- 1st—Bottom ... 11.9

R.M.P./10 m.p.h. Top Gear ... 638

CLUTCH
Type ... Langite in Oil

SPROCKETS
Engine ... 21 teeth
Gearbox ... 18 teeth
Clutch ... 43 teeth
Rear Wheel ... 43 teeth

CHAIN
Primary-Front-Pitch ... $\frac{1}{2}'' \times .335'' \times \frac{5}{16}''$
Links ... 70
Secondary-Rear-Pitch ... $\frac{5}{8}'' \times .400'' \times \frac{3}{8}''$
Links ... 98

CAPACITIES
Fuel Tank ... 3 galls. (13.5 litres)
Oil Tank ... 5 pints (3 litres)
Gearbox ... $\frac{2}{3}$ pint (400 c.c.)
Primary Chaincase ... $\frac{1}{4}$ pint (150 c.c.)
Front Forks (each leg) ... $\frac{1}{4}$ pint (150 c.c.)

TYRE SIZES
Front ... 3.25 × 19 in.
Rear ... 4.00 × 18 in.

SUSPENSION
Front ... Telescopic
Rear ... Swinging Fork

BRAKES
Type ... Internal Expanding
Front Diameter ... 8 in. (20.32 cm.)
Rear Diameter ... 7 in. (17.78 cm.)

OVERALL DIMENSIONS
Seat Height ... 30.5 in. (77.5 cm.)
Wheel Base ... 55.25 in. (140.3 cm.)
Length ... 86.25 in. (219 cm.)
Width ... 28.5 in. (72 cm.)
Ground Clearance ... 5 in. (12.7 cm.)

WEIGHT
Unladen ... 393 lbs. (178 kilos)

Technical Data

BONNEVILLE 120 (T120) TECHNICAL DATA

ENGINE
Type	O.H.V. Twin
B.H.P. at R.P.M.	46 at 6,500
Bore	2.79 in. (71 mm.)
Stroke	3.23 in. (82 mm.)
Capacity	40 cu. in. (649 c.c.)
Compression Ratio	8.5 : 1

Valve Clearance (Cold):—
Inlet	0.002 in. (0.05 mm.)
Exhaust	0.004 in. (0.10 mm.)

Valve Timing:—(with 0.020 in. (0.50 mm.) tappet clearance for checking)
Inlet Valve opens B.T.C.	34°
Inlet Valve closes A.B.C.	55°
Exhaust Valve opens B.B.C.	48°
Exhaust Valve closes A.T.C.	27°

IGNITION
Magneto Contact Point Gap	0.012 in. (0.3 mm.)
Sparking Plugs	Champion N4, K.L.G. FE100 or Lodge HLN
Sparking Plug Gap	0.020 in. (0.50 mm.)

Timing (Fully Advanced):—
Crankshaft position	39° B.T.C.
Piston position	$\tfrac{7}{16}''$ (11 mm.) B.T.C.

CARBURETTERS (2)
Type	Amal Monobloc
Main Jet	240
Needle Jet	.1065
Needle position	2
Throttle Valve	376/3½
Pilot Jet	25

Technical Data

TRANSMISSION
Gearbox—Type	Positive Selection (Foot operated)
Speeds	Four
Gear Ratios:—	
4th—Top	4.88
3rd—Third	5.81
2nd—Second	8.25
1st—Bottom	11.9
R.P.M./10 m.p.h. Top Gear	638

CLUTCH
Type	Langite in Oil

SPROCKETS
Engine	21 teeth
Gearbox	18 teeth
Clutch	43 teeth
Rear Wheel	43 teeth

CHAIN
Primary-Front-Pitch	$\frac{1}{2}'' \times .335'' \times \frac{5}{16}''$
Links	70
Secondary-Rear-Pitch	$\frac{5}{8}'' \times .400'' \times \frac{3}{8}''$
Links	98

CAPACITIES
Fuel Tank	3 galls. (13.5 litres)
Oil Tank	5 pints (3 litres)
Gearbox	$\frac{2}{3}$ pint (400 c.c.)
Primary Chaincase	$\frac{1}{4}$ pint (150 c.c.)
Front Forks (each leg)	$\frac{1}{4}$ pint (150 c.c.)

TYRE SIZES
Front	3.25 × 19 in.
Rear	4.00 × 18 in.

SUSPENSION
Front	Telescopic
Rear	Swinging Fork

BRAKES
Type	Internal Expanding
Front Diameter	8 in. (20.32 cm.)
Rear Diameter	7 in. (17.78 cm.)

OVERALL DIMENSIONS
Seat Height	30.5 in. (77.5 cm.)
Wheel Base	55.25 in. (140.3 cm.)
Length	86.25 in. (219 cm.)
Width	28.5 in. (72 cm.)
Ground Clearance	5 in. (12.7 cm.)

WEIGHT
Unladen	393 lbs. (178 kilos)

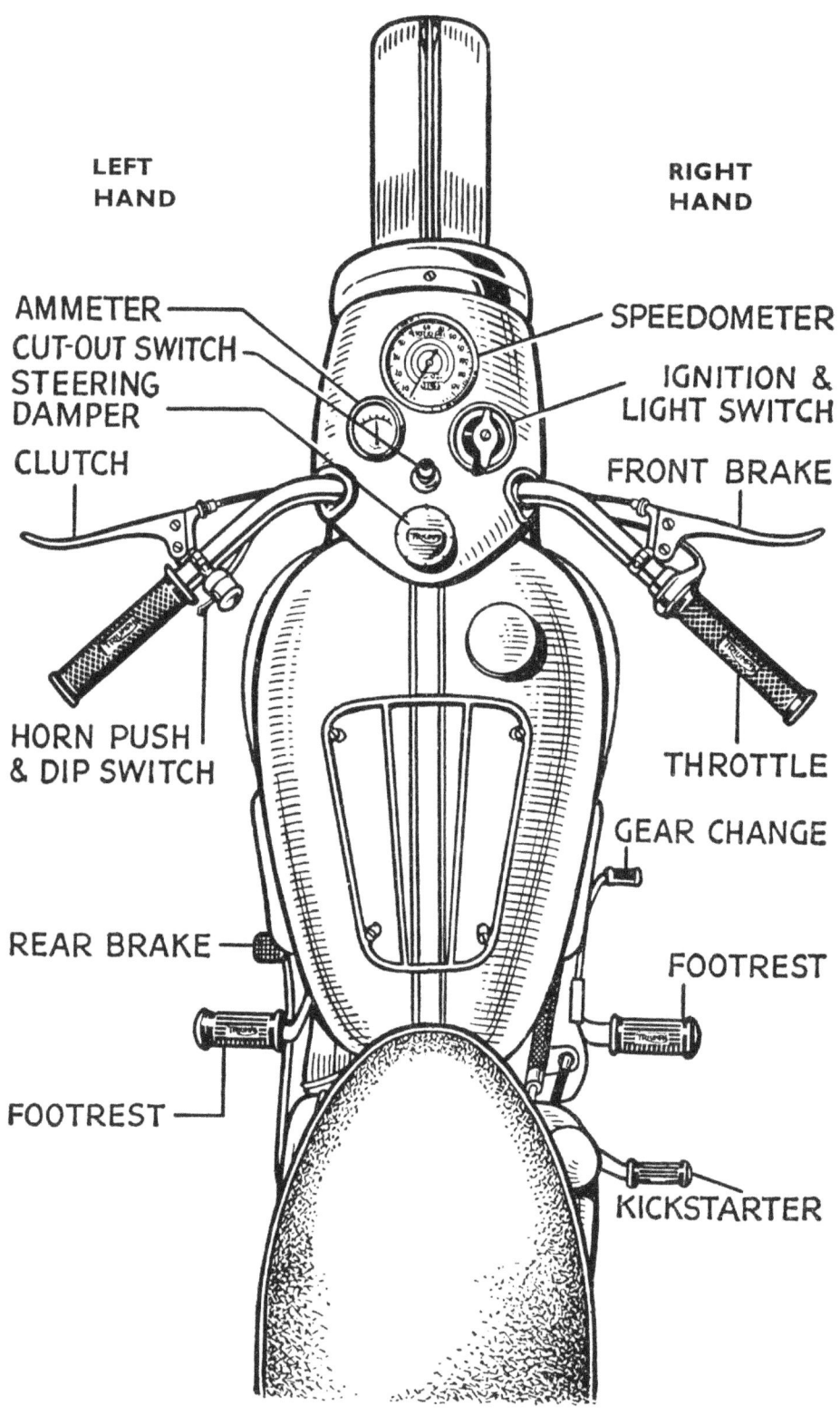

Fig. 1. Control Layout.

CONTROLS—INSTRUMENTS

The position and application of the controls is explained by assuming that the rider is sitting on the machine.

As the layout is not identical on all machines differences will be shown by inserting the model type after the caption.

Clutch Lever. On left side of handlebar. The clutch is also operated by the gearchange lever and before adjustment, see Gearbox Section, Page 71.

Front Brake Lever. On right side of handlebar. Always apply gentle pressure to the lever and use in conjunction with the rear brake.

Throttle Control. This is a twistgrip operated by the right hand. Twist towards the rider to open. There is a knurled knob which can be used to adjust the friction on the rotor to personal choice.

Magneto Control Lever (TR6). On left side of handlebar. Open the lever (clockwise) to retard the ignition.

Carburetter Air Control Lever (TR6). On right side of handlebar. Close the lever (anti-clockwise) to shut the air valve. On the 6T and T110 the air valve is controlled by a knob on the top of the carburetter. Press the knob down and twist to shut the air valve.

Horn Push and Dipper Switch. On left side of handlebar. Push the cap to sound the horn and operate the lever to raise or lower the headlamp beam.

Ignition Cut-Out Button. On left side of handlebar (TR6 and T120) or in centre of nacelle (T110). Depress to stop engine.

Speedometer. Registers speed, trip and total mileage. To return the trip indicator to zero, pull down and twist the knurled knob beneath the instrument. On the 6T and T110 the knob is carried on a flexible extension reached from the rear of the nacelle. Illumination of the speedometer is controlled by the main lighting switch.

Lighting Switch. On nacelle (T110) or on the frame beneath the nose of the twinseat (TR6 and T120). Turn the lever to operate.

OFF	ALL LIGHTS OFF
L	TAIL AND PARKING LIGHT ON
H	TAIL AND HEADLIGHT ON

Controls

Lighting and Ignition Switch (6T). Turn the lever to operate lights. Switch positions :—

        O   ...   .   ALL LIGHTS OFF
        P   ...   .   TAIL AND PARKING LIGHT ON
        H   ...   .   TAIL AND HEADLIGHT ON

Ignition Switch :—(Controlled by key)
        CENTRAL ...   ...   IGNITION OFF
        IGN ...   .   IGNITION ON (NORMAL)
        EMG ...   .   IGNITION ON (EMERGENCY)
        See page 157 *before using this switch position.*

Ammeter. This indicates the charging rate of the alternator when the engine is running, or the rate of discharge when the lights are "ON" and engine stopped.

Steering Damper. Turn the large knob in the centre of the handlebar to adjust the degree of friction.

OIL PRESSURE INDICATOR

The indicator button operates through the oil pressure release valve, which is situated in the timing cover. When the engine is running the indicator button should begin to protrude at approximately 2,000 r.p.m. (equivalent to 30 m.p.h. in top gear). The button may not protrude at all at tick-over.

GENERAL

The 6T and T110 are fitted with panels which enclose the rear of the machine. The battery, tool-roll and oil tank are beneath the twinseat, which may be lifted towards the left after pulling the knob, at the top of the right panel.

It will rarely be necessary to remove the panels as all routine maintenance can be done with them in position. If the panels must be removed, the best method is to unbolt the twinseat from its hinges and release the panel fixings which consist of one bolt at the top front, four screws on top and one bolt near each pillion footrest bracket. Remove the screws at the front panel joint, pull the front end of the panels apart and lift them off backwards and upwards.

FOOT CONTROLS

Footbrake. A flat pedal in front of the left footrest. Depress to operate. The first application should be applied gently and then pressure increased as the road speed decreases.

Gearchange. A small foot lever in front of the right footrest. The lever is moved "DOWN" to select a low gear and "UP" to select a higher gear. The neutral position is between 1st and 2nd gears (see also page 71).

Controls

Kickstarter. This is behind the right footrest. All models have the fixed pedal type with the exception of the TR6 ; this model has the folding pedal type.

ADJUSTMENT OF CONTROLS AND RIDING POSITION

When first taking over the machine, the rider should adjust the various controls to suit his own individual requirements.

Footrests. The left footrest is located by four pegs and the right footrest by two pegs. The footrests are non-adjustable and the securing nuts should be checked periodically for tightness.

Gear Change Lever. This is fitted to a serrated shaft. To re-position, slacken off the set-screw and ease the lever off the serrations. Replace in a convenient position and tighten up the set-screw.

Footbrake Pedal. The rear brake pedal is adjustable for position. The free movement is adjustable by the finned nut on the rear end of the operating rod.

Handlebars. Adjustment is made by slackening off the four "U" bolts, nuts and turning the handlebar to the desired position. The TR6 & T120 handlebar is clipped to the top lug by four set-screws and by releasing these the handlebar can be adjusted in a similar manner. Ensure that either set-screws or nuts are securely tightened to avoid handlebar slip.

Control Levers. If the clamping screws which secure the lever assemblies to the handlebar are slackened, the control can be moved to suit the rider's preference.

Twinseat. This cannot be adjusted for height, but has been designed to suit the average rider.

When placing a machine with Swinging Arm rear springing on the prop stand, pull the rear of the machine upwards. If this is not done the rear suspension units will eventually extend against the damping and the movement may cause the machine to fall over.

CONTROL CABLES
ADJUSTMENT POSITIONS

Throttle Cable. The adjuster is located in the cable, approximately 12" from the twistgrip, except on earlier 6T models where the adjustment is made on the right side of the S.U. carburetter. For Bonneville 120 adjustment, see page 142.

Starting

Air Cable (TR6). Adjust the cable abutment screw, located in the carburetter top.

Magneto Cable (T100, T110 & T120). Raise the rubber sleeve where the cable enters the magneto when the adjuster can be turned after slackening off the locknut.

Clutch Cable. Adjustment is made at the handlebar lever. (See page 91 for further details).

Front Brake Cable. An adjustable thumb nut is located on the lower cable abutment on earlier models and at the handlebar lever on later models.

TAKING OVER THE MACHINE

After taking delivery of the machine and before taking it on the road, carefully check that the oil tank, primary chaincase and gearbox levels are correct (See page 28). Ensure that the battery is in a charged condition, "topped up" to the correct level and the battery connections secured. The tyres should be checked with a pressure gauge and if necessary adjusted in accordance with the instructions on page 131. Fill the petrol tank with a premium grade of fuel and the machine is ready for starting. If premium grade petrol is not available, lower compression ratio pistons should be fitted to the TR6, T110 and Bonneville 120.

Although each machine is thoroughly checked before leaving the Works or Distributors for the security of all nuts, bolts, etc., it is advisable after the first 100 miles to re-check and again at 500 miles. This is a necessary precaution due to the bedding down of the engine and motorcycle parts.

STARTING THE ENGINE (COLD)

For machines fitted with the Amal Carburetter

Engage the gearbox in the neutral position, between first and second gear.

Turn the petrol tap ON.

Lift the clutch lever and depress the kickstarter two or three times to separate the clutch plates.

In very cold weather it may be necessary to close the air control.

Partly retard the ignition by turning the control lever away from the closed position (clockwise).

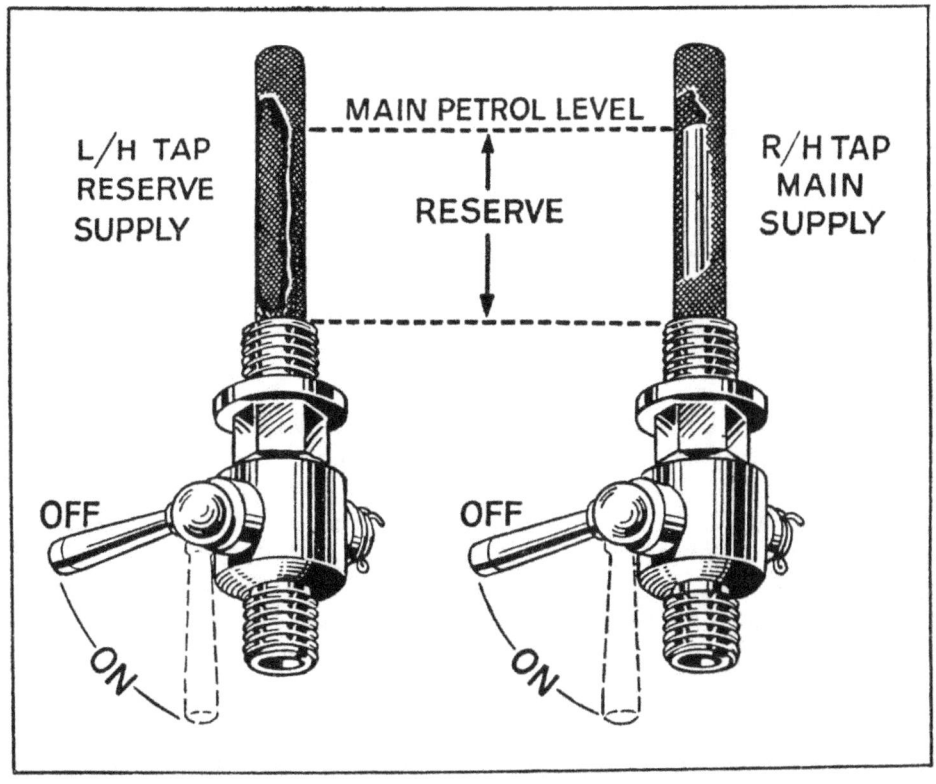

Fitted to Models TR6 and T110—Turn on the L/H tap after the supply from the R/H tap is exhausted.

NOTE.—The Bonneville 120 has no reserve and both taps should always be used.

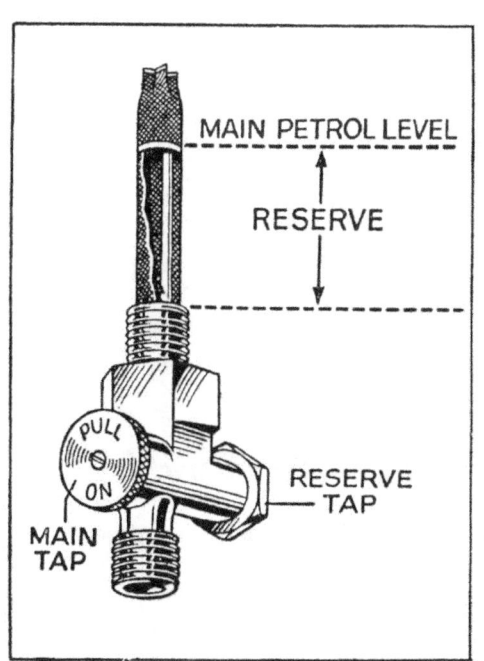

Fitted to 6T—Pull out the hexagon headed plunger for reserve supply. The main tap plunger MUST be left in ON position.

Fig. 2. PETROL TAP POSITIONS.

Starting

Flood the carburetter by depressing the tickler on the float bowl until the base of the carburetter is just wet. Do not flood the carburetter until the petrol streams out, as this may cause difficult starting.

Turn the engine over until compression can be felt on one cylinder. Re-position the kickstarter pedal to almost the horizontal position by freeing the clutch.

On the 6T model, switch the ignition key to the "IGN" position.

Open the throttle slightly by turning the twistgrip about $\frac{1}{8}$ turn and then depress the kickstarter pedal smartly when the engine should fire immediately. A second or third kick may be necessary if the controls are incorrectly set.

Failure to start the 6T model may be due to a flat battery; in this case turn the ignition key to "EMG" which is the emergency start position. Depress the kickstarter when the engine will fire. Once the engine is running the ignition key MUST be returned to the "IGN" position, as the engine should not be run longer than is absolutely necessary in the "EMG" position. (For special running conditions on the "EMG" circuit see page 157).

When the engine starts the air lever can be fully opened as it warms up. It is particularly important to open the air lever as soon as possible, otherwise the mixture strength may be too rich and the oil on the cylinder walls will be washed off, causing harmful results.

Under no circumstances allow the engine to "idle" when cold. The throttle should be adjusted to a fast "tickover" in order to warm the oil rapidly and ensure good circulation. This precaution will reduce cylinder wear.

Finally, attention must be paid to the oil pressure indicator immediately the engine starts. The indicator button MUST protrude from the release valve cap. If the button does not protrude, stop the engine at once and investigate the failure (See page 23).

Always turn the petrol taps "OFF" when parking the machine.

STARTING THE ENGINE (COLD)

For machines fitted with the S.U. Carburetter

Engage the gearbox in the neutral position, between first and second gear.

Turn the main petrol tap ON; when not in use turn it OFF.

Lift the clutch lever and depress the kickstarter two or three times to separate the clutch plates.

On the left side of the carburetter is the jet lever and to increase the mixture strength for a COLD start raise the lever. No predetermined position can be stated owing to the different starting characteristics of the various engines, but the rider will soon find the most suitable lever position. The lever should be put in the lowest position when the engine is warm.

Turn the engine over by the kickstarter until compression can be felt on one cylinder. Re-position the kickstarter pedal to almost the horizontal position by freeing the clutch.

Switch on the ignition by turning the key in the centre of the lighting switch to the position "IGN", open the throttle about $\frac{1}{8}$ turn and then depress the kickstarter pedal smartly when the engine should fire immediately, if not, re-position the throttle and jet lever.

Failure to start the engine after the controls have been re-set may be due to a flat battery; in this case turn the ignition key to "EMG" which is the emergency start position. Depress the kickstarter when the engine will fire. Once the engine is running the ignition key MUST be returned to the "IGN" position as the engine should not be run longer than is absolutely necessary in the "EMG" position. (For special running conditions on the "EMG" circuit see page 157).

When the engine starts, close the twistgrip to a brisk tickover. While the engine is COLD the jet lever should be raised sufficiently to keep the engine running fast and evenly and should remain in that position until it is warm enough to run with the lever fully depressed. It will be noted that the lever is friction loaded and can, therefore, be set in any position for any length of time according to climatic conditions. For this reason, no specific time for the RICH running condition can be stated.

Always turn the petrol taps "OFF" when parking the machine.

RUNNING-IN

For many years, motorcyclists were advised to ride their new machines at a speed not in excess of 30 m.p.h. for the first thousand miles. With a modern machine of high, or comparatively high performance, this type of running-in is entirely useless, and at the end of the one thousand miles only very little improvement will have been effected in the bearing surfaces of the engine.

Running-in should be carried out progressively, and it is necessary for the rider to make what may be termed a very definite arrangement with himself before he starts riding the new machine. He should make up his mind never to be bustled during the running-in period and to ride at his own speed entirely irrespective of the speed of other traffic. It is, naturally, annoying when one owns a high performance machine

Running-in

to be passed on the open road by a lightweight, but the rider of a new model must control his impulses, happy in the thought that the treatment he is giving his engine will mean considerably improved performance at the end of the running-in period.

When a machine is intelligently and carefully run-in, it will be faster, mechanically quieter, and will wear longer than the mount of a rider who pays no attention to the finer points of running-in. With a new machine, speed, within reason, does not greatly come into the question ; the main idea to keep in one's mind is that the engine must never be stressed. By far the best indication is the amount of throttle opening, and during the initial stages more than about a quarter throttle should not be used.

The engine must not be allowed to slog in the higher gear ratios ; it is far better to change down to a lower gear when the engine will be revving faster, but much more easily. It is a good plan to put a little spot of white paint on the twistgrip rubber, and a spot of black paint on the chromium plated twistgrip body, in such a position that these coincide when the throttle is closed. It is then easy to estimate the throttle opening during the running-in period and the "spots" can easily be removed, or the position of the white one altered.

After about 250 miles have been covered, the throttle opening can be increased to say a third, and this means that the speed will gradually increase. A further amount of throttle can be used as the running-in progresses, until the full throttle opening has been worked up to at about 1,200 miles.

Following the principle throughout that the engine must never be unduly stressed, speed bursts will be carried out progressively. With experience it may be found that at a certain throttle opening the machine will easily reach 50 miles per hour. When the speedometer needle touches that speed for the first time, the engine should immediately be throttled down. After a period of slower running, the 50 m.p.h. mark can be worked up to again, and this time held for a little longer. By gradually working up in this way, the time will come when the first of a few miles at 50 m.p.h. has been arrived at progressively. The same care should be taken when higher speeds are reached. With the higher performance machines in the Triumph range, similar care should be taken to see that the maximum speed is worked up to very carefully and is only held for a very short period initially. At really high speeds, it is advantageous to close the throttle momentarily at regular intervals, as this enables an increased amount of oil to pass up the cylinder bore. When the engine is thoroughly run-in this precaution is, of course, unnecessary.

During the running-in period great care must be taken to follow the lubrication instructions which will be found on page 28.

Lastly, do not forget that you will have plenty of time to try the paces of your new mount during the many thousands of miles you will cover after the running-in period has been completed. Never be tempted to "see what she will do" in the early stages, and do not be persuaded by your friends to test the speed of the machine against theirs until you are quite satisfied that your engine is thoroughly run-in.

ENGINE LUBRICATION SYSTEM

The dry sump lubrication system is employed on all Triumph engines. The oil is fed by gravity from the oil tank via a filter and pipe to the pressure side of the oil pump. The pump is a double plunger type, fitted with two non-return valves. From this point the oil is forced through drilled passageways to the crankshaft, and from the big end the oil issues in the form of a fog to lubricate the pistons and the other internal engine parts.

The oil pressure is controlled by means of a release valve situated in the timing cover. This valve serves two purposes, first to release excessive oil pressure and secondly to indicate the pressure by visible means. The valve consists of a piston, main spring, secondary spring, oil seal and button indicator. When the engine is running the valve is forced back by oil pressure on the secondary spring, this being indicated by the button projecting through the cover nut. Excessive pressure will move the piston back still further on the main spring and allow oil to be by-passed through the release valve body to the crankcase, from there to be scavenged to the oil tank.

After lubricating the engine, oil falls to the bottom of the crankcase where it is filtered. The crankcase oil return pipe which can be seen protruding through the filter after the sump plate has been removed, then returns the oil to the suction side of the oil pump to be returned to the oil tank. The suction oil pump plunger has twice the capacity of the pressure side, in order to make certain that no surplus oil remains on the floor of the crankcase. To lubricate the valve rockers, oil is taken from the return scavenge pipe by tapping the supply just below the oil tank. The oil, after being forced through the rocker spindles, lubricates the valve stems and push rod cups. The oil drains from the valve wells in the cylinder head into the push rod cover tubes, where it then lubricates the tappets and finally drains into the sump.

LUBRICATION MAINTENANCE

ENGINE

The system employed is simple and will function over a long period of time without attention to the actual pumping mechanism. On the other hand, failure to observe the elementary precautions of changing the oil and cleaning the filters at regular intervals, may cause a complete breakdown due to foreign matter entering the system.

If the oil tank cap is removed after the engine has been started, it will be noted that the return of oil to the tank via the stack pipe (seen just inside the filler aperture) is intermittent. The reason for this is that the scavenge side of the oil pump has a greater capacity than the feed side. Therefore, the crankcase sump is kept free of oil under normal running conditions and the scavenge pump will draw air until the crankcase scavenge pipe is again submerged in oil. The air which is forced into the oil tank is vented out via an outlet pipe into the primary chaincase.

Lubrication System

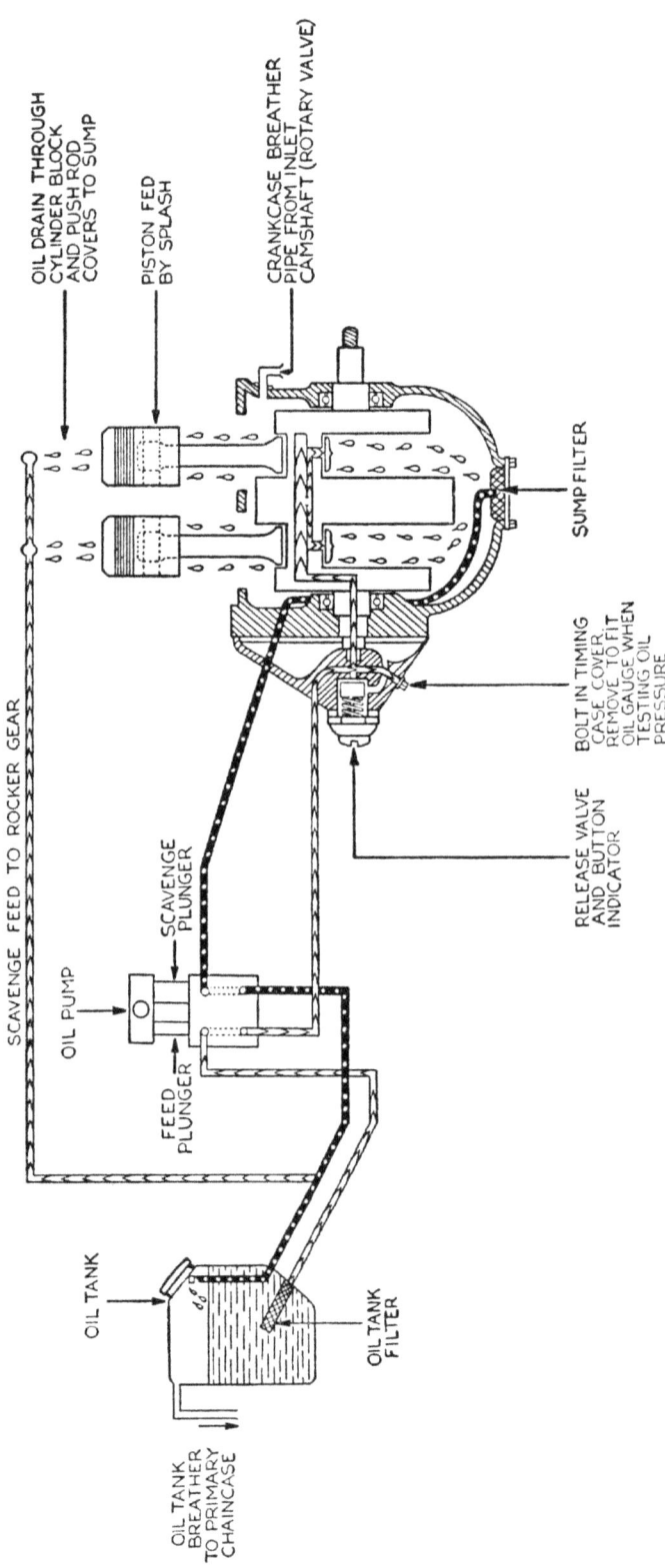

Fig. 3. ENGINE LUBRICATION DIAGRAM.

Lubrication Maintenance

In the event of a lubrication fault, the following causes have been listed diagnosing trouble:—

OIL TANK

The level in the oil tank should be 1½ in. (4 cm.) below the filler cap. Further addition of oil will cause excessive venting into the primary chaincase due to lack of air space. Always ensure that the vent pipe is clear as any obstruction will cause a back pressure in the oil tank, which in turn will prevent adequate scavenging by the oil pump, resulting in an oil flooded crankcase.

OIL PUMP

The only part likely to show wear after a considerable mileage is the oil pump block which can be replaced very cheaply. The plungers and the pump body being constantly immersed in oil, wear is negligible. It is unnecessary therefore, to suspect these parts if the lubrication is at fault. Should the non-return valve balls not be seating properly, the pump will not function satisfactorily. The remedy is to remove the oil pump and unscrew the two plugs situated under the oil pump body to remove the balls and springs. All parts should then be washed in petrol to remove any foreign matter, and when replacing the balls they should be given a sharp tap onto their seatings before re-assembly. Prime the pump with oil before fitting.

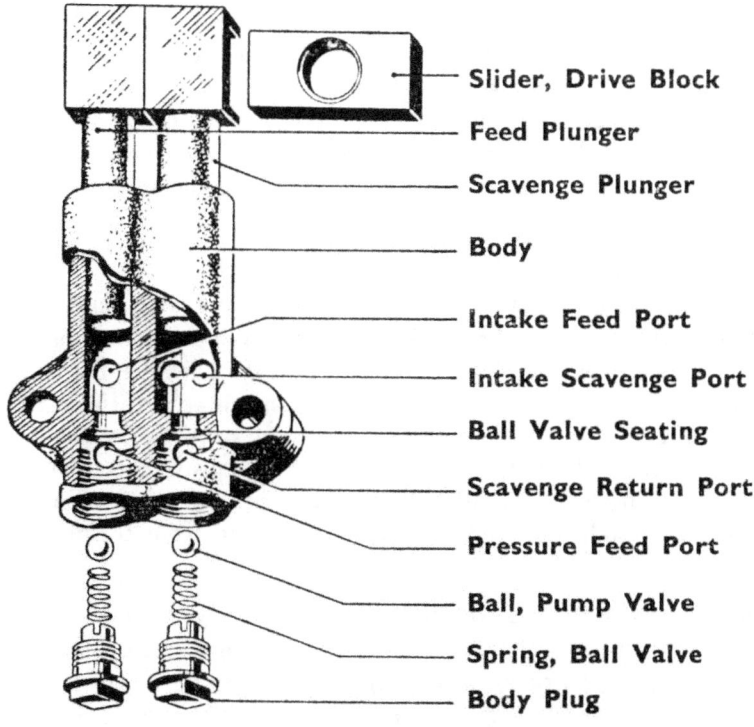

Fig. 4. OIL PUMP.

Lubrication Maintenance

OIL RELEASE VALVE AND INDICATOR

This unit is very reliable and should require no maintenance other than cleaning. When the oil is changed it is advantageous to dismantle this unit and thoroughly wash it in petrol to ensure that the piston works freely in the release valve body. Under no circumstances should the release valve springs be tampered with as the spring poundage is set to give the correct oil pressure. Should it be necessary to replace these springs at any time, genuine Triumph spares should be obtained.

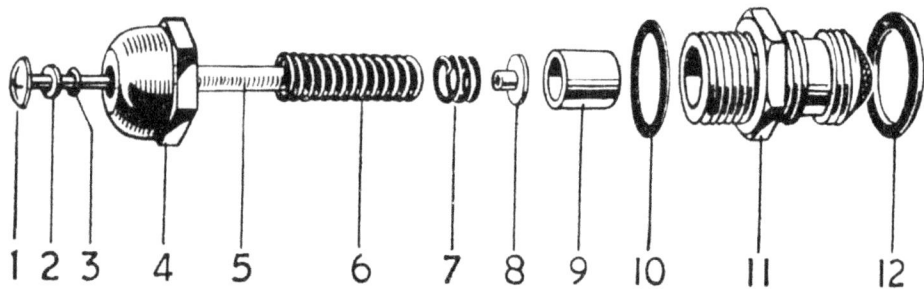

Fig. 5. OIL PRESSURE RELEASE VALVE.

1 Indicator Shaft
2 Cup
3 Rubber "O" Ring
4 Valve Cap
5 Rubber Sleeve
6 Main Spring
7 Auxiliary Spring
8 Nut
9 Piston
10 Fibre Washer
11 Valve Body
12 Fibre Washer

OIL PIPES (TANK TO ENGINE)

When replacing the oil pipes to the rubber connections, care must be exercised to prevent chafing the inside of the rubber connection. Failure to observe this may result in a small piece of rubber entering the oil system, which, on reaching the oil pump would cause lack of pressure to the crankshaft. Foreign matter in the scavenge pipe line above the pump would be returned to the tank (in exceptional cases it may block the rocker oil feed) and is prevented from entering the oil system by the tank filter.

CRANKCASE SCAVENGE PIPE

In the unlikely event of this cracking or an air leak between the pipe and the crankcase, the oil will not scavenge from the crankcase. Trouble of this kind would only make itself known when the engine is hot. A simple method by which the tube can be tested is to first remove the crankcase sump plate and filter and then attach a length of rubber tubing over the scavenge pipe. Place the open end of the rubber tube in the mouth and suck. If the tubing collapses, this will prove the air tightness of the scavenge pipe. On the other hand if the tube does not collapse, a leak is evident. To rectify this fault, the engine must be removed from the frame and stripped.

VALVE ROCKERS, ROCKER SPINDLES AND PUSH RODS

The oil feed to the rocker spindles is supplied from the scavenge side of the main oil supply. Lack of lubricant to the rockers can only be caused by a stoppage in the oil pipe line. The obvious course is to remove the pipe and check by forcing air through it. To check the oil supply at the spindle, run the engine till it is warm to increase the oil temperature and then slacken off the two acorn nuts, which secure the oil pipe banjos to the rocker spindles, when a steady drip of oil should emerge. It is advantageous to flood the rocker mechanism if the machine has been "laid up" for an appreciable time, or even after de-carbonising, etc. To do this, start the engine and then remove the oil tank filler cap, when a finger can be placed over the scavenge outlet pipe, thus forcing the oil through the rocker spindles, rockers and to the push rods. NOTE:—Always use the correct grade of oil as recommended on page 180. Cheap, inferior or the incorrect grade of oil will shorten the life of the engine.

GEARBOX
The gearbox is lubricated by oil and under no circumstances should a heavy viscous oil or grease be employed. Splash oil is fed to all parts including the enclosed gearchange and kickstarter mechanism to ensure complete lubrication. For oil changing and routine maintenance see page 28.

PRIMARY CHAINCASE
The primary chaincase houses the clutch, primary drive chain, engine sprocket and the alternator unit. Care should always be taken to ensure that the correct oil level is maintained ; the lubricant qualities are not reduced by condensation if the correct grade oil (SAE 20) is employed. Failure to observe these elementary instructions may result in a burnt out clutch, chain failure, and possibly damage to the alternator unit. If an oil of a higher viscosity than SAE 20 is used, the clutch plates will be difficult to separate, thus causing extremely noisy gear changing. For oil changing and routine maintenance see page 28.

CYCLE PARTS
The steering head races and wheel bearings are packed with grease on assembly. They should be dismantled and repacked with the correct grade of grease every 10,000 miles (15,000 kms.). The swinging fork pivot should be lubricated with a high-pressure grease gun every 1,500 miles (2,500 kms.) until grease is forced from each end of the pivot bearing. The front and rear brake cam spindles also should be given one shot at the above intervals.

CHAINS
The front chain is enclosed and positively lubricated (See Primary Chaincase, page 28). The rear chain however is lubricated by controlled oil splash from the primary chaincase. The method used is an oil trough in the rear of the inner chaincase and a hole drilled to atmosphere. In the outer cover a corresponding hole is drilled and tapped, into which a tapered needle valve is screwed, the taper entering the hole in the inner cover. By screwing the valve in or out the oil supply to the rear chain is decreased or increased accordingly.

CONTROLS
The control cables require lubricating at intervals, as, if they become dry, stiffness in operation will result. A good plan is to remove the cable at the handlebar end, wrap a piece of brown paper around the top end of the casing to form a funnel, securing it in position by a rubber band. If thin machine oil is then fed into the funnel and allowed to remain overnight, it will trickle down the casing and lubricate the inner wire.

CHANGING THE OIL

When the machine is new the oil should be changed frequently during the running-in period in order to make certain that any foreign matter which the oil picks up in the course of its circulation shall be eliminated.

ENGINE

The oil should be changed at 250, 500 and 1,000 miles (400, 800 and 1,500 kms.) during the running-in period and thereafter every 1,500 miles (2,500 kms.) regularly. When changing the oil it is essential that the oil filters are thoroughly cleaned in petrol.

Oil Tank Filter. To remove, unscrew the union nut attaching the feed pipe to the tank and then the large hexagonal nut to which the filter is fitted.
(6T and T110). It is not necessary to remove the panels to drain the oil tank or remove the filter. Disconnect the union nut and feed pipe below the filter and allow to drain. The filter can then be removed by using a socket spanner or thin box spanner.

Crankcase Filter. This filter is located in the base of the crankcase, to remove, unscrew the four nuts. Withdraw the filter carefully to avoid damage to the gauze.

It is advisable to flush out the oil tank with a flushing oil which is obtainable from most garages or accessory dealers. The flushing oil can be filtered through a piece of muslin and retained for further use. If the tank is very dirty it should be removed from the machine and thoroughly cleaned.

After the lubrication system has been drained and re-filled, all the joints which have been disconnected and the oil tank drain plug should be gone over again with a spanner to make certain that they are perfectly tight before the engine is started up. When the engine is again started, immediately check to see that the oil indicator is projecting and that the oil is returning to the tank. Inspect all joints for oil tightness.

PRIMARY CHAINCASE

The oil in the primary chaincase should be changed every 1,000 miles (1,500 kms.), or every month if a thousand miles has not been covered. The correct quantity is $\frac{1}{4}$ pint (150 c.c.). By carefully maintaining the oil level and changing the oil at regular intervals, the primary chain will be kept in excellent condition and will run for a long mileage without attention. If the oil is allowed to become dirty and partially broken down, wear will develop on the primary chain, which will require constant adjustment. (See Oil Chart, page 180).

GEARBOX

The oil in the gearbox should be drained and the gearbox flushed out after the machine has run 500 miles (800 kms.). Thereafter, the oil should be changed every 5,000 miles (8,000 kms.), but it is advisable to check the oil level at thousand mile intervals.

TELESCOPIC FORKS: See page 96 or 106.

ROUTINE MAINTENANCE AFTER RUNNING-IN PERIOD

	APPROXIMATE MAINTENANCE PERIODS		PAGE No.
	Miles.	*Kilometres.*	
ENGINE			
Check oil and replenish if necessary	250	400	25
Drain oil tank when warm and re-fill	1,500	2,500	28
Clean oil filters	1,500	2,500	28
Check and adjust tappets	3,000-4,000	5,000-6,000	34
Clean and adjust sparking plugs	2,000-3,000	4,000-5,000	172
Decarbonise and top overhaul	10,000-12,000	15,000-18,000	35
GEARBOX			
Check oil and replenish	1,000	1,500	83
Drain oil (when warm) and re-fill	5,000	6,000	83
Check clamp bolts	1,000	1,500	92
PRIMARY CHAINCASE			
Drain oil and re-fill (if the mileage is not covered, change monthly)	1,000	1,500	28
Check cover security screws	1,000	1,500	91
FORKS			
Drain oil and re-fill	5,000	8,000	96
Renew bushes, bearings and oil seals	20,000	30,000	100
Check play in headraces	5,000	8,000	96
Re-pack headraces with grease	10,000	15,000	96
SWINGING FORK			
Apply grease with gun	1,500	2,500	134
WHEELS			
Re-pack with grease	10,000	15,000	115
Check wheel bearings	2,000-3,000	4,000-5,000	115

See pages 180 and 181 for recommended lubricants.

Routine Maintenance after Running-in Period

	APPROXIMATE MAINTENANCE PERIODS		PAGE No.
	Miles.	Kilometres.	
CHAINS			
Adjust tension if necessary	1,000	1,500	92
Lubricate rear chain	1,000	1,500	93
BRAKES			
Grease cable and rod mechanism	1,000	1,500	183
Adjust (normal running)	1,000	1,500	114
BATTERY			
Check level of acid solution and add distilled water to bring level just above plates monthly. In very hot weather check more frequently.			169
TYRE PRESSURES			
Check and correct weekly			131
CARBURETTER			
Dismantle and clean	1,500	2,500	140
AIR FILTER			
Clean and re-oil filter element (Where machine is used in extremely dusty conditions the servicing period should be at more frequent intervals).	2,000	3,000	143
MAGNETO OR DISTRIBUTOR			
Check and adjust contact points	2,000-3,000	4,000-5,000	155
Clean and lubricate contact breaker	5,000	8,000	163
GENERAL			
Lubricate all cables, check security of all nuts and bolts	1,000	1,500	183

See pages 180 and 181 for recommended lubricants.

THE ENGINE

CRANKCASE

The crankcase is cast in two halves from aluminium alloy and is designed to provide maximum rigidity. The crankshaft is supported by two heavy duty ball bearings one in either crankcase half. The camshafts are housed transversely in the upper part of the crankcase and they operate in phosphor bronze bushes. The camshaft fitted to operate the inlet push rods is so designed that crankcase pressure is released to atmosphere through a rotary disc valve. Located in the timing side crankcase are the timing gears and the oil pump.

FLYWHEEL AND CRANKSHAFT

The balanced two throw crankshaft and flywheel are bolted together to make a complete unit. The "H" section connecting rods are forged from RR56 Hiduminium alloy and the bottom caps are steel stampings, the two parts being bolted together with two high-tensile bolts. Insert bearing shells are fitted, and are also available in .010 in. and .020 in. undersizes.

CYLINDER BLOCK

The cylinder block is made from high grade cast-iron. The bottom flange locates and retains the fixed tappet guide blocks.

PISTONS

The pistons are die-cast "LO-EX" aluminium alloy, each fitted with two compression and one scraper ring. The gudgeon pins are a tight push fit in the pistons and are held in position by spring steel circlips.

CYLINDER HEAD

The cylinder head houses the inlet and exhaust valves. Two separate rocker boxes complete with the rockers are bolted to the head to operate the valves. The heads are made from either cast-iron or die-cast aluminium alloy. The latter have cast-iron valve seats cast into the head during the manufacture.

LUBRICATION

Dry sump lubrication is employed. The system is operated by a twin plunger reciprocating oil pump. See page 23 for further information.

CARBURATION

Either by Amal or S.U. carburetter.

IGNITION

Either by Lucas magneto or Lucas alternator.

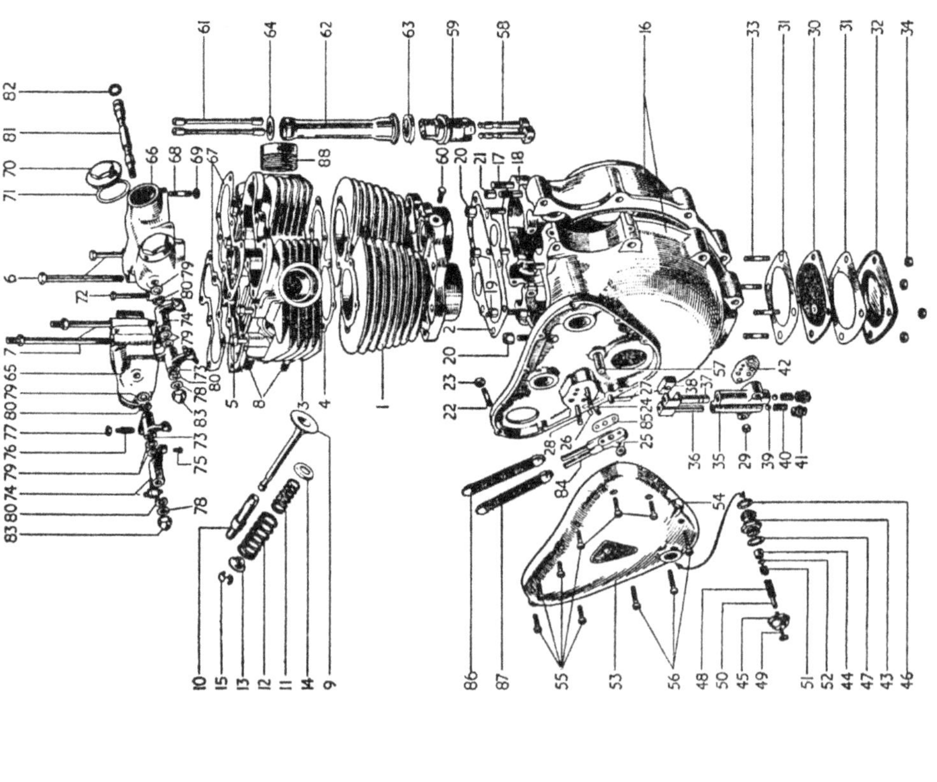

The Engine

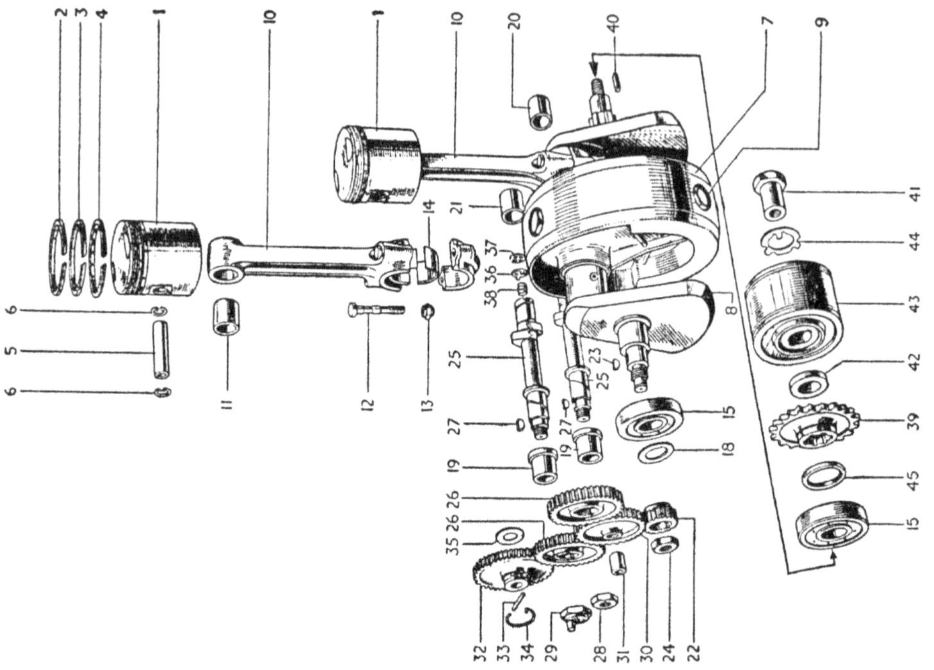

Fig. 7. CRANKSHAFT ASSEMBLY

Fig. 6. CRANKCASE ASSEMBLY.

INDEX TO FIG. 6 CRANKCASE ASSEMBLY 6T

Index No.	Description.	Index No.	Description.	Index No.	Description.
1	Block, cylinder.	24	Stud, oil junction block.	46	Washer, body.
2	Washer, cylinder base.	25	Nut, stud.	47	Washer, cap.
3	Head, cylinder.	26	Dowel, oil junction block.	48	Spring, main.
4	Gasket, cylinder head.	27	Dowel, timing cover.	49	Shaft, indicator.
5	Bolt, short.	28	Stud, oil pump.	50	Tube, rubber.
6	Bolt, medium.	29	Nut, stud.	51	Spring, auxiliary.
7	Bolt, long.	30	Filter, oil.	52	Nut, shaft.
8	Stud, inlet manifold.	31	Washer, filter cover joint.	53	Cover, timing.
9	Valve.	32	Cover, filter.	54	Plug, timing cover.
10	Guide, valve.	33	Stud, filter cover.	55	Screw, short.
11	Spring, valve inner.	34	Nut, stud.	56	Screw, long.
12	Spring, valve outer.	35	Body, oil pump.	57	Spindle, intermediate wheel.
13	Collar, valve.	36	Plunger, oil pump feed.	58	Tappet.
14	Cup, valve spring.	37	Plunger, oil pump scavenge.	59	Block, guide.
15	Cotter, valve split.	38	Block, oil pump slider.	60	Screw, lock.
16	Crankcase.	39	Ball, oil pump valve.	61	Rod, push.
17	Stud, cylinder base.	40	Spring, oil pump valve.	62	Tube, cover.
18	Stud, cylinder base (Dowel).	41	Plug, oil pump.	63	Washer, lower.
19	Nut, stud.	42	Washer, oil pump.	64	Washer, upper.
20	Nut, stud.	43	Body, oil release valve.	65	Box, inlet rocker.
21	Dowel, cylinder base stud.	44	Piston, valve.	66	Box, exhaust rocker.
22	Stud, magneto to crankcase.	45	Cap, release valve.	67	Gasket, rocker box.
23	Nut, stud.				

Index No.	Description.
68	Stud, rocker box.
69	Nut, stud.
70	Cap, inspection.
71	Washer, cap.
72	Bolt, rocker box.
73	Rocker, valve R.H.
74	Rocker, valve L.H.
75	Ball pin, rocker.
76	Adjusting pin.
77	Locknut.
78	Washer, thrust.
79	Washer, thrust.
80	Washer, spring.
81	Spindle, rocker.
82	Seal, spindle.
83	Nut, dome.
84	Pipes and block, oil tank to engine.
85	Washer, oil pipe block.
86	Connection, oil pipe (rubber).
87	Connection, oil pipe (rubber).
88	Exhaust adaptor.

INDEX TO FIG. 7 CRANKSHAFT ASSEMBLY 6T

Index No.	Description.	Index No.	Description.	Index No.	Description.
1	Piston.	12	Bolt, rod to cap.	25	Camshaft.
2	Ring, top compression.	13	Nut, rod to cap.	26	Wheel, camshaft.
3	Ring, centre compression.	14	Bearing, T/S.	27	Key, camshaft wheel.
4	Ring, scraper.	15	Bearing, D/S.	28	Nut, exhaust camshaft.
5	Gudgeon pin.	18	Clamping washer.	29	Nut, inlet camshaft (pump drive).
6	Circlip.	19	Bush, camshaft, T/S.	30	Wheel, intermediate gear.
7	Flywheel.	20	Bush, camshaft, D/S.	31	Bush, intermediate wheel.
8	Crankshaft.	21	Bush, camshaft D/S (Breather).	32	Pinion, distributor.
9	Bolt.	22	Pinion, timing.	33	Pin, distributor pinion.
10	Rod, connecting.	23	Key, timing pinion.	34	Circlip, distributor pinion.
11	Bush, small end.	24	Nut, timing pinion.		

Index No.	Description.
35	Washer (Brass).
36	Valve, crankcase rotary.
37	Disc, rotary valve.
38	Spring, rotary valve.
39	Sprocket, engine.
40	Key, rotor.
41	Nut, sprocket and rotor.
42	Clamping washer.
43	Rotor.
44	Washer, locking.
45	Oil seal.

TAPPET ADJUSTMENT

(Model 6T and Later T110)

These models are fitted with camshafts employing a Ramp-Cam form which makes it necessary to maintain a 0.010" (0.25 mm.) clearance (COLD) between the valve rocker adjusting pin and the valve tip in order to ensure silent operation and maximum efficiency. If the clearance is appreciably less the valve timing will be affected resulting in loss of power and the possibility of burnt valves. All machines with ramp camshafts have a mark :—
alongside the engine serial number.

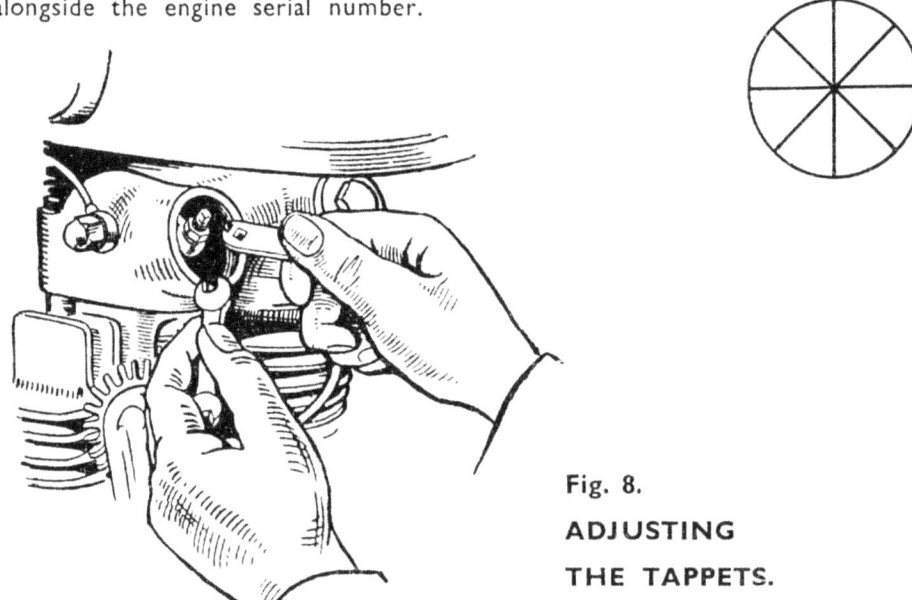

Fig. 8.

ADJUSTING THE TAPPETS.

(Models TR6, T110 & Bonneville 120)

These models have high-lift camshafts and no silencing ramps are incorporated in the cam form. The tappet adjustment, therefore, differs from the other models, the inlet being set at 0.002" (0.05 mm.) and the exhaust at 0.004" (0.10 mm.).

ADJUSTMENT (COLD)

Rocker Box Inspection Caps. Remove all four from the rocker boxes.

Positioning the Valves. First remove both sparking plugs. Turn the engine by means of the kickstarter until the left exhaust valve is fully open. The right exhaust tappet is now on the base of the cam, and the clearance at the right exhaust rocker should be adjusted to the appropriate figure. Turn the engine until the right exhaust valve is fully open and adjust the left exhaust rocker. Follow a similar sequence for the inlet valves.

Tools. In the toolkit, two spanners are provided for this adjustment. (See Fig. 8)

Rocker Adjuster Pin. Slacken off the adjuster pin locknut and screw down the adjuster until it just contacts the valve tip. For remaining details on model 6T read (a) and (b) and for TR6, T110 & T120 read (a) and (c).

(a) When the adjuster contacts the valve tip, hold the adjuster firmly with the spanner and tighten up the locknut with the other spanner. Grip the rocker adjuster between thumb and forefinger and move the rocker sideways to test for freedom of movement. Now test the up and down movement where the clearance between the adjuster and valve tip should be just perceptible.

(b) In order to obtain the 0.010" (0.25 mm.) clearance, first take particular note of the squared end of the adjuster and with both spanners in position, slacken the locknut slightly, taking care not to move the adjuster whilst doing so. Now slacken off the adjuster ONE FLAT ($\frac{1}{4}$ turn) and, maintaining it in the new position, re-tighten the locknut.
Carry out the same procedure with each tappet.

(c) The clearance on the exhaust valve can be estimated by first adjusting the tappet as in (2), paragraph (one). To obtain the 0.004" (0.10 mm.) clearance, slacken back the adjuster HALF A FLAT ($\frac{1}{8}$ turn). This may be slightly in excess of the clearance figure but the error is on the right side. For the inlet clearance, only slightly slacken off the adjuster so that when the rocker is held between thumb and forefinger and operated in an up and down movement, a distinct "click" can be heard when the adjuster strikes the valve tip.

DECARBONISING

The engine should be decarbonised only when it shows definite signs of requiring this attention. Falling off in power, loss of compression, noisy operation, and more difficult starting are all signs that the engine needs decarbonising. The engine will probably run at least ten thousand miles (15,000 kms.) between the decarbonising periods.

It should be noted that it is entirely unnecessary to remove the cylinder block when decarbonising the engine. We strongly recommend that this part is not taken off unless it is proposed to fit new piston rings or do some other work on the engine which necessitates the removal of the block. The engine will run more smoothly and give better service if the piston rings are left undisturbed.

Gasket sets are available for all models, and it is recommended that the correct set for the model is obtained before commencing the work.

Before commencing the operation, clean off any dirt, grease, etc., with paraffin or a suitable degreasing agent. Secondly obtain two boxes : one for the cylinder head, etc., and the other for nuts, washers, etc. By doing this the operator will not have to search the four corners of the garage for the vital nut to complete the job.

Decarbonising

DISMANTLING

Petrol Tank. Turn off the petrol tap or taps and disconnect the petrol pipes. Slacken the nut which secures the front of the retaining strap and then remove the rear cross bolt. Lift off the tank and collect the four rubber buffers.

Exhaust System. Slacken the exhaust pipe finned clip bolts, remove the pipe to bracket bolts, the silencer steady nuts and silencer hanger bolts. Remove each pipe and silencer as an assembly. (TR6. Also slacken the branch pipe clip bolt).

Torque Stays. Detach the torque stays by removing the two nuts and frame bolts (T120). The torque stay is a flat plate which supports the float chamber and plate, float chamber and pipes should be removed as an assembly.

Electrical Equipment. Disconnect the H.T. leads and remove the sparking plugs.

Carburetter—Amal. Remove the air cleaner connection and unscrew the two flange nuts. Withdraw the carburetter from the fixing studs and tie it to the frame. If it is desired to clean the unit, unscrew the knurled ring securing the throttle and air slides and take away the mixing chamber assembly. Carefully tie the slide assembly to the frame, out of harm's way.

Rocker Feed Pipe. Unscrew the acorn nuts holding the pipe to the rocker spindles. If the banjos tend to turn, use a spanner on the flats to retain them. Ease the pipe off the spindles.

Rocker Drain Pipe (6T). Slacken the adaptor bolts at the push rod covers and remove the adaptor bolts at the cylinder head.

Rocker Boxes. First remove the rocker inspection caps while the boxes are fixed to the head. Now remove the six nuts which hold the rocker boxes to head. (6T, four nuts). FAILURE TO DO THIS FIRST MAY RESULT IN BROKEN CYLINDER HEAD LUGS. Remove the four small bolts and unscrew the four central cylinder head bolts. The bolts cannot be lifted past the top tube with the rocker box resting on the head, but if the box is raised as far as possible and tilted to either side the bolts can be removed.

Cylinder Head. Unscrew the four remaining bolts and lift off the head and push rod cover tubes.

Inspection and Preparation. The method of decarbonising the parts and removing the valves and grinding-in, etc., is fully explained under the above heading on page 44.

Decarbonising

RE-ASSEMBLY

First anneal the head gasket and copper washers by heating to cherry redness and plunging into cold water.

Push Rod Covers. Place in position with new rubber washers. The locating discs must have the push rod holes across the machine.

Cylinder Head. Place the head on the block and screw the four outer bolts finger-tight.

Inlet Rocker Box. Stick the gaskets to the rocker boxes with a smear of grease and fit new push rod cover washers. Place the inlet push rods on the tappets and turn the engine with the kickstarter until both tappets have dropped as low as possible. Hold the box above the head and insert the torque stay bolts singly while tilting the box. Lower the rocker box into position, making sure that the rocker ends engage with the push rods and screw down the bolts. Insert the two short bolts and FINALLY THE THREE NUTS (6T TWO NUTS).

Rocker Drain Pipes (6T). Fit the adaptors with annealed copper washers and tighten carefully.

Exhaust Rocker Box. Fit this in the same way as the inlet rocker box.

Cylinder Head Bolts. Tighten the cylinder head bolts diagonally, starting with the central four. The correct torque loading is 18 ft./lbs. The short rocker box bolts and nuts should also be tightened. Turn the engine with the kickstarter and watch each valve as it opens to check that the push rods are correctly fitted.

Tappet Adjustment. Adjust the tappet clearances as detailed on page 34 and replace the rocker inspection caps.

Torque Stays. Replace the torque stays and tighten the fixings.

Carburetters. If the carburetter has been dismantled, complete the re-assembly and test the operation of the slide. On models with alloy cylinder heads fit a new paper washer and the insulating block. On all models fit a new "O" ring seal in the groove in the carburetter body. Replace the carburetter and tighten the nuts alternately. Check the operation of the carburetter slide again, and if sticking now occurs, suspect over-tightening of the nuts or distortion of the flange.

Rocker Feed Pipe. Replace the rocker feed pipe with new or annealed copper washers. If the banjos tend to turn, use a spanner on the flats to retain them.

Petrol Tank. Place the three small and one large rubber buffers in position and then fit the tank. Be careful that the tank does not trap the control cables or rocker feed pipe. Replace the rear cross bolt and tighten the front securing nut just sufficiently to hold the tank on the buffers. The strap must NOT be so tight that all movement is prevented. Connect the petrol pipes.

Decarbonising

Exhaust System. Replace the exhaust system and ensure that all fixings are in position before finally tightening them.

Testing. Start the engine and run for a short while to warm it. If necessary adjust the slow running settings on the carburetter. When the engine has cooled check the external nuts and bolts for slackness, but do not tighten further than the original settings.

REMOVING THE ENGINE FROM THE FRAME

Petrol Tank. Turn off the petrol tap or taps and disconnect the petrol pipes. Slacken the nut which secures the front of the retaining strap and then remove the rear cross bolt. Lift off the tank and collect the three rubber buffers.

Exhaust System. Slacken the exhaust pipe finned clip bolts, remove the pipe to bracket bolts, the silencer steady nuts and silencer hanger bolts. Remove each pipe and silencer as an assembly. (TR.6. Also slacken the branch pipe clip bolt).

Torque Stays. Detach the torque stays by removing the two nuts and frame bolt. (T120, torque stay is a flat plate which supports the float chamber and plate, float chamber and pipes should be removed as an assembly).

Carburetter—Amal. Remove the air cleaner connection and unscrew the two flange nuts. Withdraw the carburetter from the fixing studs.

Rocker Feed Pipe. Unscrew the acorn nuts holding the pipe to the rocker feed pipe. If the banjos tend to turn, use a spanner on the flats to retain them. Ease the pipe off the spindles.

Control Cables. Disconnect the magneto cable at the handlebar end and coil it neatly close to the magneto.

Footrests. Remove both footrests leaving the fixing rod in position.

Brake Pedal. Take out the split-pin securing the rod to the pedal. Unscrew the pedal spindle nut and withdraw the pedal.

Primary Chaincase, Alternator, Engine Sprocket and Clutch. Remove these parts as described on page 84.

Oil Pipes. Place a tray under the engine and disconnect the oil pipes junction block from the crankcase.

Front Engine Plate. (6T & T110) First remove the cover plate which is secured by one screw. (All Models) Support the crankcase underneath the sump and remove the two studs and two bolts and lift off the front engine plate. Also remove the long crankcase to frame stud.

Rear Engine Plates. Remove the two upper studs holding the crankcase to the engine plates. Slacken the bottom stud and those holding the engine plates to the frame. Tilt the engine to the rear of the machine to release the bottom stud from the slots and then lift the engine out of the frame.

Dismantling the Engine

DISMANTLING THE ENGINE

Having removed the engine from the frame, it should be mounted on the bench in such a manner that the work can be conveniently carried out. The Fig. 9 shows a useful and simple method of holding the engine firmly to enable dismantling.

DISMANTLING

Oil Pressure Release Valve. Unscrew from the timing cover.

Timing Cover. Remove the securing screws and tap around the edge with a hide hammer to break the cover joint. Withdraw the cover.

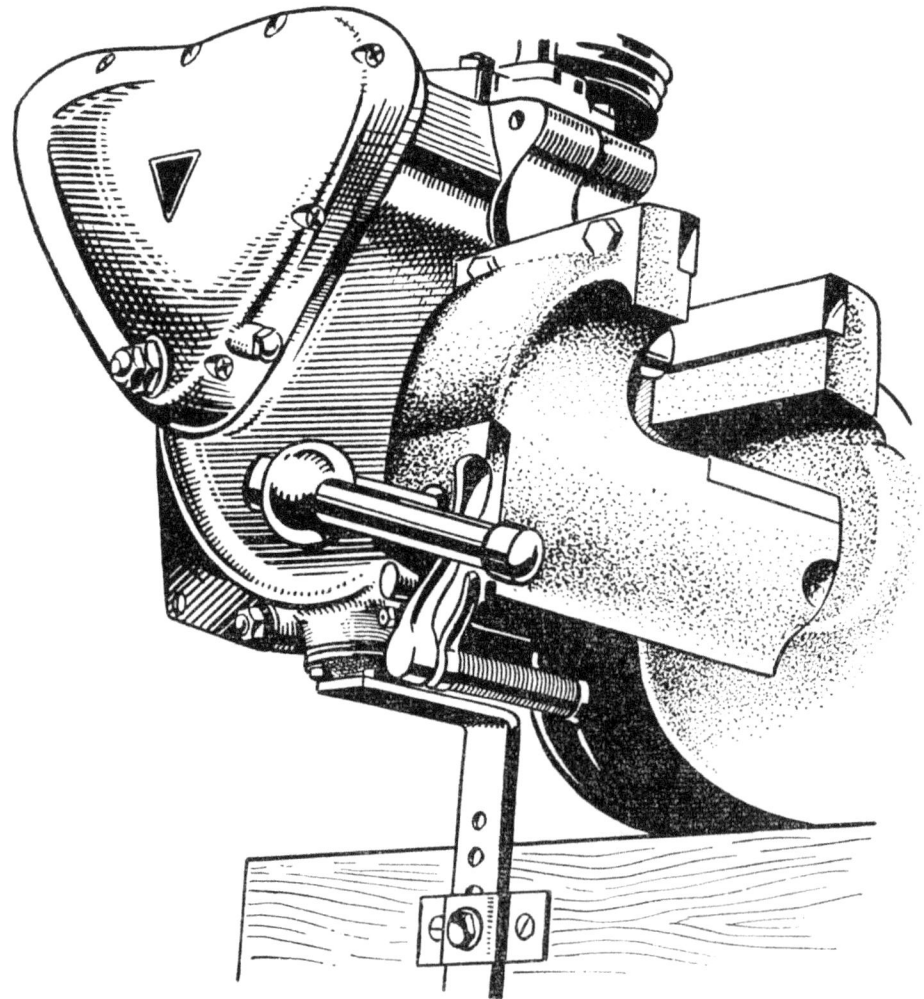

Fig. 9. ENGINE IN VICE.

Dismantling the Engine

Oil Pump. Take off the two securing nuts and slide the pump off the studs.

Crankshaft and Camshaft Nuts. Remove these nuts. Note that the camshaft has a L.H. THREAD (turn clockwise to unscrew) and the crankshaft nut has a R.H. THREAD (turn anti-clockwise to unscrew).

Distributor Gear (Coil). Remove the circlip from the drive pinion boss groove, which retains the pin locking the drive gear on the shaft. Remove the pin when the gear and steel thrust washer can be withdrawn.

Magneto Gear. Unscrew the securing nut and screw into the gear centre the withdrawal tool (DA50/1) which is supplied with the tool kit. When the tool is in position, tighten the centre bolt when the gear will be withdrawn from the shaft.

Automatic Timing Device. To remove, unscrew the centre bolt which has a self-extracting thread.

Camwheels. If the bushes in the timing side crankcase are not worn, it is unnecessary to remove the camwheels as the crankcase can be split without detaching them. The removal of these gears necessitates the use of the special withdrawal tool Z89. Screw the body of the tool "C" on to the threaded portion of the camwheel (See Fig. 11), and by screwing the extractor bolt "A" in the camwheel is withdrawn from the shaft.

Intermediate Gear Wheel. Remove from the spindle.

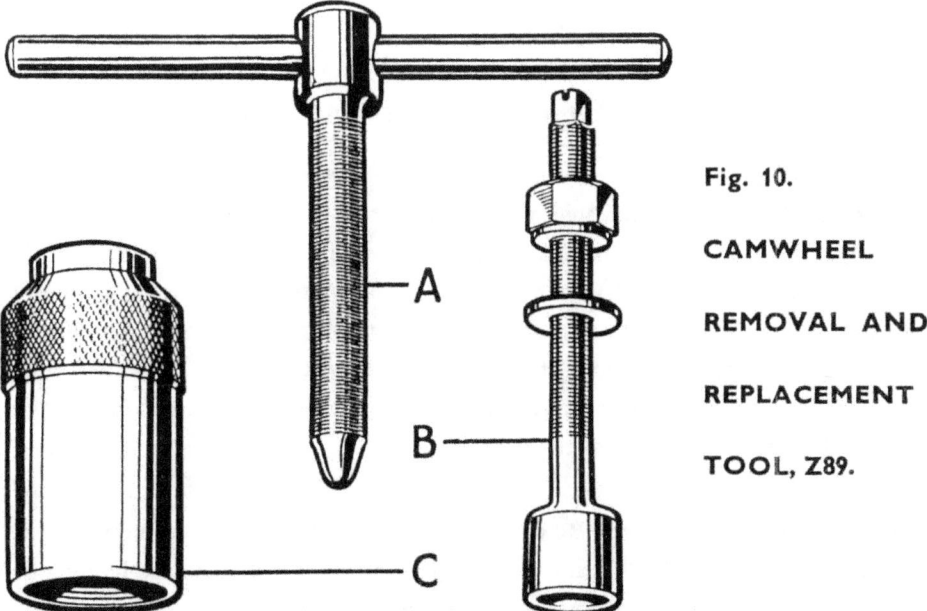

Fig. 10.

CAMWHEEL REMOVAL AND REPLACEMENT TOOL, Z89.

Removing Camwheels

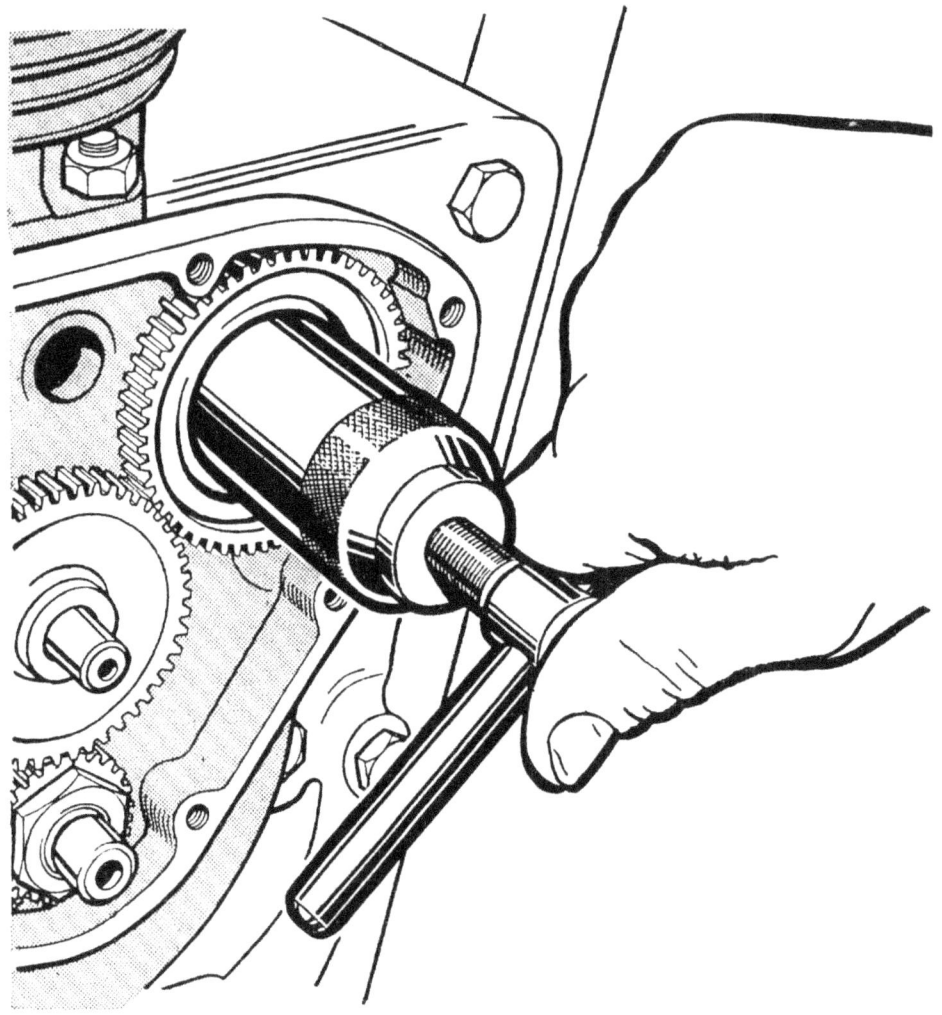

Fig. 11. REMOVING THE CAMWHEEL.

Crankshaft Pinion. Again a special tool, part No. Z121, must be employed to withdraw this gear from the crankshaft. Fig. 12 clearly illustrates its application. Place the end cap over the crankshaft and fit the body of the tool over the pinion. Rotate the body of the tool through a few degrees until the locating wire can be pushed towards the pinion to the full extent of its travel. Hold the tool body, with a tommy-bar through the hole if necessary, and turn the screw clockwise to draw off the pinion. Remove the key from the shaft.

Cylinder Head and Rocker Boxes. This unit should be removed as an assembly. Unscrew the four rocker oil drain adaptors and the eight cylinder head holding bolts, when the unit can be removed from the cylinder block.

Removing Crankshaft Pinion

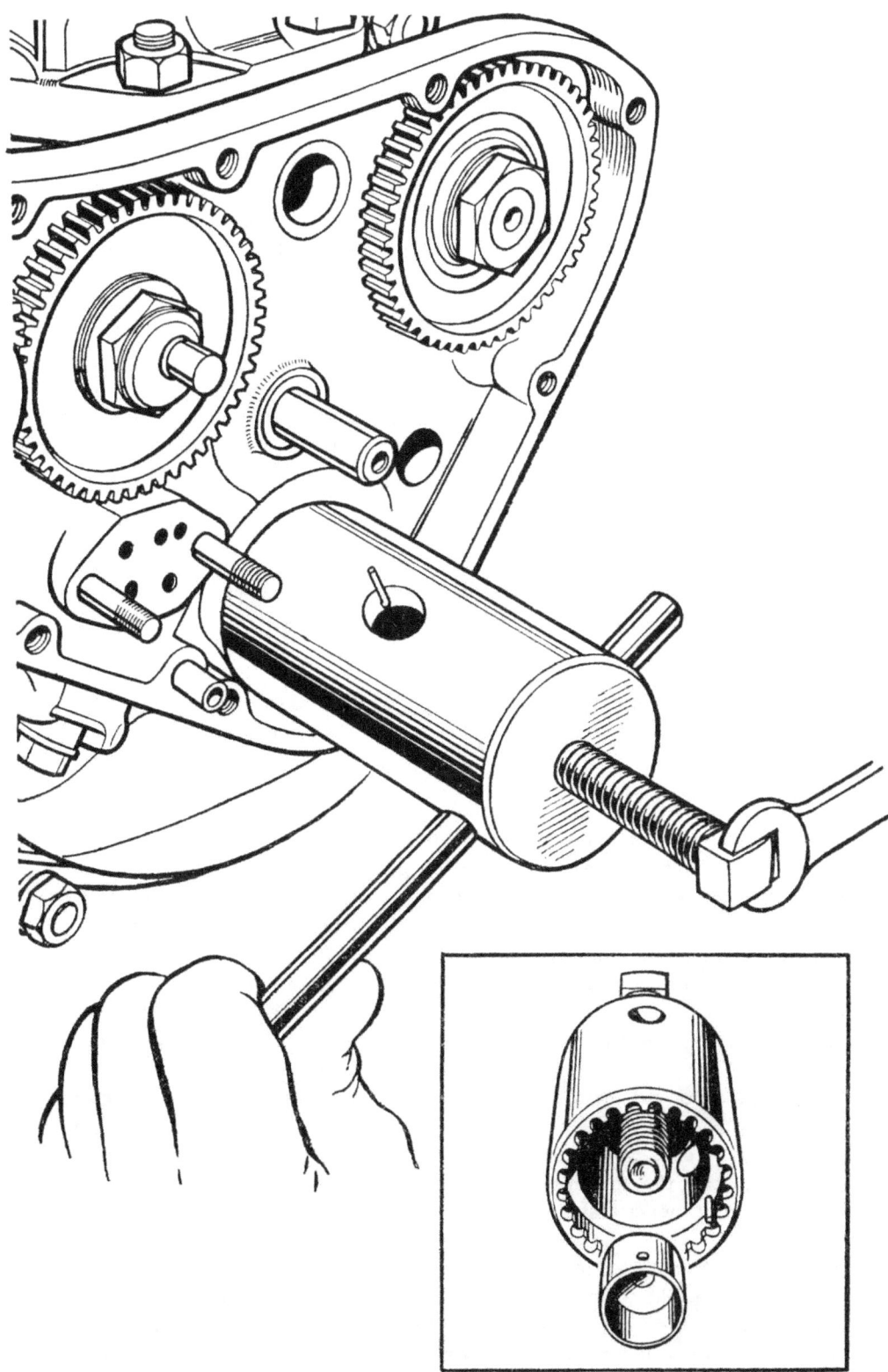

Fig. 12. REMOVING THE CRANKSHAFT PINION WITH TOOL Z121.

Dismantling Cylinder Head

Push Rods and Covers. Remove from the tappet blocks.

Cylinder Block. Unscrew the eight nuts ; secure the tappets in the blocks by placing a rubber wedge between them, taking care not to use undue force. Carefully lift the cylinder block off the pistons.

Pistons. Remove a circlip from each piston and then press the gudgeon pins out from the opposite end. The fit of the gudgeon pins in the pistons is fairly tight ; if a gudgeon pin extractor is available, it should be employed. The pistons should be suitably marked on the inside to ensure replacement to their original positions.

Magneto or Distributor. Unscrew the securing nuts and remove the unit.

Crankcase Bolts. Remove the remaining bolts and screws. NOTE.—Do not forget to remove the two screws from the internal bosses.

Crankcase Filter. Slacken off the vice jaws and remove the crankcase. Unscrew the four nuts holding the filter base and remove the base and filter gauze.

Crankshaft and Camshafts. To split the crankcase, bump the drive shaft onto a piece of wood when the two halves will readily part. The crankshaft and camshafts can now be removed.

In the drive side crankcase the breather rotary valve and spring are located in the camshaft bush. Care should be taken not to lose these.

DISMANTLING, PREPARATION AND ASSEMBLY OF THE ENGINE UNITS

CYLINDER HEAD

Rocker Boxes. Unscrew the four or six nuts and then the four screws when the rocker boxes can be removed from the head. Wash the rocker boxes thoroughly and inspect the parts for wear. Check the ball ends, adjuster pins, and rockers on the spindles for wear. Examine the rocker boxes for cracks or pulled studs. Normally, wear on the rocker spindles is negligible as they are fully lubricated. The adjuster pins sometimes show slight wear or indentation which can be removed by lightly stoning the hardened pad. If the markings are too deep, the pins should be replaced. Carefully inspect the ball ends, if the spheres are mis-shapen the ball ends must be changed. This operation will necessitate dismantling the rocker box or boxes. To do this, knock out the rocker spindle from the threaded end using a hide hammer or similar soft tool to prevent damage to the thread. After withdrawing the rocker levers the ball ends can be pressed out of the housings and the new ball ends fitted. When replacing the spindles, a new rubber seal must be employed ; Fig. 6 shows the position of the various washers.

Valves and Springs. Compress the valve springs sufficiently with a compressor tool, when the split cotters can be eased away with a narrow screwdriver or similar tool. Release the tool and withdraw both valve and valve springs. Repeat the operation to the other valves ; mark the valves for replacement. Inspect the springs for signs of fatigue and compare with new springs. If in doubt always fit new springs.

Servicing Cylinder Head

Clean the valves and remove any burnt oil from the stems; if the valve faces are pitted they can be re-ground, but excessive grinding by machine is not advisable as the heat transference of the valve will be adversely affected. The stem of the valve should be inspected for wear and scuffing and if either is pronounced, it should be replaced.

Removing Carbon from Cylinder Head. Remove the carbon with a flat round headed scraper from the head spheres and ports. Take particular care when cleaning around the valve seatings to avoid damage to the faces. Inspect the valve seats for pitting or pocketing and the valve guides for ovality. Remember, if the valve guides are changed, the valve seatings must be re-cut. The same applies to a valve replacement or a valve which has had the seating face re-ground.

Replacing the Valve Guides. To remove the old guide place a shoulder drift into the guide from the inside of the combustion chamber and drive out. When fitting the new guide, grease the outer diameter and drive into the cylinder head from the top. Always use a shoulder drift when doing this operation and drive in the guide carefully to avoid damage.

Re-cutting the Valve Seats. A job such as this can normally be undertaken by your dealer at a moderate cost. After the seats have been re-cut, they should be blended to give an even seating of approximately $\frac{3}{32}$ in. (2.38 mm.).

Grinding-in the Valves. This should be done with a fine carborundum grinding-in paste. First smear a little around the valve face and insert the stem into the new valve guide. Attach the valve grinding tool to the stem tip and commence to grind the valve face to the valve seating, using a semi-rotary movement, occasionally lifting the valve and turning through 180°. Continue this process until a uniform seat results. Remove the valve and wash thoroughly in petrol or paraffin and examine the seating. A surer method is to apply a thin even smear of "Engineer's marking blue" to the face of the valve. Rotate the valve one complete revolution and then remove it for inspection.

A thin uniform line, free from pit marks or other surface blemishes on valve face and valve seat indicates that the seating is satisfactory. After completion, the part must be thoroughly washed to remove all traces of the grinding-in compound.

Assembling the Cylinder Head. First ensure that all parts are thoroughly clean, then oil the valve stems and guides. Place a valve into its respective guide (Note, inlet are marked "IN" and exhaust "EX") and holding the valve head against the seat, turn the head on its side and fit the lower spring cup over the guide and then the inner and outer spring and finally the top collar. Compress the springs with a compressor tool until the split cotters can be fitted into the collar and around the valve stem cut-away. Release the pressure on the compressor tool and remove. Tap the stem head of the valve smartly to ensure correct replacement of the cotters. Repeat the operation to the other valves. The exhaust pipe stubs on the alloy heads are screwed into the exhaust ports and tightness must be ensured before replacing the cylinder head. Do not replace the rocker boxes at this stage.

CYLINDER BLOCK AND PISTONS

Cylinder Block. Remove all traces of carbon from the upper wall of the bores and then wash thoroughly in a cleaning solvent. Check the amount of wear in the upper part of the bore by comparing it with the measurements in the lower. Anything over 0.005" (0.13 mm.) will denote that re-boring is necessary. A rough check can be made by checking the piston ring gap in various sections of the cylinder bores, and dividing by 3. Normally, the wear at the bottom of the bore is very light.

$$63 \text{ mm.} = 2.4798 - 2.4803 \text{ in.}$$
$$71 \text{ mm.} = 2.7948 - 2.7953 \text{ in.}$$

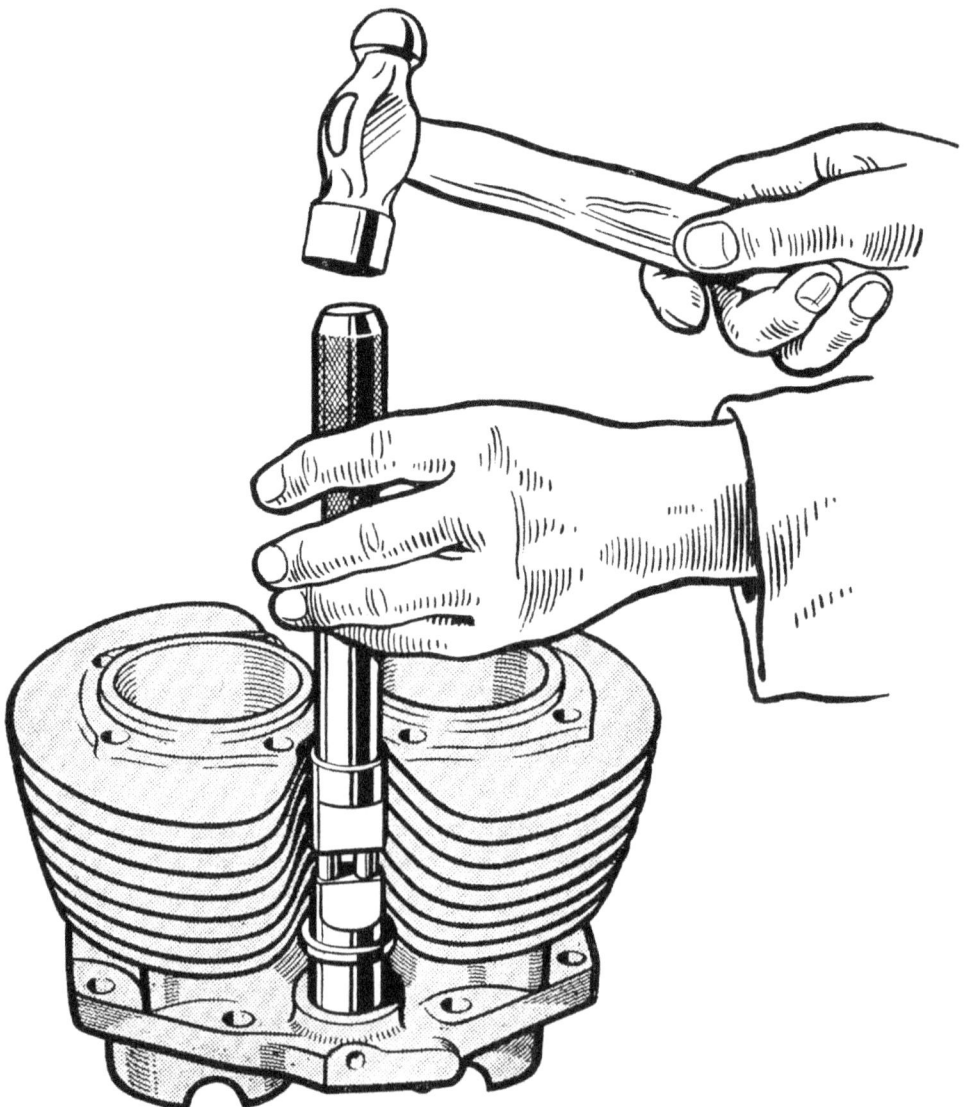

Fig. 13. ASSEMBLING THE TAPPET BLOCK.

Inspection of Pistons and Tappets

RECOMMENDED REBORE OVERSIZES ARE AS FOLLOWS:—

Cast Iron Block	+.010"/+.020"/+.040"	500 c.c.
Cast Iron Block	+.010"/+.020"	650 c.c.
Alloy Block	+.010"/+.020"	500 c.c.

It will be noted that the alloy block can only be re-bored to a maximum of +.020", this is due to the fact that cylinder liners are fitted. Further re-boring would thin down the liner beyond safety limits. It is possible to change the liners, but work such as this should only be entrusted to a competent engineering concern, who will have the necessary equipment.

Tappets. The base of the tappets have a "Stellite" tip fitted; this material has great resistance to wear and under general running conditions, the tappets will not require changing until a considerable mileage has been covered. The centre of the tip may show signs of indentation which is caused by the peak of the cam. This does not however indicate wear and the tappet can be re-installed.

Tappet Blocks. It is not necessary to remove the tappet blocks from the cylinder base for inspection; the amount of wear can be estimated by rocking the tappet head. The tappet stem should be a sliding fit in the tappet block bores and the tappet base must fit snugly in the block base. Slackness at these points will cause excessive mechanical clatter. To remove the tappet blocks from the cylinder base flange, place the cylinder block downwards on the bench, remove the locking screw and drift the tappet block out of the cylinder flange. When fitting the new tappet block, grease the outer surface and if possible support the cylinder flange (See Fig. 13). Do not forget to line up the locking screw hole in the tappet block to that in the flange. Replace the locking screw.

Pistons. If the pistons are to be further employed, the rings and gudgeon pins when removed from each piston should be kept separate to ensure correct replacement. Carefully clean away the carbon deposit from the piston crown, taking particular care not to scratch the metal surface. The light deposit of burnt oil on the piston skirt should be removed by rubbing with a rag which has been dipped in petrol. Never in any circumstances use an emery cloth. To clean the ring grooves, it is advantageous to use an old broken ring by inserting the broken end into the groove and working it around the circumference. Clean out the oil drain holes in the scraper ring groove and thoroughly wash the piston. On the inside surface of the piston rings will be found a light deposit of carbon which must be removed if the rings are to be re-fitted.

Now roll each ring around its respective groove to ensure that it does not stand proud of the piston after being fitted correctly and compressed. Before fitting new rings, the gap must be checked in the lowest part of the cylinder bore. The ring must lie square to the bore for checking purposes and to ensure this, place the bottom of the piston skirt onto the ring and ease it down the bore. Check the gap with feeler gauges.

Piston Rings

PISTON RING GAPS WHEN NEW

	Min.	Max.
Compression Ring Gap	0.010″ (0.25 mm.)	0.014″ (0.35 mm.)
Scraper Ring Gap (500 c.c.)	0.007″ (0.18 mm.)	0.011″ (0.28 mm.)
,, ,, ,, (650 c.c.)	0.010″ (0.25 mm.)	0.014″ (0.35 mm.)

When replacing the piston rings, note that the second compression ring has a taper-face and must be fitted in the middle piston ring groove. The face with (TOP) etched on it must be towards the piston crown. Later models are fitted with two taper-faced compression rings, which must both be fitted with the marking TOP uppermost.

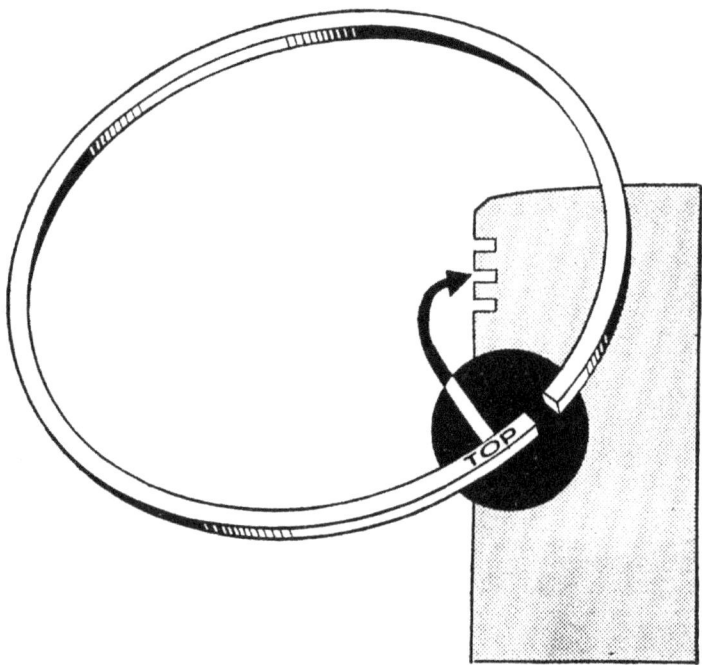

Fig. 14. Taper Faced Piston Ring Position.

VALVE PUSH RODS AND COVER TUBES

Push Rods. Examine the end cups for chips around the edge, slackness on the tube and general wear inside the cups. For any of these faults, the push rods must be renewed. Bent push rods can cause undue noise and loss of power, so before replacing them to the engine, examine each one for straightness by rolling them on a true surface which could show up any irregularity.

Cover Tubes. If oil leakage is to be avoided after an overhaul, always ensure that the ends are tight on the tubes and in no way damaged.

CRANKCASE UNIT

Main Bearing. Press out the timing and driving side main bearings and oil seal. This can be more easily accomplished by warming the crankcase. Wash thoroughly and dry out with compressed air if possible as this will tend to remove any small particles of foreign matter. Spin the outer race to test the bearing for roughness and then inspect the balls and track for signs of indentation or pitting. Finally, test the end float which should be negligible in a good bearing. Replace if any fault is shown.

Crankcase. Wash the crankcase halves and inspect all stud fixings for security and the casting for cracks or damage. Remember, if one half of the crankcase is damaged, a complete new crankcase must be purchased as these are machined in pairs. The camshaft bushes normally show very little signs of wear until a considerable mileage has been covered. To make a rough check, fit the camshaft into the bearing and ascertain the up and down movement. If it is desirable that the bushes are changed, proceed as in the following paragraph.

Camshaft Bushes. To remove the bushes in the timing side half, heat (100°C approx.) the crankcase around the bush housing when the bushes can be easily pressed out. While the case is still warm, press in the new bushes, ensuring that the oil hole is lined up with the drillway in the housing. The removal of the drive side bushes is a little more difficult and it is necessary to cut a thread in the bushes with a tap before heating the crankcase. When this is done, re-insert the tap and hold the square end in the vice when the crankcase can be gently tapped away with a hide hammer leaving the bush attached to the tap. Located behind the rear bush is the breather valve porting disc. Before replacing the new bush, ensure that this disc is correctly positioned on the locating peg.

If the temperature of the crankcase half has dropped, re-heat and then press in the new bushes. The phosphor bronze bushes are machined to size before pressing in, and only the smallest amount of metal need be removed when reaming. To ensure accurate alignment, the two halves should be bolted together before reaming.

Scavenge Pipe. Check this pipe for security and ensure that a perfect oil seal is made where it enters the crankcase in the pump position. Failure at this point would reduce oil scavenge to the minimum.

Servicing Crankcase

Refitting the Main Bearings. Make sure the main bearing housings are perfectly clean. Heat the crankcase to approximately 100°C. and press the bearings fully home. Press in the oil seal with the lip outwards.

Timing Cover. This cover houses a very important bush which seals the crankshaft oil supply. If this bush is worn, the pressure from the oil pump will be released directly into the timing cover, thus reducing the quantity and pressure of oil to the big ends. The bush should always be changed when overhauling the engine. Press out the old bush and press in the new bush. Ream in position. (New crankshaft end diameter $=0.622 - 0.623"$. Bush internal diameter $=0.6235 - 0.624"$). Reground crankshaft $=0.600 - 0.601"$. Bush internal diameter $=.6015 - .6020"$.

Timing Gears. Timing gear wear is negligible; the only part which will require changing after considerable mileage is the intermediate gear bush. To change, push out the old bush and insert the new. It may be necessary lightly to ream the bush to suit the spindle diameter. If the timing gears are noisy, it is futile to purchase an odd gear to overcome this fault. A far better plan is to consult your Triumph dealer who will be able to remedy this trouble by selective assembly of gears from his stocks.

Oil Pump. As previously stated under "Lubrication Maintenance", Page 23, only the oil pump block will show signs of wear after considerable mileage. When doing an engine overhaul however, completely dismantle the pump by removing the two plungers and the two body plugs when the non-return ball valves and springs will be released. Wash the pump body and examine the ball seatings; if these show signs of heavy indentation, pitting or wear to one side of the seat, they can be re-cut with a 45° cutter or drill suitably sharpened. Inspect the balls and springs and if in doubt about their condition, new ones should be fitted. When replacing the balls, they should be given a sharp tap onto their seatings to ensure a good seat. After assembling the pump, submerge the body in oil and operate the plungers. This will prime the pump and at the same time give some indication of its pumping ability.

Oil Release Valve and Indicator. The illustration, Fig. 5, indicates the construction of the valve and indicator and should be closely followed during the dismantling and assembly procedure. First remove the valve cap and indicator assembly by unscrewing from the main body when the piston valve can be withdrawn. To remove the indicator, grip the shaft nut and unscrew the shaft from it. Withdraw the shaft to release the springs and rubber sleeve. Carefully clean all parts and ensure that the piston valve works freely in the body. Do not tamper with the springs by stretching to increase the tension as the spring poundage is set to give the correct pressure. When replacing the indicator always fit a new sleeve, cut to length if necessary. Assemble in the following manner: Place indicator shaft into the cap and slide the new sleeve over the shaft followed by the main spring (large) and auxiliary spring (small) and finally screw on the shaft nut. Oil the piston valve and enter into the body, position the joint washer on the body and screw on the cap assembly. Later models have an "O" ring in the cap which can be changed after prising out the small steel cup.

Servicing Crankshaft

Crankshaft and Connecting Rod Assembly. The dismantling, overhaul and assembly of this unit is a job that is normally undertaken by the dealer, or at the works. If the owner wishes to carry out this work, he must have a certain amount of mechanical ability and a good workshop.

Dismantling.
Remove the three radial bolts securing the flywheel and slide the flywheel off the shaft, inverting it to clear the crank webs. Remove the plug in the right hand end of the shaft and take out the sludge trap tube for cleaning.

Inspection and Identification. Wash all parts thoroughly and examine the bearing surfaces.

	New	
Crank big-end journal size	1.6235"	(4.1237 cm.)
	1.6240"	(4.1250 cm.)
Connecting rod big-end size	1.6250"	(4.1275 cm.)
	1.6255"	(4.1288 cm.)
Connecting rod small end	0.6885"	(1.7488 cm.)
	0.6890"	(1.7501 cm.)
Gudgeon pin size	0.6882"	(1.7480 cm.)
	0.6885"	(1.7488 cm.)
Connecting rod side float	0.0290"	(0.737 mm.)
	0.0320"	(0.813 mm.)

Light score marks on the crank big-end journals can be carefully eased down with smooth emery but after this operation the parts must be carefully washed again. If the cranks are scored, the connecting rod big-end shells will also be scored and must be changed. These bearings are completely prefinished and under no circumstances may the bearings be scraped or the connecting rod joint faces filed. If the damage is beyond repair, service re-ground cranks and big-end shells can be obtained from a dealer in the following UNDERSIZES:—

Cranks	—0.010"—0.020"
Connecting rod big-end shells	—0.010"—0.020"

The small end bush wear can be detected by inserting the gudgeon pin into the bush. If in good condition the pin should be a smooth working fit in the bush, no rock being in evidence. To replace the bush, press out the old one and at the same time insert the new. Ensure that the oilways are aligned. When reaming the bush, care must be taken to ensure that the bore is parallel with the big-end.

The final examination is the fit of the main bearings on the crank timing and driving shafts. The bearings should be a tight push fit; a loose fitting bearing would tend to cause crankcase "rumble". Worn shafts may be built up with copper plating.

Servicing One-piece Crankshaft

TO ASSEMBLE THE CRANKSHAFT

Place the oil tube in the crankshaft with the larger end at the right hand side and the larger hole in the middle of the tube away from the centre of the shaft. Insert one of the flywheel bolts through the top hole until it engages with the tube. Fit the plug at the right side, fully tighten it and then peen metal into the screwdriver slots to secure it. Now remove the bolt. The flywheel should be heated to approximately 80°C. There is a punch mark on the right hand side of the flywheel and the flywheel should be placed over the shaft facing in the correct direction but inverted at first to clear the crank web. Turn the flywheel the right way up and slide it over the centre portion of the shaft so that the bolt holes are in alignment. Fit a new shakeproof washer to each bolt and start each bolt a few turns, tightening each alternately to a final torque loading of 330/350 lb. in.

If a new or re-ground crankshaft or flywheel has been fitted, the assembly must be re-balanced, using balance weights part number Z.120 (2 off per set) 595 grams each. Place the assembly on truly horizontal knife edges. Mark the lowest point with chalk and turn the assembly through 90°; if it returns to the same position drill at the chalk mark on the centre line of the flywheel with a $\frac{1}{2}$ in. diameter drill. Drill a little at a time and then test the effect, but do not drill deeper than $\frac{1}{2}$ in. If more drilling is required start a new hole $\frac{3}{4}$ in. between centres distant. When the balancing is complete the assembly should rest in any position and if disturbed should rest in the new position. Finally wash the assembly with paraffin or kerosene to remove all swarf and dirt.

TWO PIECE CRANKSHAFT (Earlier Models)

Dismantling. Grip the bottom end of the flywheel in the vice and carefully mark each rod so that they can be replaced in exactly the same position relative to the cranks and the connecting rod cap to the rod itself. Unscrew the two nuts securing each rod and remove the rods from the cranks. Replace the cap to the rods for the time being. Identify the cranks to the flywheel and then remove the six bolts and nuts, when the assembly can be parted. The inspection procedure and all measurements are exactly as detailed on page 51.

Assembly. Press the oil tube into the timing side crankshaft so that the cut-away engages with the spigot on the oil drillway plug. **The hole in the centre of the oil tube will now be pointing to the middle of the flywheel.** Offer up the crank complete with oil tube to the flywheel, which is best held by clamping a vice on to it at the balance weight portion. Offer up the drive side crank so that it passes over the oil tube and then fit six NEW high-tensile bolts and nuts. Secure the nuts when fully tightened by centre-punching the periphery of the bolt thread.

Servicing One-piece Crankshaft

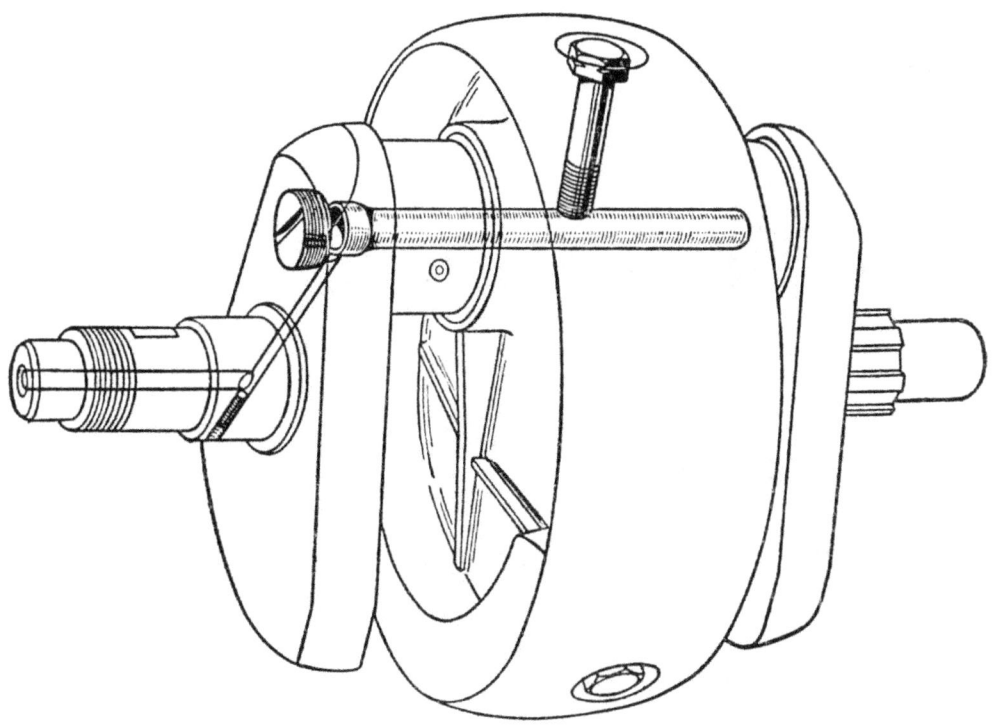

Fig. 15. ONE-PIECE CRANKSHAFT, SHOWING OIL TUBE.

Fitting Connecting Rods

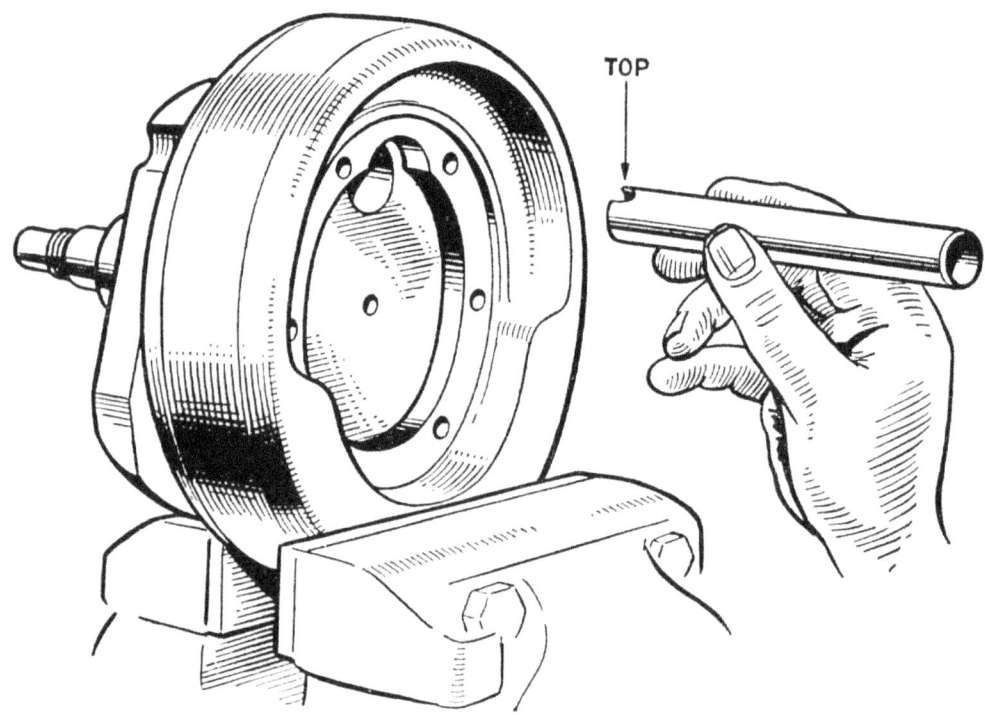

Fig. 16. TO ASSEMBLE THE TWO PIECE CRANKSHAFT

TO FIT THE CONNECTING RODS

Make sure the connecting rod, end cap and bearing shells are scrupulously clean. Fit one shell in the rod with the tab in the notch and the other shell in the cap. Make sure the journal is clean and oil it lightly. The rod, cap, bolt and nut are punch dotted so that the cap may be correctly fitted with reference to the rod, i.e. bearing tabs at the same side (see Fig. 17). Tighten the nuts evenly until the punch marks are in line. If replacement bolts are fitted, the correct tension is a torque loading of 320/330 lb. in. or a bolt stretch, measured with a micrometer, of .004-.005 in. (.102-.127 mm.). Apply the nozzle of an oil gun to the timing side oilway and pump oil until it passes both big-end bearings.

Fitting Connecting Rods

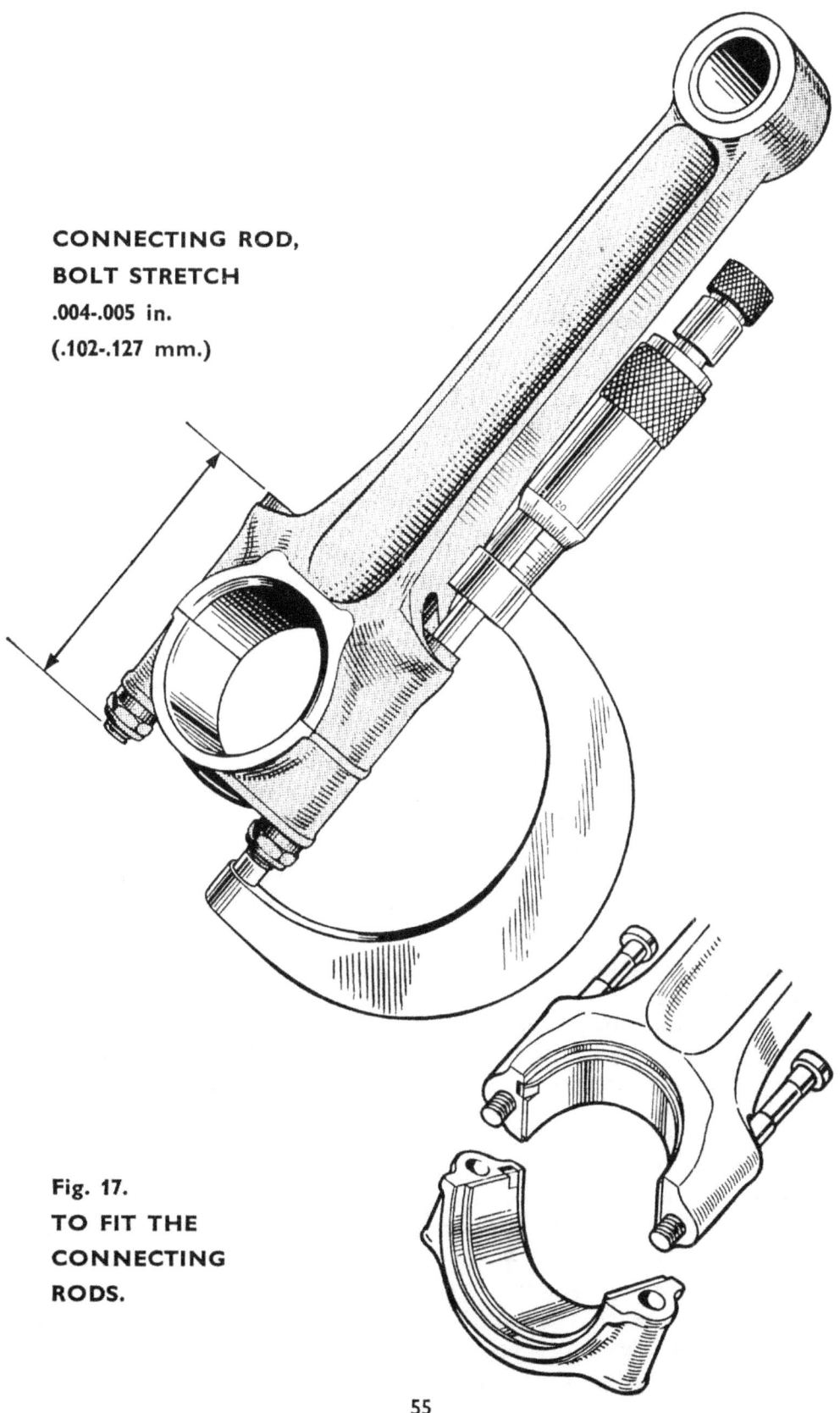

CONNECTING ROD, BOLT STRETCH
.004-.005 in.
(.102-.127 mm.)

**Fig. 17.
TO FIT THE CONNECTING RODS.**

ASSEMBLING THE ENGINE

Before commencing this operation, clean down the work bench and lay out the engine units and parts in assembly order. Also check the nuts, bolts and washers, etc., and have the gaskets and jointing compound available. When the engine is being erected, each working surface must be liberally oiled. This can be done with the use of a clean paint brush or an oil can. The operator should not rub on the oil with his fingers, otherwise a certain amount of grit, etc. may be picked up during the process.

Crankcase, Driving Side. Lubricate the main bearing and the camshaft bushes.

Crankshaft Assembly. Enter the driving side shaft into the ball-race in the drive side crankcase. Ensure that the shaft is fully located. (It is advantageous to allow the shaft to protrude vertically through a convenient hole in the bench and then the outer face of the drive side crankcase will take the weight on the flat surface of the bench).

Camshafts. The breather valve must be fitted in the inlet (rear) camshaft. On all models except the Bonneville 120 and TR6, the camshafts are identical; on these the inlet camshaft is Part No. E3134. First insert the spring and then the breather disc valve engaging the projections into the camshaft slots. Enter this assembly into the inlet (rear of engine) camshaft bush and test the engagement of the disc valve by depressing the camshaft. Insert the other camshaft into the exhaust (front of engine) camshaft bush.

Crankcase Timing Side. Lubricate the main bearing and camshaft bushes. Lightly smear jointing compound on the inner mating face, then thread this half over the crankshafts and camshafts. Bolt the two halves together, ensuring that these meet without undue force being applied. If any difficulty is encountered, suspect the breather disc in the inlet camshaft being out of position. To remedy, rotate the camshaft until the slot is engaged. Two internal screws are located in the crankcase just above the camshaft; be sure to replace these.

Aligning the Crankcase Halves. The top of the crankcase must present a perfectly flat face to the cylinder base. There must be no step between the halves. If a step is evident, a sharp tap on the stud boss nearest to the proud face with a hide hammer, will bring it flush. Do not strike the base face itself. When the two faces are properly mated, the bolts and screws should be fully tightened. Rotate the crankshaft to check for freedom of movement.

Sump Filter. Fit the filter with a new joint washer to the sump and over the scavenge pipe, then the cover with a joint washer. Replace the four washers and nuts but do not over-tighten, otherwise a broken stud may result, a trouble which can be well avoided at this stage.

Crankcase. Place the crankcase in the vice as in the dismantling procedure and pour into it an egg-cupful of engine oil (100 c.c.).

Replacing Camwheels

Crankshaft Pinion. Fit the plain washer and Woodruff key to the engine shaft and assemble the pinion (shoulder side to the engine) to the shaft. When the pinion is correctly positioned to the key it must be fully located by tapping it onto the shaft with a hollow punch. Do not fit the nut at this stage.

Camwheels. To fit these, special tool Z89, Fig. 10, must be employed. First assemble the keys to the camshafts, then screw on the centre tool (B). Slide the camwheel over the tool and engage the keyway onto the key. Screw onto the camwheel thread the outer tool (C), and onto (B), the left hand nut. Screw down the nut until it contacts the outer tool, then, to prevent the camshaft turning when the nut is screwed down, hold the end of the rod (B) with a suitable tool. When the camwheel is fully located remove the tool and then fit the opposite camwheel. Do not attempt to punch the camwheels onto the shafts, as the key will be brought into contact with the shaft bushes and may cause considerable damage.

If the operator cannot avail himself of the special tool, the camshafts and camwheels can be assembled before the two halves of the crankcase are fitted together. Fit the camshafts to the timing side crankshaft half and then support them, when the camwheels can be aligned to the keys and punched into position.

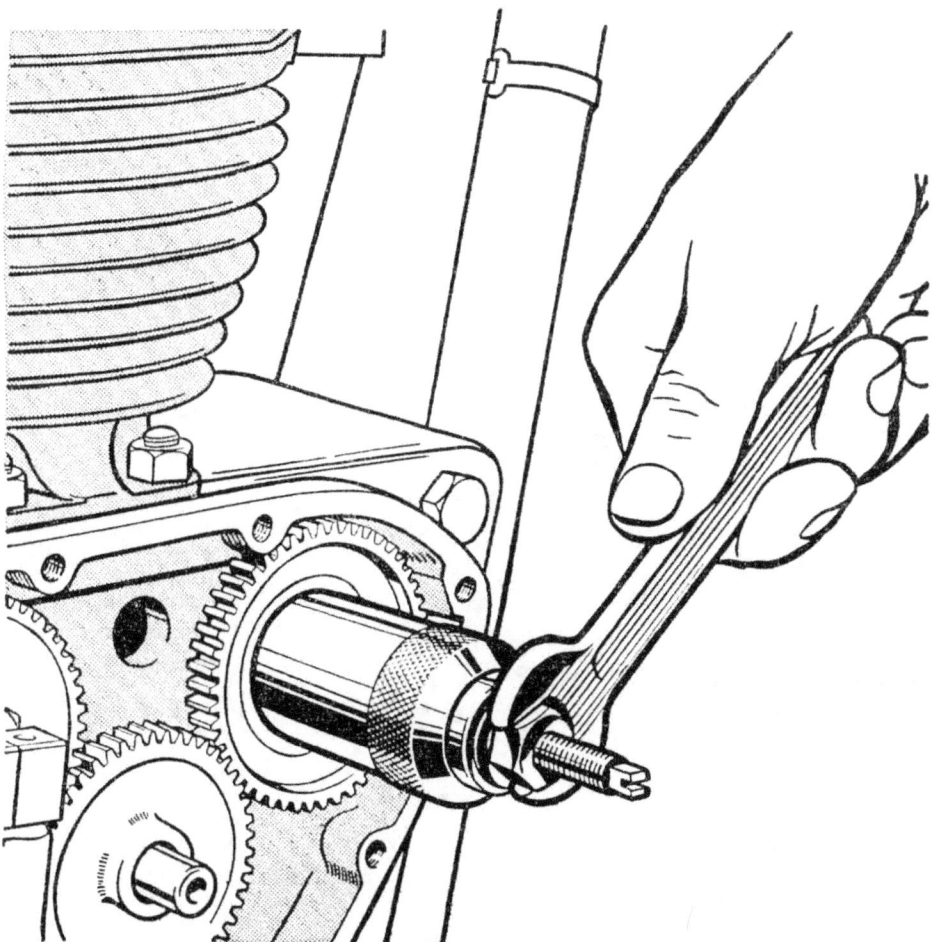

Fig. 18. REPLACING THE CAMWHEEL.

Timing Gear Markings

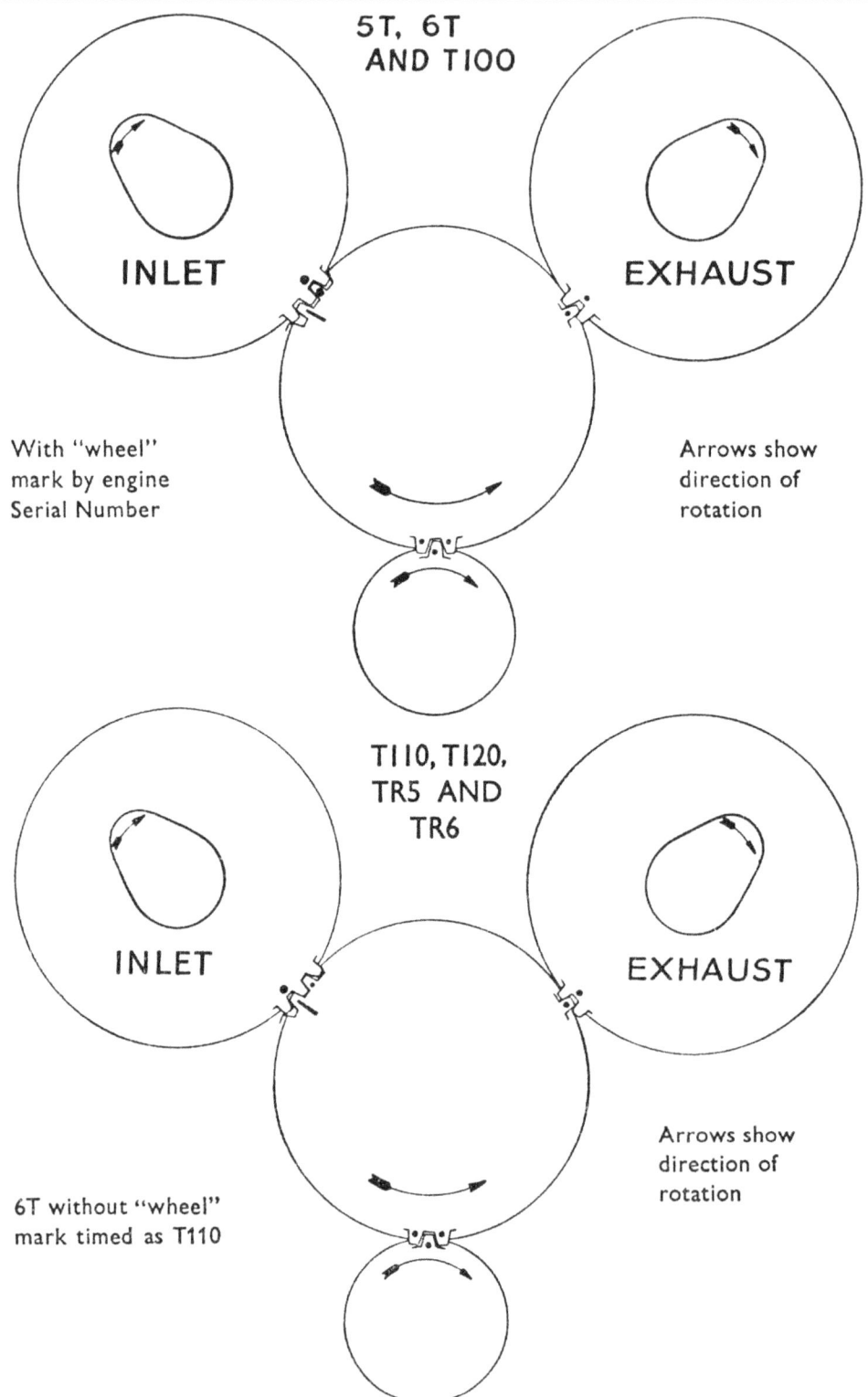

Fig. 19.
Position of Timing Pinion in relation to Camwheels and Crankshaft Pinion.

Timing Diagrams

Valve Timing. Assemble the intermediate wheel in the position shown on page 58 for your particular model.

Pinion and Camwheel Nuts. Replace the pinion nut (R.H.), followed by the exhaust camshaft nut (L.H.), and finally the inlet camshaft nut (L.H.), which has the eccentric drive peg for the oil pump. Ensure that these nuts are well secured.

Oil Pump. Prime the pump with oil and fit to the crankcase with a new joint washer. Ensure that the washer is positioned correctly and not covering any oilways.

Magneto. Assemble the magneto to the crankcase and secure with the three nuts.

Magneto Driving Gear. Fit the gear to the magneto shaft and loosely screw on the nut.

Distributor. See Ignition Timing, page 67.

Pistons. If replacing the old pistons, they must be fitted to their appropriate connecting rods. Lubricate the small end bushes and fit the pistons to the rods. Carefully insert the gudgeon pins until they abut against the circlips already in the piston boss. Now fit the two remaining circlips and ensure that they are in grooves. If in doubt regarding the serviceability of the circlips, always fit new ones, the cost of

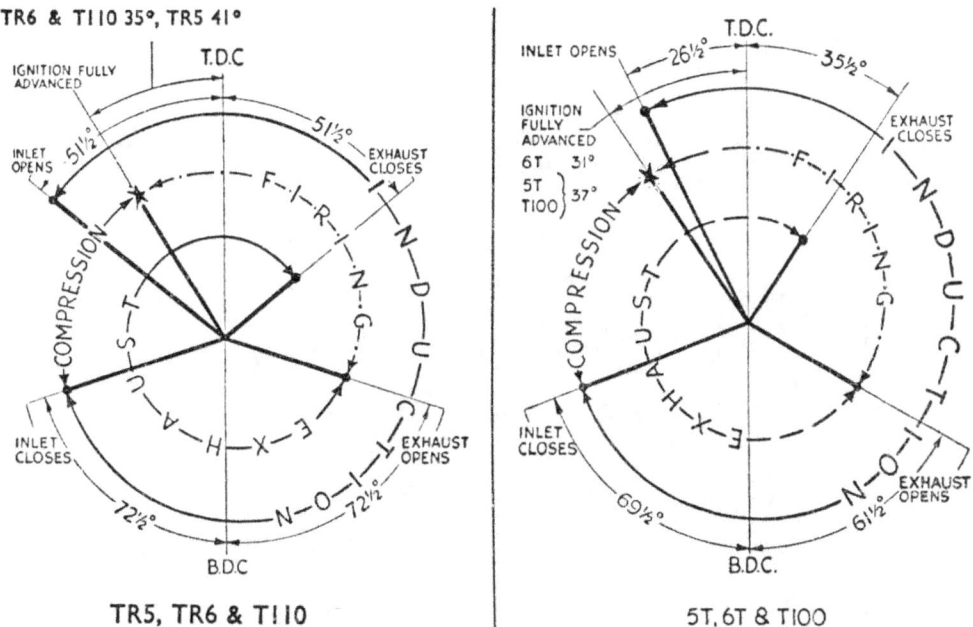

Fig. 20. **TIMING DIAGRAMS.**

See pages 6-13 and 176-179 for checking figures, including T120.

Fitting Cylinder Block

which is extremely small when compared with the damage which can result from a badly fitting circlip. Lubricate the piston rings and skirts and turn the ring so that the gaps do not coincide. Place the piston ring clip over the rings and allow the base of the pistons to rest on the forward top face of the crankcase (see Fig. 21).

Cylinder Block. Grease the cylinder block base washer and fit to the block. Lubricate the tappet blocks and assemble the tappets. Place a rubber wedge between the tappet stems to prevent them falling into the crankcase during assembly (see Fig. 21). Liberally oil the cylinder bores and then lower the block over the pistons until the piston rings enter the bores.

Support the block in one hand and turn the crankshaft with the other, forcing the piston up into the bores. As the pistons enter the bores, the piston ring clips will fall clear and can be withdrawn over the connecting rods. Guide the block over the base studs and then remove the wedges from the tappets. Fit the eight holding nuts and securely tighten.

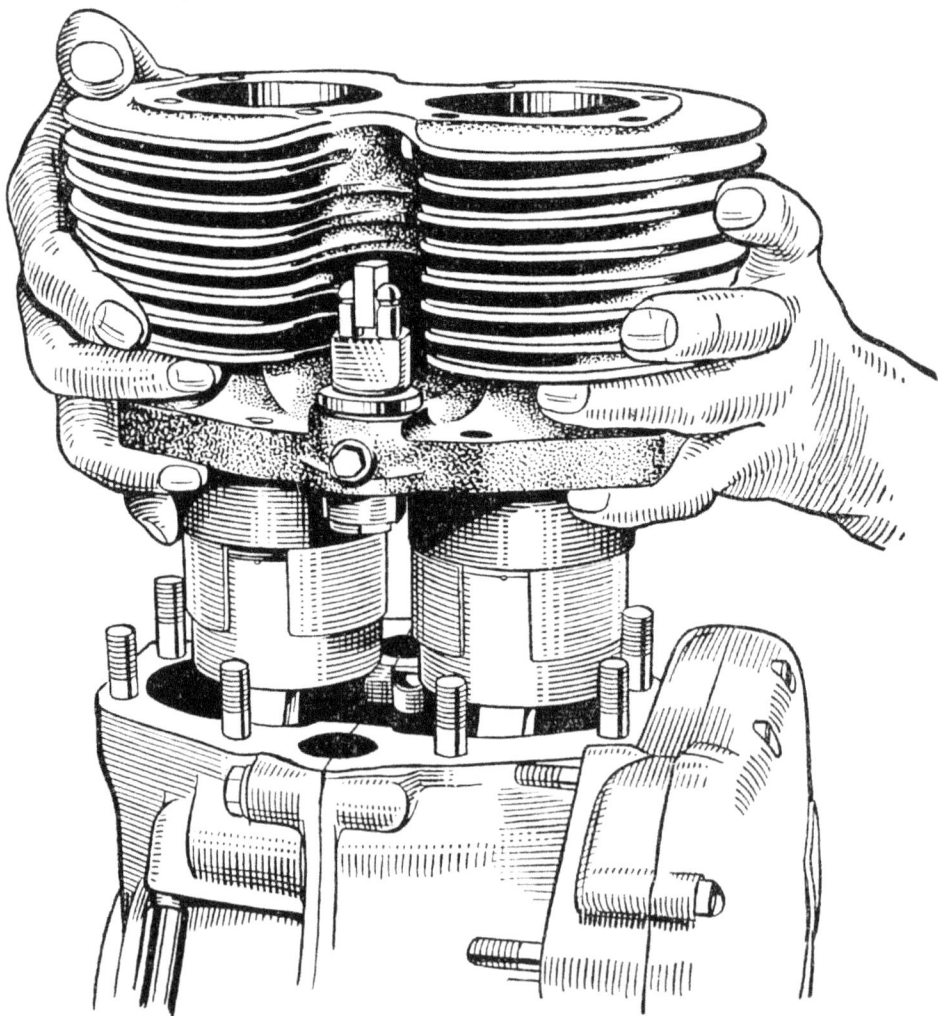

Fig. 21. FITTING THE CYLINDER BARREL.
(Note the rubber wedge holding the tappets).

Fitting Cylinder Block

Ignition Timing. The timing of the engine can be carried out at this stage if desired. The information given on page 67 (Magneto) and page 68 (Coil) applies when the cylinder head is fitted. The marked timing stick should be discarded in favour of a depth gauge, by which means an accurate measurement can be made directly on top of the piston.

RE-ASSEMBLY

First anneal the head gasket and copper washers by heating to cherry redness and plunging into cold water.

Inlet Manifold. Assemble the inlet manifold to the cylinder head with the new joint washers. In the case of the cast-iron cylinder head, we recommend the use of jointing compound with the joint washers. The reason for this is that as the manifold and cylinder head are manufactured from dissimilar metals, a slight amount of "weave" takes place between them which may cause the washer to become dislodged.

Push Rod Covers. Place in position with the new rubber washers. The locating discs must have the push rod holes across the machine.

Cylinder Head. Place the head on the block and screw the four outer bolts finger tight.

Inlet Rocker Box. Stick the gaskets to the rocker boxes with a smear of grease and fit new push rod cover washers. Place the inlet push rods on the tappets and turn the engine with the kickstarter until both tappets have dropped as low as possible. Hold the box above the head and insert the torque stay bolts singly while tilting the box. Lower the rocker box into position, making sure that the rocker ends engage with the push rods and screw down the bolts. Insert the two short bolts and FINALLY THE THREE NUTS (6T TWO NUTS).

Rocker Drain Pipes (6T). Fit the adaptors with annealed copper washers and tighten carefully.

Exhaust Rocker Box. Fit this in the same way as the inlet rocker box.

Cylinder Head Bolts. Tighten the cylinder head bolts diagonally, starting with the central four. The correct torque loading is 18 ft. lbs. The short rocker box bolts and nuts should also be tightened. Turn the engine with the kickstarter and watch each valve as it opens to check that the push rods are correctly fitted.

Ignition Timing. If the timing has been left until this stage is reached, reference should be made to page 67 (Magneto) and page 68 (Coil).

Timing Cover. Smear the joint face with jointing compound and assemble the cover to the crankcase. Employ a well fitting screwdriver when tightening the screws.

Oil Release Valve Indicator. Fit the joint washer and screw the assembly into the timing cover.

Tappet Adjustment. Adjust as described on page 34 and replace the four inspection caps.

INSTALLING THE ENGINE

Engine. When the engine has been prepared for installation, ensure that the rear lower stud is fitted in position with the nuts loosely assembled. Check that the footrest spindle is positioning the distance piece between the rear engine plates. Now lift the engine into the frame and engage the rear lower stud into the rear engine plates. A box placed under the engine will retain it in this position. When the stud is engaged, fit the remaining two studs and loosely assemble the nuts and washers.

Front Engine Plate. Insert the long stud which secures the crankcase to the frame tubes. Assemble the front engine plate with two studs to the crankcase and two nuts and bolts to the frame. Now tighten all the front and rear engine plate bolts and nuts. (6T and T110). Replace the front engine plate cover and tighten the securing screw.

Torque Stays. Replace the torque stays and tighten the fixings.

Right Footrest. Place the adaptor and footrest on the spindle.

Primary Chaincase, Alternator, Clutch and Engine Sprocket. Place the short distance piece on the footrest spindle and a new paper joint washer on the crankcase. Fit the inner chaincase and secure to the crankcase with three screws. Fit the engine sprocket, primary chain, clutch, alternator and outer chaincase as described on page 91.

Left Footrest. Make sure the dowels are in position between the chaincase and footrest, replace the footrest and tighten the spindle nuts.

Brake Pedal. Replace the brake pedal on the spindle and secure it with the spring washer, plain washer and nut. Connect the operating rod and secure it with a plain washer and split pin.

Carburetter. If the carburetter has been dismantled, complete the re-assembly and test the operation of the slide. On models with alloy cylinder heads, fit a new paper washer and the insulating block. On all models fit a new "O" ring seal in the groove in the carburetter body. Replace the carburetter and tighten the nuts alternately. Check the operation of the carburetter slide again, and if sticking now occurs suspect over-tightening of the nuts or distortion of the flange.

Control Cables. Connect the air or magneto control cables and test their operation.

Oil Pipes. Connect the oil pipe junction block to the engine. Replace the rocker feed pipe with annealed copper washers at the rocker spindles. REPLENISH THE OIL TANK.

Installing the Engine

Exhaust System. Fit the exhaust pipes and silencers to the machine and connect up all fixings before finally tightening.

Petrol Tank. Place the three small and one large rubber buffers in position and then fit the tank. Be careful that the tank does not trap the control cables or rocker feed pipe. Replace the rear cross bolt and tighten the front securing nut just sufficiently to hold the tank on the buffers. The strap must NOT be so tight that all movement is prevented. Connect the petrol pipes.

Testing. Start the engine and immediately check that the oil pressure indicator button is protruding. If it is not starting to protrude, stop the engine at once and then proceed to investigate the cause. Run for a short while and if necessary adjust the slow running settings on the carburetter.

NOTE

When the motorcycle has covered the first 250 miles after its overhaul, it is wise to check all nuts and bolts to ensure that they have not become loose due to the engine "bedding down".

TIMING THE ENGINE

VALVE TIMING

The camwheels, timing pinion and intermediate wheel which mesh together are suitably marked; when these marks coincide with each other, the valve timing is correct. Fig. 19 clearly illustrates the timing for the respective models. NOTE: When the engine crankshaft has been rotated the marks on the gears will not coincide due to the uneven number of gear teeth until the crankshaft has been turned a considerable number of times. The timing of course, is not affected.

MODELS FITTED WITH RACING CAMS E.3134

The marking on the camwheels may not be sufficiently accurate for timing the valve operation for racing purposes. It will be noted that the camwheel (E.1486R), has three keyways provided to enable the operator to obtain accuracy of plus or minus $2\frac{1}{2}$ degrees. An initial setting can be made by using the "dash" timing mark as shown in Fig. 19 for the T101 model.

The following valve timing instructions are given assuming that the engine has been fitted with racing cams and is now installed in the vice (Fig. 9, page 40) with the rocker boxes, timing gears and timing cover still to be fitted.

Exhaust Rocker Box. Assemble the exhaust rocker box and the timing side push rod to the cylinder head. Fit the holding bolts and nuts and tighten down.

Tappet Adjustment. Ensure that the tappet is on the base of the cam and then adjust the rocker pin to give 0.020in. (0.50 mm.) clearance between the pin and the valve tip. The most accurate method of determining the opening and closing points is to mount a Dial Test Indicator with the button resting on the top collar of the valve. Failing this, adjust the clearance to 0.025 in. (0.62 mm.) and use a 0.005 in. (0.12 mm.) feeler to gauge when the clearance has been taken up.

Checking T.D.C. Fit a degree timing disc to the drive side engine mainshaft and fix a pointer in any convenient location. Turn the crankshaft until the pistons are at T.D.C., then set the disc and pointer to read 0 degrees and clamp up firmly. To ensure that the pistons are at true T.D.C., turn the crankshaft backwards until the piston is say $1\frac{1}{2}$in. (4 cm.) down the stroke. Note the reading on the disc. Now turn the crankshaft forward until the pistons are again $1\frac{1}{2}$in. (4 cm.) down the stroke. The disc reading should be equal. If not correct, re-adjust the disc or pointer. Particular care should be exercised to ensure accurate T.D.C. setting.

EXHAUST CAMSHAFT TIMING

Setting the Crankshaft. Turn the crankshaft forward until the disc reading is 55 degrees before B.D.C.

Setting the Exhaust Camshaft. Rotate the camshaft "CLOCKWISE" until all play between the rocker adjuster pin and valve tip is taken up.

Timing the Engine

Fitting the Camwheel. First fit the intermediate wheel. It is now necessary to fit the camwheel to the shaft without disturbing it or the intermediate wheel. This is made possible by aligning one of the three keyways with the camshaft key and the teeth in line with the teeth on the intermediate wheel. When aligned, press on the camwheel (See Fig. 18), page 57.

Checking the Valve Closing. Turn the crankshaft backwards until the rocker adjuster clearance is nil, which should give the point of closing of the valve as 34 degrees after T.D.C.

It should be appreciated that due to tolerances in manufacture, wear, etc., it may not be possible to obtain the exact degree figures quoted. Points of opening and closing should be within 3 degrees either way, if the error is more, the camwheel must be extracted and one of the remaining two keyways tried. Do not forget to mark the keyway already tried with an indelible pencil to prevent it being accidentally tried again.

INLET CAMSHAFT TIMING

Repeat the exhaust procedure by fitting the inlet rocker box, timing side push rod and adjusting the clearance between rocker adjuster and valve to give 0.020in. (0.50 mm.).

Setting the Crankshaft. Turn the crankshaft backwards until the exhaust valve closes and the disc reading is 55 degrees after B.D.C.

Setting the Inlet Camshaft. Rotate the camshaft "ANTI-CLOCKWISE" until all play between the rocker adjuster pin and valve tip is taken up (valve closing).

Fitting the Camwheel. Assemble in the same manner as in the exhaust camshaft procedure.

Checking Valve Opening. Rotate the engine forward until there is no play between the rocker adjuster and valve tip when the point of opening should be approximately 34 degrees before T.D.C. (The exhaust valve is now open).

As a final check, the drive side cylinder push rods may be fitted and the timing of the drive side cylinder checked. If any discrepancy (up to 4 degrees) is found between the two cylinders, it should be equalised. To do this, it will be necessary to remove the camwheel and select another keyway. When the timing has been corrected, insert the new figures in the "Record Table" overleaf, thereby obviating this last operation for subsequent assemblies. Mark the camwheels to ensure correct re-assembly.

Timing the Engine

VALVE TIMING RECORD TABLE

.... INLET VALVE OPENS ... ... B.T.D.C.

.... INLET VALVE CLOSES ... ... A.B.D.C.

.... EXHAUST VALVE OPENS ... ... B.B.D.C.

.... EXHAUST VALVE CLOSES ... ... A.T.D.C.

TAPPETS SET AT 0.020 in. (0.50 mm.)

Remove the timing disc and pointer. Detach the rocker boxes and push rods for final assembly (See page 61).

TAPPET ADJUSTMENT

When the rocker boxes and push rods are finally assembled, RE-ADJUST THE TAPPET CLEARANCE TO :—

INLET ... ... 0.002 in. (0.05 mm.)

EXHAUST ... ... 0.004 in. (0.10 mm.)

IGNITION TIMING (RACING)

In order to ensure accuracy, a degree timing disc should be employed when timing the ignition for racing purposes. Fit the disc to the engine shaft and find the true T.D.C., then clip the pointer to indicate ZERO degrees. Set the magneto with the contact points just breaking and the cam ring in the fully advanced position ; turn the crankshaft to give the following readings on the compression stroke :

500 c.c. models ... ... 42° before T.D.C.

650 c.c. models ... ... 39° before T.D.C.

Accuracy of the ignition timing can be finally checked by running the engine at full throttle under load and moving the ignition lever slowly from the fully advanced position and noting the increase or decrease in R.P.M.

IGNITION TIMING (MAGNETO)

(Assuming that the magneto is in position and the timing cover is removed).

Magneto Wheel. Unscrew the securing nut and screw into the gear centre the withdrawal tool DA50/1 which is supplied with the toolkit. When the tool is in position, tighten the centre bolt and the gear will be withdrawn from the shaft. The automatic timing device is released by unscrewing the central bolt which has a self-extracting thread. Next, set the contact breaker points to .012 in. fully open.

Sparking Plugs. Remove both plugs.

Piston Positioning. Unscrew the rocker inspection caps. Engage TOP gear and then rotate the rear wheel in the correct direction for forward travel, watching the valve operation in the L.H. (DRIVE SIDE) cylinder. When the INLET valve closes, continue gently to rotate the rear wheel until the piston reaches the top of the stroke (This is known as "TOP DEAD CENTRE"—T.D.C.). The correct piston position can be felt with the timing stick by rocking the rear wheel to and fro. When the T.D.C. has been found, mark the lowest part of the timing stick which is visible at eye level and remove the stick; make a further mark (the correct distance for the particular model, see pages 6-13) above the first mark. Now re-insert the timing stick into the cylinder and rotate the rear wheel backwards until the piston has fallen about 1 in. (2.5 cm.), then reverse the rotation and slowly bring the piston up to the desired mark on the timing stick. This procedure eliminates any error due to backlash in the timing gears.

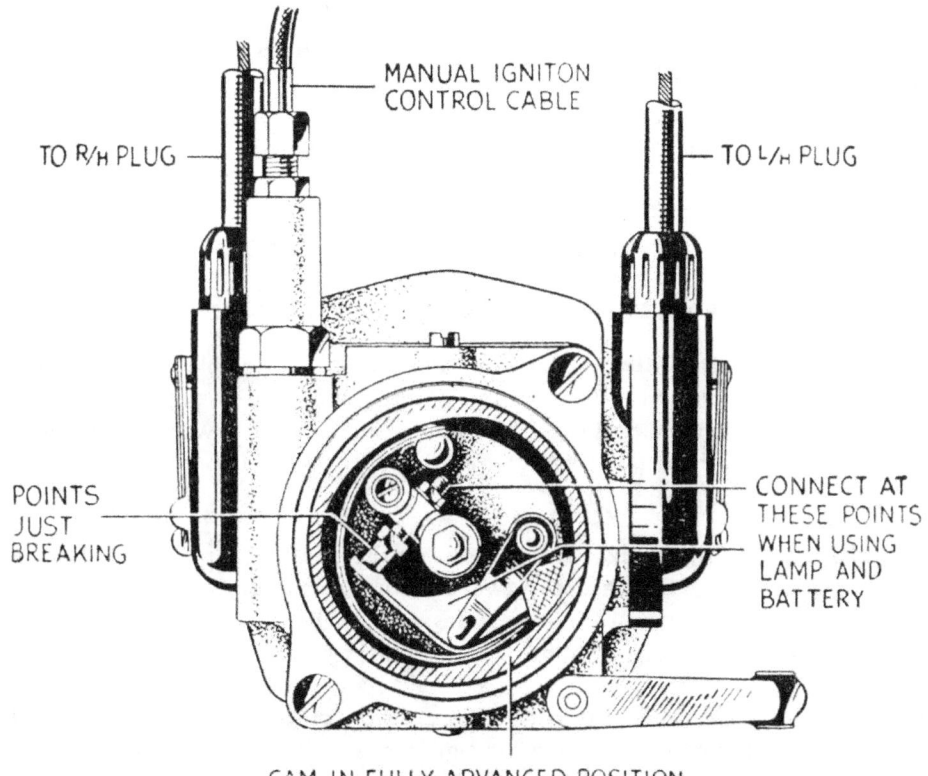

CAM IN FULLY ADVANCED POSITION

Fig. 22. MAGNETO IN TIMING POSITION.

Coil Ignition Timing

Positioning the Contact Breaker. Remove the contact breaker cover and advance the manual control lever on the handlebar (Close anti-clockwise to advance). Rotate the contact breaker until the points are in the upper position and just breaking (See Fig. 22). In order to ascertain accurately the exact point of opening, slip a 0.0015 in. (0.04 mm.) feeler gauge or a piece of tissue paper between the points. Rotate the contact breaker and the gauge will be released immediately the points start to open.
Another method of ascertaining the opening point is to connect a battery and lamp across the points as shown in Fig. 22, but the central bolt must be removed or insulated from the contact breaker body.

Magneto Gear. Carefully retain the contact breaker in the set position and fit the gear to the magneto shaft (ensure that the shaft and gear bore is free from oil). Tap the gear gently to engage the taper and fit and secure the washer and nut.

Automatic Timing Device. If this is fitted the procedure is the same, but the unit must be lightly wedged against the spring into the fully advanced position. The self-extracting centre nut should be screwed almost fully home and the unit may then be tapped home on the taper and the nut tightened securely.

Final Operation. Re-check the timing and if correct, replace the timing cover, contact breaker cover, sparking plugs, H.T. lead (See Fig. 22) and the four rocker inspection caps.

Sparking Plug Leads. If the timing operation has been carried out correctly, join the plug leads as follows:—
    The lead nearest the engine to the right cylinder.
    The opposite lead to the left cylinder.

IGNITION TIMING (COIL)

REPLACING THE DISTRIBUTOR AND DRIVING PINION

Replacing the Distributor, Adaptor and Coil. Assemble the distributor complete with the clamping lever to the adaptor and tighten the retaining bolt. Fit the adaptor to the crankcase with the clamping nut and bolt towards the crankcase and with the slotted head pointing downwards. Fit the lower retaining nut but do not tighten at this stage.

Clamp the coil onto the bracket and ensure that the two bolts are tight. Assemble the coil and bracket onto the upper two distributor adaptor studs and fit the remaining nuts. Tighten up all three retaining nuts. The distributor clamp nut and bolt should be loose enough to allow the distributor to rotate for final positioning.

Replacing the Distributor Drive. The position of the distributor should be adjusted to give the easiest position for timing the ignition, and subsequent maintenance. Rotate the distributor body until the contact breaker points are approximately at 11 o'clock when looking from the left hand of the machine. Tighten the

Distributor

lever clamping bolt in this position. If a long screwdriver is held against the slotted head of the clamping bolt from the underside of the engine, the nut can be tightened more easily. With R.H. cylinder (Timing Side) at T.D.C. on compression stroke (both valves closed) rotate the rotor arm clockwise until the contact breaker points are just beginning to open, when the rotor arm is pointing to the rear of the machine, Holding the rotor arm in this position, slide the thrust washer, followed by the drive pinion, onto the distributor shaft so that the hole in the pinion boss lines up with the hole in the distributor shaft. Mesh the pinion into the nearest position on the mating pinion and slide the locking pin through the wheel and shaft, retaining it in position by placing the circlip in the groove in the pinion boss. The distributor is now in the best position for final timing and adjustment of the contact breaker points.

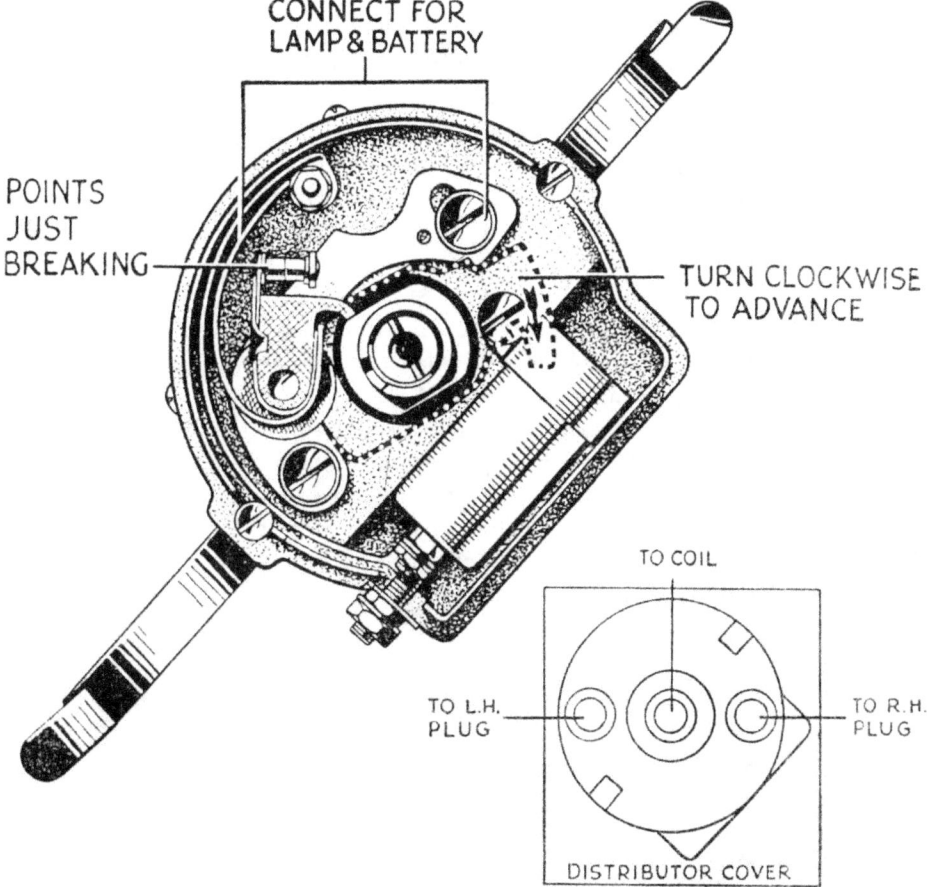

Fig. 23. DISTRIBUTOR IN TIMING POSITION.

Coil Ignition Timing

TIMING

Setting the Contact Breaker Points. Slacken the distributor clamp bolt and rotate the distributor slowly until the contact breaker heel is on the peak of the cam lobe, when the point should be separated. To adjust the points, slacken off the two screws securing the fixed contact plate and move the plate to give a 0.014-0.016 in. (0.36 mm.-0.40 mm.) gap between the contact points. Tighten up the screws and re-check the gap adjustment.

Piston Positioning. Unscrew the rocker inspection caps. Engage TOP gear and then rotate the rear wheel in the correct direction for forward travel, watching the valve operation in the right cylinder. When the INLET valve closes, continue gently to rotate the wheel until the piston reaches the top of the stroke (This is known as "TOP DEAD CENTRE"—T.D.C.). The correct piston position can be felt with the timing stick by rocking the rear wheel to and fro. When the true T.D.C. has been found, mark the lowest part of the timing stick which is visible at eye level and remove the stick; make a further mark $\frac{1}{32}$ in. (0.80 mm.) above the first mark. Now re-insert the timing stick into the cylinder and rotate the rear wheel backwards until the piston has fallen about $\frac{1}{4}$ in. (6 mm.), then reverse the rotation and slowly bring the piston up to the desired mark on the timing stick. This procedure eliminates any error due to backlash in the timing gears.

Correct Positioning of the Distributor. Switch on the ignition. Stand over the right hand side of the machine and place the left hand under the distributor, holding it in such a manner that it can be freely turned to the left or right. Now lean across the saddle or twinseat and rotate the distributor housing slightly (contact breaker points nearly vertical) until the points just open. This is shown by the ammeter, which will no longer show a discharge. Retaining the distributor in position tighten up the clamp bolt and make a further check. Finally check that the lever clamp bolt is fully tightened. A long screwdriver should be held against the slotted head of the clamping bolt from the underside of the engine to prevent it from rotation when the nut is being tightened.

Sparking Plug Leads. If the timing operation has been carried out correctly, join the plug leads as follows:—

    The lead nearest to the engine the left cylinder.
    The opposite lead to the right cylinder.

Distributor Protective Cover. Fit the P.V.C. sheet over the distributor with cut-away hole on the left of the engine. Fit the H.T. leads from the distributor cap into the cut-away.

GEARBOX WITH SLICKSHIFT

The gearbox employed has four speeds and is very robustly constructed. It will require very little attention, and, if its oil change intervals are strictly adhered to and the security of its clamping bolts occasionally checked, the life of the gearbox will be greatly prolonged.

For the rider who wishes to use his machine in one or more of the various competitions or for road racing, a set of gears can be made available to suit the particular conditions. To change from STANDARD to WIDE ratio, four gears are required, namely—mainshaft high, mainshaft second, layshaft high and layshaft second. The speedometer driven gears will also have to be changed to correct the speedometer to gearbox ratio. To fit CLOSE ratio gears a complete set is required and as no provision is made for the speedometer gears, a sealing plug is supplied. A tachometer driven off the cam gear is employed for the purpose of checking the engine revolutions when close ratio gears are fitted. On page 182 an "Engine Revolution" and "Gear Ratio" chart will be found which will assist the rider in choosing a suitable combination of gears.

Briefly, the gearbox operates in the following manner:

Gear selections are made by depressing or raising the pedal. The pedal is attached to the plunger quadrant which is spring loaded on either side of its axis. After the pedal has been operated, it will automatically return to the central position for the next selection. When the pedal is depressed the upper quadrant plunger moves under the guide plate, whereas the lower one, being released, connects with the gear operating quadrant which is geared to the camplate.

The camplate is rotated by the gear quadrant, the movement being arrested by a spring loaded plunger which is sprung into a notch in the camplate periphery. As the camplate rotates, the gear selector forks which are connected, move along their spindle and in turn shift the gears. Fig. 25 shows clearly all the working parts and before attempting to dismantle the gearbox, the illustration should be carefully studied.

The Slickshift gearchange mechanism automatically disengages the clutch when the gearchange pedal is operated. The principle of operation is illustrated in Fig. 24. A cam is connected to the pedal and whenever the pedal is operated either for an upward or downward gearchange, the cam contacts a roller attached to the clutch operating lever. The clutch lever is also connected by cable to a lever on the left handlebar and may be operated in the normal manner if desired. It is recommended that the Slickshift is used for gearchanging on the move and the handlebar lever used to make standing starts. It is suggested that the rider acquaints himself with the following paragraphs before using the Slickshift on the machine, as a few moments' study of the principles involved will be amply repaid. The Bonneville 120 is not fitted with Slickshift, although the gearbox is similar externally.

To Move Off. To secure a clean engagement of bottom gear, it is necessary that the controls should be adjusted so that the machine idles slowly and reliably. On models equipped with manual ignition control, the lever should be retarded for $\frac{3}{4}$ to $\frac{1}{2}$ of its travel. The handlebar lever gives a larger movement at the clutch than the foot pedal and should be used for selecting bottom gear and moving off.

Gearbox with Slickshift

To Change Gear Upwards. When the road speed is sufficient to change to the next higher gear, ease the throttle very slightly and simultaneously raise the pedal upwards to the limit of its travel and then allow it to return to the central position. Until the pedal is released the clutch is disengaged and no drive is transmitted. The technique is identical to that previously used by many riders when changing from third to top gear.

To Change Gear Downwards. When the road speed has fallen sufficiently to warrant a change to a lower gear, press the gearchange pedal downwards gently but firmly to the limit of its travel. Before allowing the pedal to return, slightly open the throttle to synchronise the engine speed with the road speed in the lower gear.

To Halt the Machine. It is possible to bring the machine to a halt in any gear, and then by use of the handlebar clutch lever to select neutral between first and second. However, with practice it is more convenient to change into bottom gear while the machine is still moving slowly and then into neutral just before the machine comes to a halt.

HINTS AND TIPS

The instructions on page 82 must be followed for the sequence of adjustment. If the cable adjustment is made before that at the operating arm, the clutch may remain partially disengaged and slipping and rapid wear of the friction material and operating mechanism will follow.

Riders with small feet and those who use their machines in heavy traffic with frequent gearchanging may prefer more pedal leverage. A heel-and-toe lever Part No. T1564 is available, which will fit all Triumph twin gearboxes. With this upward gear changes can be made by pressing down the rear half of the lever with the heel. To secure a clean engagement of bottom gear after the machine has been parked, depress the kickstarter pedal to free the clutch before starting the engine.

FAULTY GEAR SELECTION

A badly adjusted clutch is one of the chief causes of faulty gear selection. Always ensure that the clutch plates spin true and that the correct grade of oil is employed (See page 180 for further information).

Footchange pedal springs may be fatigued or broken, thus preventing the pedal from centralising itself. Remedy—change both springs.

Quadrant Plunger Sticking. To remedy, remove the plunger and polish the bearing surface with smooth emery until the plunger will move freely in its housing. It is a good plan to renew the plunger springs if this fault occurs.

Camplate Plunger Sticking. To remedy, remove the domed nut from the bottom of the gearbox casing and apply the same remedy as for Quadrant Plungers.

Slackness of the nuts securing the kickstarter assembly or clutch centre. As both these parts are attached to the gearbox mainshaft, either becoming loose would allow the mainshaft to float and cause a faulty gear selection. Remedy—obvious.

Gearbox with Slickshift

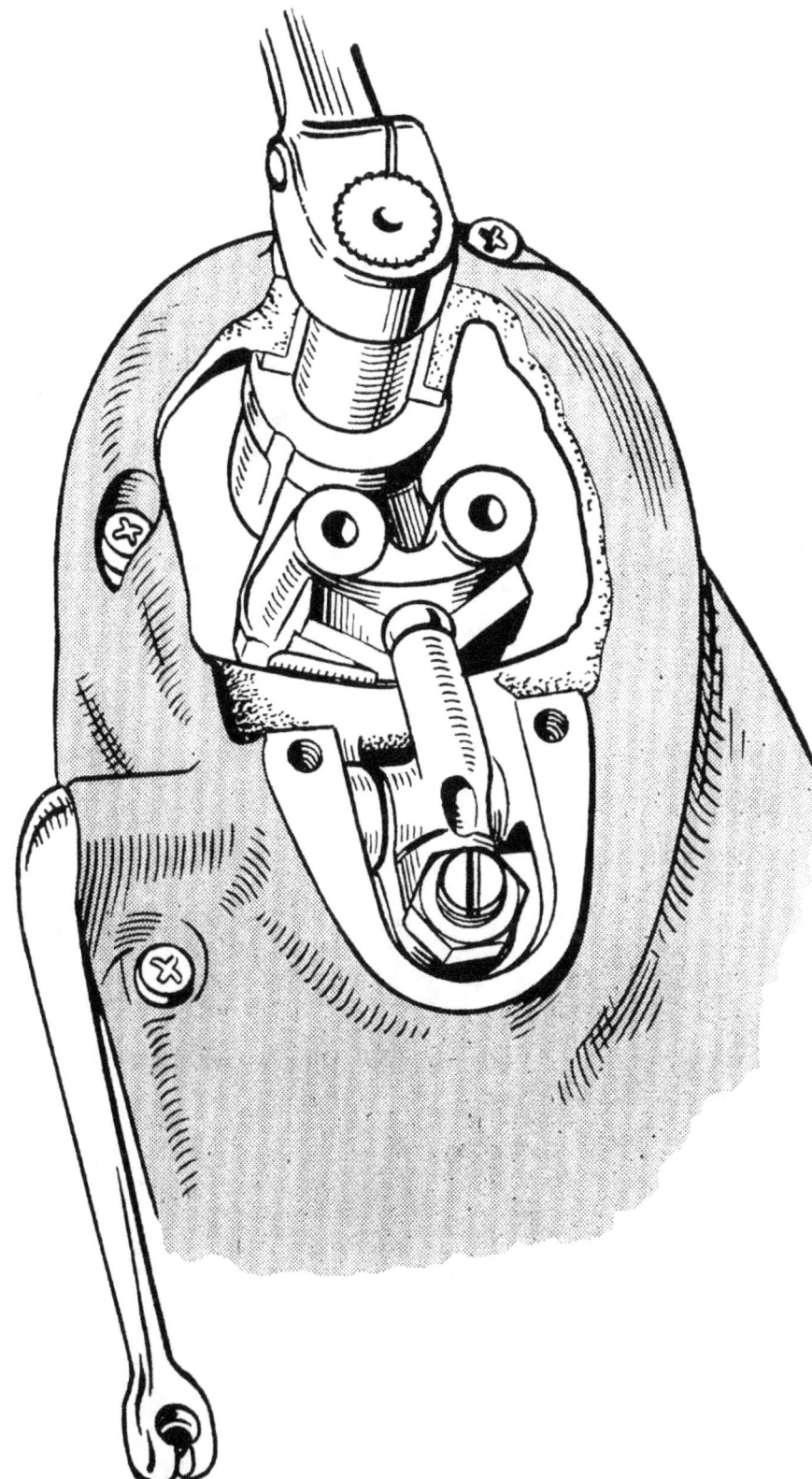

Fig. 24. SLICKSHIFT GEARCHANGE MECHANISM.

Gearbox

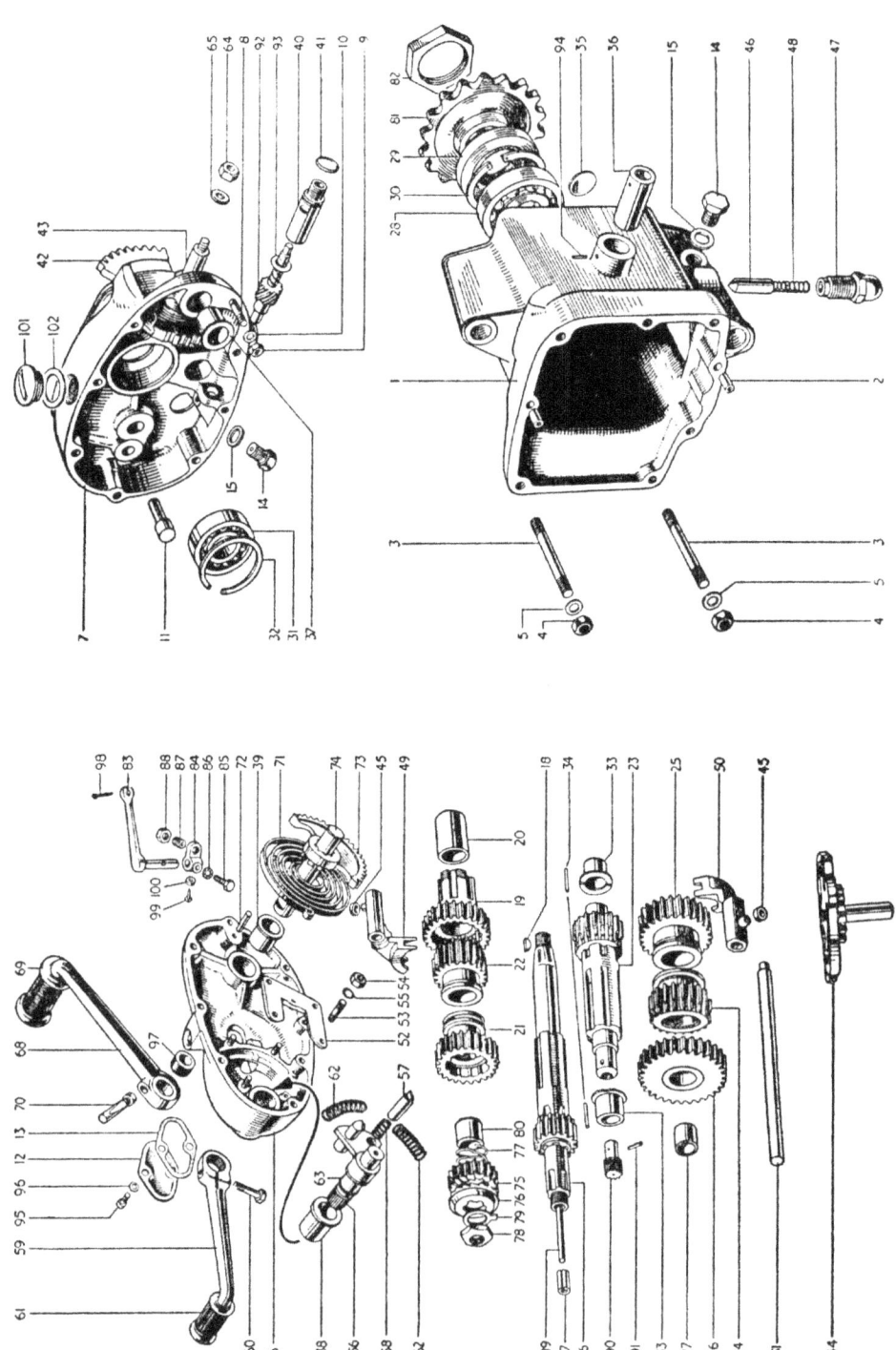

Fig. 25. GEARBOX (COMPONENT PARTS).

INDEX TO FIG. 25. GEARBOX (COMPONENT PARTS).

Index No.	Description.	Index No.	Description.
1	Casing.	51	Rod, selector forks.
2	Dowel.	52	Plate, plunger guide.
3	Stud.	53	Stud.
4	Nut.	54	Nut.
5	Washer.	55	Washer.
6	Cover, outer.	56	Quadrant, gearchange.
7	Cover, inner.	57	Plunger, gearchange.
8	Stud.	58	Spring.
9	Nut.	59	Pedal, gearchange.
10	Washer.	60	Bolt.
11	Stop, kickstarter.	61	Rubber, gearchange.
12	Cover, inspection.	62	Spring, pedal return.
13	Joint washer.	63	"O" ring.
14	Plug, level and drain.	64	Nut.
15	Washer.	65	Washer.
16	Mainshaft.	68	Crank, kickstarter,
17	Bush.	69	Rubber, kickstarter.
18	Key.	70	Cotter, kickstarter.
19	High gear.	71	Spring, kickstarter return.
20	Bush.	72	Peg, spring anchor.
21	Third gear.	73	Quadrant, kickstarter.
22	Second gear.	74	Axle, kickstarter.
23	Layshaft.	75	Pinion.
24	Third gear.	76	Ratchet.
25	Second gear.	77	Spring, ratchet.
26	Bottom gear.	78	Nut.
27	Bush.	79	Tab washer.
28	Bearing.	80	Sleeve.
29	Oil seal.	81	Sprocket.
30	Circlip.	82	Nut.
31	Bearing.	83	Lever, clutch operating.
32	Circlip.	84	Arm, clutch operating.
33	Bush, layshaft.	85	Peg, arm to lever.
34	Peg.	86	Washer, serrated.
35	Blanking disc.	87	Adjuster, clutch rod.
36	Bush, camplate.	88	Nut, adjuster, locking.
37	Bush, gearchange spindle.	89	Rod, clutch operating.
38	Bush, gearchange spindle.	90	Pinion, speedometer drive.
39	Bush, kickstarter.	91	Peg.
40	Bush, speedometer.	92	Gear, speedometer drive.
41	Sealing ring.	93	Thrust washer.
42	Quadrant, selector.	94	Peg, camplate bush.
43	Spindle.	95	Screw.
44	Camplate.	96	Washer.
45	Roller.	97	Rubber, kickstarter spindle.
46	Plunger, indexing.	98	Split pin.
47	Domed nut.	99	Peg, roller to arm.
48	Spring.	100	Roller, clutch operating.
49	Selector fork, mainshaft.	101	Filler plug.
50	Selector fork, layshaft.	102	Joint washer.

REMOVING THE GEARBOX FROM THE FRAME

Exhaust System. Remove both exhaust pipe and silencer assemblies by slackening the finned clip bolts, the bracket to frame bolts and the silencer bolts when assembly can be eased off the exhaust stubs.

Footrests. Remove the left footrest, withdraw the right footrest and spindle as an assembly. Take care not to lose the distance piece between the primary chaincase and the left rear engine plate and the distance piece between the engine plates.

Footbrake Pedal. Take out the split pin securing the operating rod to pedal, unscrew the pedal spindle nut, when the pedal can be withdrawn.

Primary Chaincase, Clutch and Engine Sprocket. Remove these parts as described on page 84.

Clutch Cable. Disconnect the cable nipple at the gearbox end and detach the cable.

Speedometer Cable. Unscrew the attachment nut at the gearbox, when the cable can be withdrawn.

Rear Panels (6T and T110). Remove as detailed on page 16.

Oil Tank. Disconnect the oil pipe block at the engine and plug the feed hole in the block to prevent loss of oil. Remove the oil tank's three fixings and withdraw the oil tank from the frame.

Battery Carrier to Engine Plate Bolt. Remove.

Rear Engine Plate Studs. Slacken the nuts on the front lower studs and remove all other nuts from the right hand engine plate. (The gearbox adjuster can be left in position). Remove the studs by drifting with an aluminium rod. Remove the cover plate, slacken the pivot bolt and ease the gearbox back, when both plates can be removed.

Pivot Bolt. Remove the nut and withdraw the pivot bolt. The gearbox can now be taken out of the frame.

Dismantling the Gearbox. Before attempting to dismantle the gearbox, wash it thoroughly to remove dirt, oil and grease, etc. Drain the oil by removing the plug in the front of the casing. Place the gearbox in the vice, with the pivot lug gripped between the jaws.

Gearbox Outer Cover. Unscrew the five screws and three nuts holding the outer cover to the inner cover and tap the joint gently with a hide hammer to break the jointing compound seal. Grip the gearchange lever and kickstarter crank and withdraw the cover from the gearbox.

Gearbox Inner Cover. Bend back the tab on the kickstarter ratchet and pinion lockwasher and, placing a block between the gearbox sprocket and the vice to prevent the sprocket revolving, undo the securing nut. Withdraw the ratchet and pinion assembly complete. Remove the four screws securing the inner cover to the shell. Tap to break the joint seal and remove the cover. Care should be taken to prevent the contents of the gearbox from coming away with the inner cover.

Gear Cluster. Remove the gear selector fork rod. Slide the mainshaft from the case until the clutch end comes free from the high gear. Taking care not to lose the rollers from the selector forks, remove the gear clusters from the gearbox in one assembly. The only gear remaining is the high gear which is held in position by the sprocket nut (See page 79).

The gearbox is now completely broken down into units and it is proposed to deal with these units separately in such a way that the fitter can dismantle, overhaul and re-assemble the major unit assemblies.

By doing the work in this manner the assembly of the gearbox is simplified in that there is no sub-assembly to bother about while concentrating on the correct assembly of the complete unit.

DISMANTLING, PREPARATION AND ASSEMBLY OF UNITS

GEARBOX OUTER COVER

Kickstart Assembly. Remove the kickstarter crank cotter pin and slide the pedal off the shaft. Withdraw the quadrant and spring assembly from the bush. Check the quadrant for chipped teeth and spindle wear, and the spring for fatigue cracks especially at the centre. Change if necessary. Replace the assembly in exactly the opposite way, making sure that the centre of the spring re-engages with the same spline on the quadrant spindle shaft (See Fig. 26, page 78).

Replace the shaft and quadrant assembly in the outer cover and place the rubber sealing tube over the shaft on the outside of the cover. Wind back the shaft one turn to pre-load the spring and insert the cotter with the threaded end towards the front of the machine.

Clutch Operation Mechanism. The internal arm is secured to the clutch operating lever by a peg screw, which has a shakeproof washer beneath the head. The roller on the forward end of the arm engages with the cam on the gearchange quadrant and the roller must turn freely. If it is desired to dispense with Slickshift for special purposes such as competition use, this may be done by removing the roller. The ball in the adjuster screw should be free to turn and undamaged. N.B.—The clutch operating rod used with the Slickshift is shorter than previously used and is chamfered at the adjuster end.

Dismantling Gearbox

Gearchange Mechanism. Provided that this mechanism has been working satisfactorily, there is no need to disturb it. If, however, it should become necessary, release the quadrant plungers and springs by raising and depressing the gearchange pedal. Remove the four nuts on the guide plate and slide the plate off the studs.

Slacken the gearchange pedal set screw and slide the pedal off the splined shaft. Withdraw the plunger quadrant from its bush. The cam track on the plunger quadrant must be smooth and free from indentations. The gear selector plungers should move freely in the quadrant and if rusty, they may be lightly polished with fine emery cloth. A rubber "O" ring seal is fitted in an annular groove in the gearchange shaft and since the cost is very small it is advisable to renew it whenever the gearbox is dismantled. Replace the springs if they have become rusty due to condensation, examine the guide plate for wear and relieve any high spots with fine emery cloth.

Replace the guide plate if the knife edges are worn. If it is necessary to remove any of the bushes, the casing should be heated before they are pressed out. Reassemble the mechanism in the opposite way to dismantling.

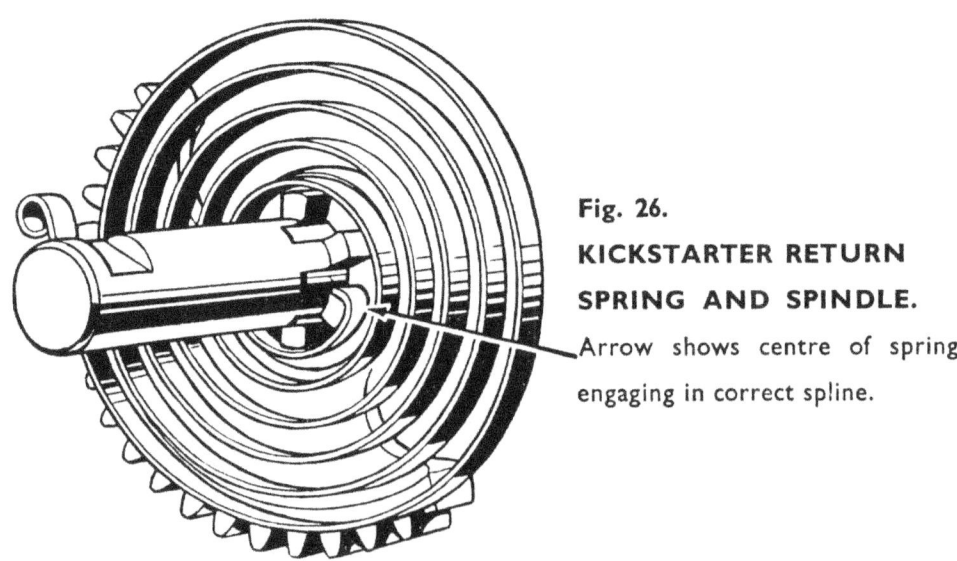

Fig. 26.
KICKSTARTER RETURN SPRING AND SPINDLE.
Arrow shows centre of spring engaging in correct spline.

GEARBOX INNER COVER

Gear Operating Quadrant. This quadrant can be inspected for wear on the teeth while still in position. The freedom of the spindle can also be checked. It is, therefore, unnecessary to remove the quadrant unless it requires changing. To do this, remove the split pin or pins and withdraw the spindle. Replace in the opposite way, using new split pins.

Bearing. Remove the retaining circlip and press the bearing out; thoroughly degrease it and dry with compressed air if possible. Check for roughess, pitting, indentation and end float; make sure that the inner race is a tight push fit on the mainshaft. When replacing, heat the casing and then press the bearing into position. Re-fit the circlip, ensuring correct engagement in the groove. Liberally oil the bearing.

Speedometer Drive. Using a soft metal drift against the spindle gear, gently tap the drive gear and bush out of its housing. Examine the gear for worn teeth and check the fit in the bush. To replace, fit the thrust washer over the gear spindle and thread the spindle into the bush. Fit the assembly into the cover, gear first. Fit the oil seal into the annular groove in the bush and press the bush into position until the keyway in the bush lines up with the screw hole.

Kickstarter Ratchet and Pinion. This assembly has already been removed to take off the inner cover. The pinion and ratchet should be checked for chipped or broken teeth and the spring for fatigue. Replace after the inner cover is back in place.

GEAR CLUSTER

Gears. Examine all the gears thoroughly for chipped, fractured or worn teeth. Check the internal splines and bushes, making sure that the splines are free on their respective shafts, with no tendency to bind, and the bush in the layshaft low gear is not worn.

GEARBOX CASING

Camplate and Plunger Assembly. Unscrew the acorn nut at the base of the main casing and withdraw the camplate plunger and spring. Remove the camplate from the bush. Make sure that the plunger works freely in its housing. Check the spring for fatigue. Examine the camplate carefully for signs of wear in the roller tracks as such wear will make gear selection difficult and damage to the gears may result. Change the camplate if a worn track is evident. To replace, fit the camplate spindle into the bush and screw the plunger assembly (pointed end engaging the camplate) into the plunger housing. Secure the camplate in the TOP (4th) gear position (see Fig. 27).

Chain Sprocket. Place a small aluminium block between a sprocket tooth and the vice, to stop the sprocket rotating, and unscrew the sprocket nut. It may be necessary to tap the end of the spanner with a hammer to free the nut. Ease away the sprocket.

High Gear, Oil Seal and Mainshaft and Layshaft Bearings. Remove the two long casing to outer cover studs and the two dowels, casing to inner cover and press the high gear out and into the casing. Ease the oil seal from the housing and discard.

Assembling Gearbox

Test the condition of the layshaft bush by using the end of the layshaft as a gauge. There should be no perceptible vertical play. Check the condition of the blanking disc for possible leakage. To renew the bush, knock out the blanking disc and press the bush into the casing. Align the cutaway on the new bush with the peg on the casing and press it into position. Support the bush and smear the rim of the blanking disc with jointing compound. Insert the disc and seal it by striking it with a flat ended drift.

Test the mainshaft high gear bush for wear by using the mainshaft as a gauge. If the bush is worn, press it out and press in the new one with the oil flinger groove on the inner end.

Remove the bearing retaining circlip and press the bearing out of the housing. Check the gear for chipped or worn teeth and the shaft bearing for wear. Thoroughly clean and degrease the journal bearing and dry with air. Check for roughness, pitting, indentation and float, make sure that the mainshaft high gear is a good fit in the inner race. When replacing, first warm the casing and then press the bearing into the housing, securing it with a circlip. Lubricate with oil when in position. Press a new seal into the housing with the part number on the outside and the leather "rolling" towards the inside of the case. Insert the high gear from inside the housing, through the bearing, and press it fully home.

Replacing the Chain Sprocket and Nut. Support the high gear from inside the casing and press the sprocket on to the high gear splines. Secure the casing in the vice and with a block between the sprocket and teeth and the vice, tighten the locknut to the sprocket. Centre punch the nut into the splines in two or three places.

ASSEMBLING THE GEARBOX

Secure the gearbox casing in a vertical position with the open end facing upwards (see Fig. 27). Slide the mainshaft third gear over the mainshaft, followed by the mainshaft second gear, with their selector grooves towards the centre. Grease the camplate roller and fit on to the smaller selector fork peg. Position the smaller selector fork in the second and third gear grooves with the shaft of the selector fork below the mainshaft and the roller towards the clutch end of the casing. Lower the assembly into the case. When the gear cluster is correctly located, turn the selector fork until the camplate roller rests in the selector camplate track. Withdraw the mainshaft slowly, leaving the second and third gears and selector fork in position to assist the assembly of the layshaft gears.

Assembling Gearbox

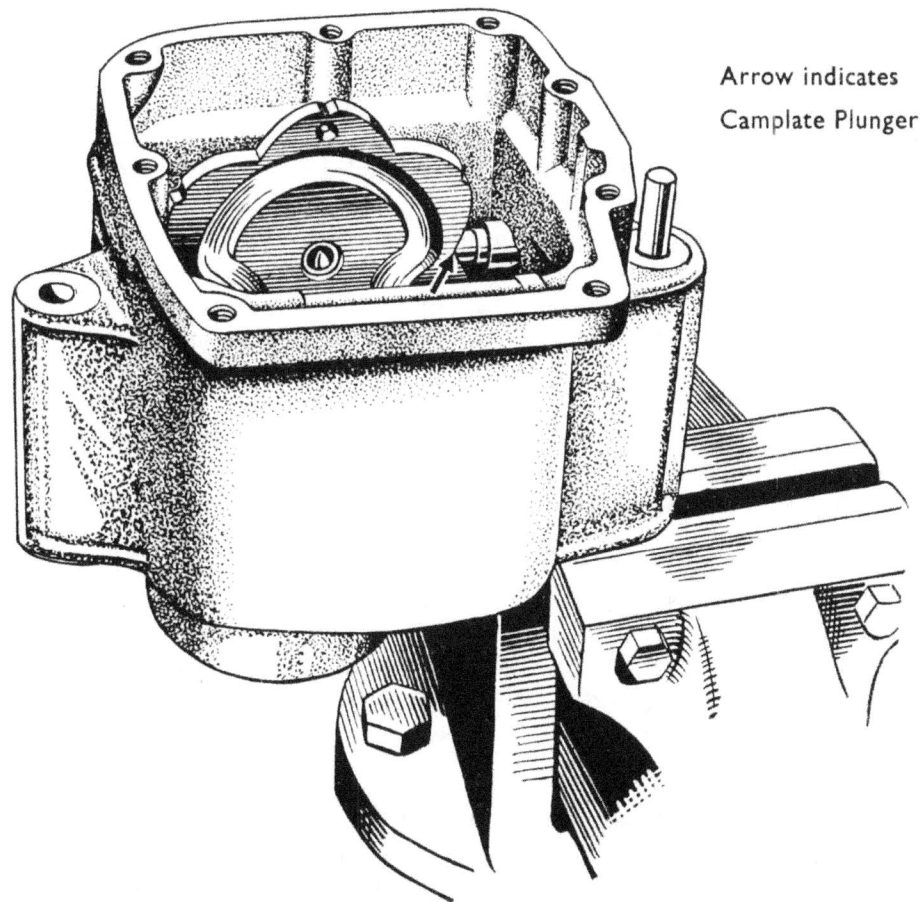

Arrow indicates Camplate Plunger

Fig. 27. GEARBOX CASING IN VICE.
Showing the Camplate in the top (4th) gear position.

Layshaft Gears. Assemble the third and second gear with the selector fork grooves facing inwards to the layshaft and high gear. Apply grease to the roller and fit to the larger selector fork peg. Fit the larger selector fork into the grooves, with the shaft of the selector above the layshaft and the camplate roller towards the open end of the gearbox. Lubricate the layshaft bush and lightly smear the shaft with oil. Install the thrust washer if the box is fitted with needle roller layshaft bearings. Lower the layshaft assembly into the gearbox, small gear first, until the camplate roller can be engaged on the camplate track. Oil the selector rod and thread it very carefully through the selector forks, shoulder end first, and engage it in the locating hole in the clutch end of the casing. Oil the mainshaft and thread it through the mainshaft gears. Place the layshaft low gear over the layshaft end with the internal teeth facing inwards. Place a straight edge over the gearbox end and test the clearance between the running face of the layshaft low gear and the outer face of the inner casing. Minimum allowable clearance is 0.005 in. (0.13 mm.) If the clearance is less than specified, the layshaft bush cannot have been fully located, or, if it has, the face of the bush must be cleaned up. Remember that a layshaft seizure means a locked rear wheel. Fit the second thrust washer to a needle roller box.

Installing Gearbox

Gearbox Inner Cover. Fit the hollow dowels and long casing studs to the casing and lightly smear jointing compound onto the cover inner face. With the selector quadrant held in the high (4th) gear position, assemble the inner cover to the casing. Tighten the casing screws ; do not omit the screw adjacent to the selector quadrant inside the cover. The action of the selector assembly can be checked if the quadrant is operated by a screwdriver and the high gear and mainshaft are rotated at the same time. With the selector in high gear, fit the kickstarter ratchet and pinion assembly onto the mainshaft in the following order : plain washer, sleeve, spring, pinion with ratchet face facing outwards, ratchet, lockwasher and nut. Lock the gears by placing a block between the chain sprocket and the vice and tighten up the ratchet nut. Bend the locking washer tab over when the nut is tight.

Gearbox Outer Cover. Smear jointing compound onto the face of the inner cover. Grasp the gearchange pedal in one hand and the kickstarter lever in the other. Wind the kickstarter pedal anti-clockwise to prevent the quadrant fouling the stop on the inner cover, when the outer cover is slid into position. Fit and tighten up the nuts and screws. Test the action of the kickstarter pedal, making sure that there is sufficient tension in the spring to return the pedal smartly and that it is not becoming "coil bound" when the pedal is depressed fully. Check that the gear selection is correct. Re-fill with $\frac{2}{3}$ pint (400 c.c.) of S.A.E. 50 grade oil. Do not use multi-grade oil. Screw the level plug into the hole and replace the filler cap.

ADJUSTMENT

Fit the outer cover but do not connect the clutch cable. The clutch pressure plate should first be trued as described on page 91. Slacken the locking nut on the adjuster screw and turn the adjuster until there is $\frac{1}{16}$ in. (1.5 mm.) free movement at the end of the clutch operating lever. Tighten the lock nut and only then fit the clutch cable and use the adjuster at the handlebar lever to obtain a total of $\frac{1}{8}$ in. (3 mm.) free movement in the cable. Secure the cable to the operating lever with $\frac{1}{8}$ in. (3 mm.) diam. split pin.

INSTALLING THE GEARBOX

Frame (Earlier Models). Ensure that the link securing the centre stand spring is correctly positioned in the frame lug.

Pivot Bolt. Fit the gearbox into the frame and insert the pivot bolt from the left.

Rear Engine Plates. Re-position to engine and frame (plate with adjuster fitted on the right). Fit the plate cover and then enter the studs (nut fitted at one end) from the left side. Do not omit the footrest spindle and lower rear stud distance pieces. Fit the right stud nuts and securely tighten all except the adjuster securing nut which should be only finger tight at this stage.

Oil Tank. Replace the oil tank and secure it to the frame with the three nuts and bolts. Remove the plug from the junction block and fit it to the crankcase with a new joint washer if necessary.

Installing Gearbox

Rear Panels (6T & T110). Replace as detailed on page 16.

Air Filter. Replace the air filter connection.

Speedometer Cable. Insert the cable end into the gearbox, ensuring that it mates with the driving spindle, and then tighten up the attachment nut.

Clutch Cable. Connect cable nipple to clutch operating arm.

Right Footrest and Spindle. Insert the spindle through the engine plates from the right side, ensuring that the distance piece is correctly located. Fit the short distance piece over the footrest spindle between the primary inner cover and engine plate.

Primary Chaincase, Alternator, Clutch and Engine Sprocket. Replace as described on page 90, but before replacing the chaincase outer cover, check the primary chain adjustment as described on page 92.

Left Footrest. Fit to spindle and securely tighten the nut.

Footbrake Pedal. Grease the pedal spindle and fit the pedal. Replace the spring washer, plain washer and securing nut. Connect operating rod to pedal, placing the plain washer over the rod end, and secure with a split pin.

Exhaust System. Refit the exhaust pipe and silencer assemblies.

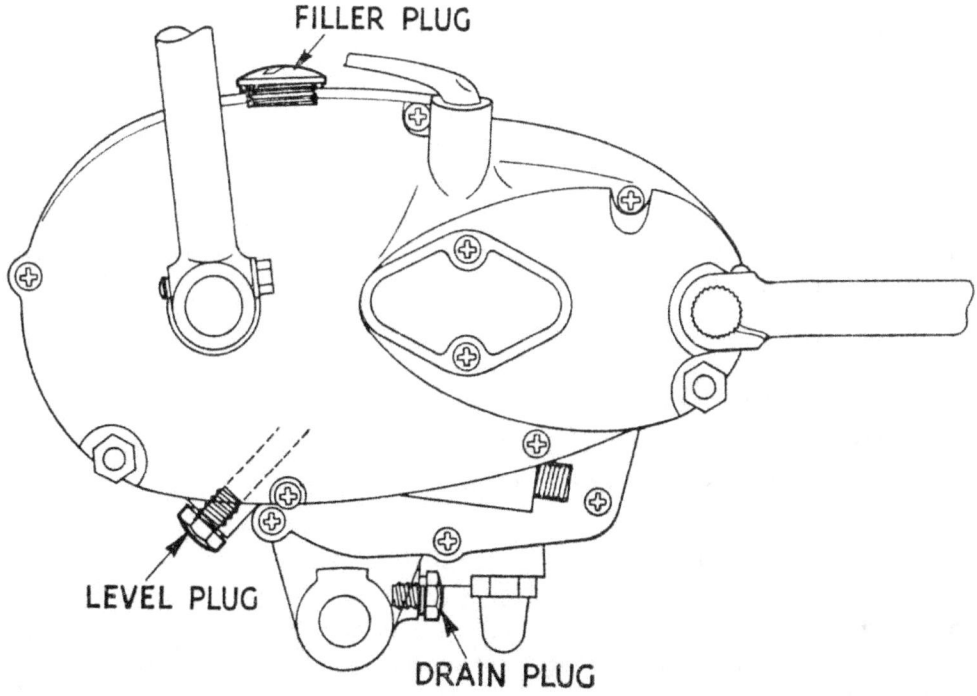

CLUTCH AND SHOCK ABSORBER UNIT

The clutch is of the multi-plate type, using synthetic friction material & incorporating a transmission shock absorber. The pressure on the plate is maintained by four springs and can be varied by screwing in or out the slotted nuts which secure them. The clutch is designed to operate in oil and it is essential that the oil level in the chaincase is maintained, otherwise the friction inserts may burn and disintegrate under heavy loading. Always use the recommended grade of oil (S.A.E. 20), see lubricant chart, page 180. If a heavier grade of oil is used, the clutch plates will not readily separate when disengaged, which will cause difficult and noisy gear selection when the gearchange pedal is operated. Even with the thinner grades of oil, the kickstarter should always be operated a few times with the clutch extracted before attempting to start the engine. This procedure ensures that the plates separate freely when a gear selection is made.

The shock absorber unit which is incorporated in the clutch is robustly constructed and is designed to give many thousands of miles of trouble-free service. Briefly, it operates in the following manner : the drive is transmitted through the clutch plates in the normal manner, then through the drive rubbers to the four armed spider which is keyed to the gearbox mainshaft. The spider is free to oscillate inside the clutch centre but is restrained by eight rubber pads, one on either side of each arm. The larger of these pads is the drive rubber, the smaller the rebound. The drive and rebound rubber effectively level out all the engine speed variations at low speeds, providing an extremely smooth and pleasant torque, which reduces transmission wear due to the absence of "snatch".

REPLACEMENT OF THE FRICTION MATERIAL

The friction material is bonded to the steel plates and cannot be renewed by the owner ; service replacement plates are available at all Triumph Dealers. The linings are unaffected by petrol, oil or paraffin. The plates must NOT be placed in a "trike" vat, as boiling trichlorethylene attacks the bonding. The thickness of the plates over the linings is 0.140 in., the lining thickness being $\frac{1}{32}$ in. Provided that the linings are not charred or peeling from the plate and there is no metal-to-metal contact due to wear, the linings are fit for further use.

OVERHAULING THE CLUTCH
DISMANTLING

Left Exhaust Pipe and Silencer. Remove as an assembly.

Footrest. Remove the left footrest.

Brake Pedal. Remove the pedal from the spindle. On 6T and T110 models, slacken or remove the finned adjuster nut on the rod to allow the pedal to drop sufficiently.

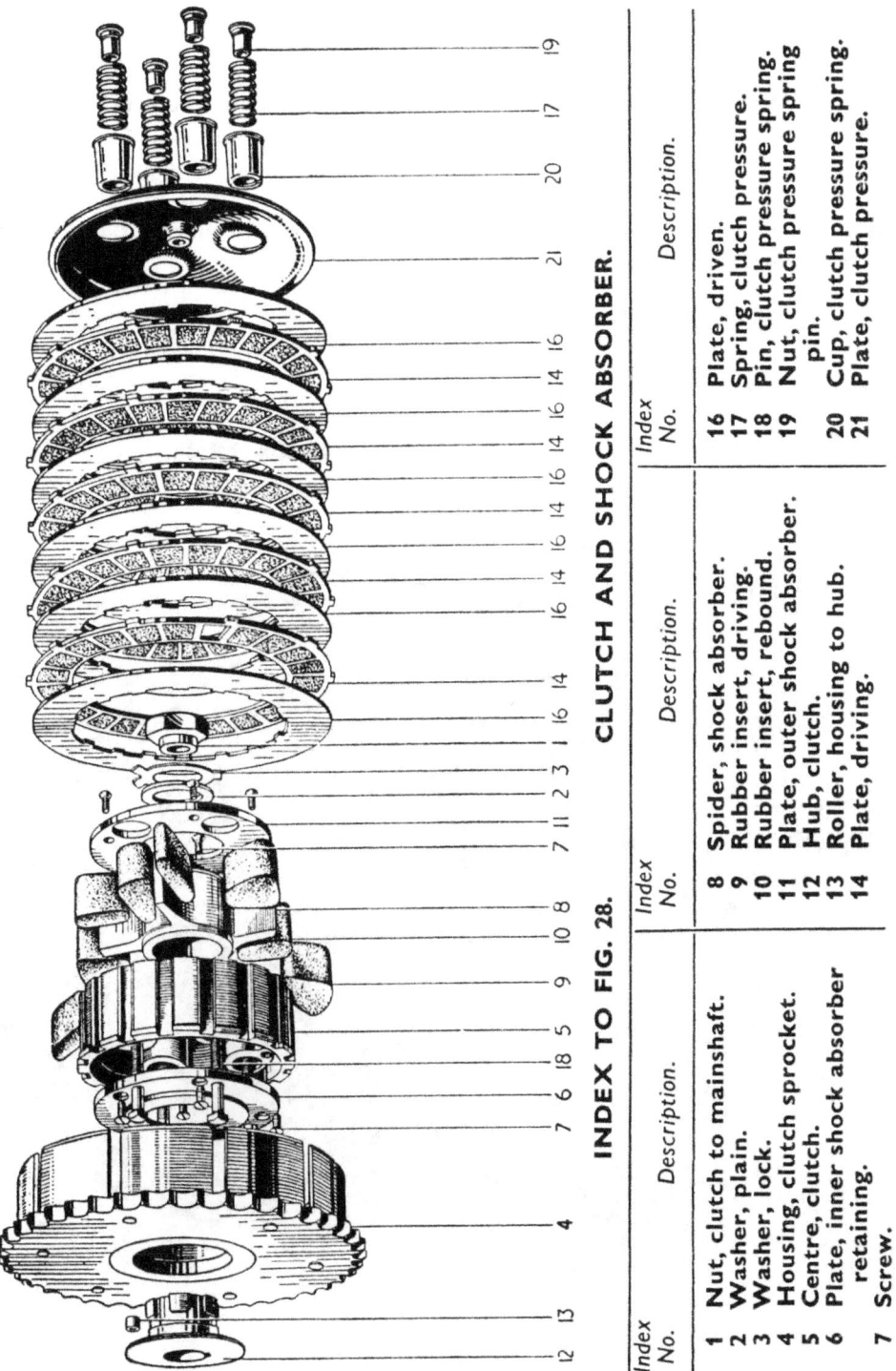

INDEX TO FIG. 28.

Index No.	Description.	Index No.	Description.	Index No.	Description.
1	Nut, clutch to mainshaft.	8	Spider, shock absorber.	16	Plate, driven.
2	Washer, plain.	9	Rubber insert, driving.	17	Spring, clutch pressure.
3	Washer, lock.	10	Rubber insert, rebound.	18	Pin, clutch pressure spring.
4	Housing, clutch sprocket.	11	Plate, outer shock absorber.	19	Nut, clutch pressure spring pin.
5	Centre, clutch.	12	Hub, clutch.	20	Cup, clutch pressure spring.
6	Plate, inner shock absorber retaining.	13	Roller, housing to hub.	21	Plate, clutch pressure.
7	Screw.	14	Plate, driving.		

CLUTCH AND SHOCK ABSORBER.

Dismantling Clutch

Primary Chaincase. Place an oil drip tray under the chaincase and proceed to remove the securing screws. Ease the outer casing away and where an alternator is fitted take care to avoid damaging the stator windings.

Clutch Slotted Nut (See Fig. 29). Unscrew these by using the special key "B" provided in the toolkit. On the underside of the nut head is a small "pip" which contacts the end of the spring coil, thus making an effective locking device which prevents the nut unscrewing when in service. To facilitate removal, insert a knife blade "A", under the head of the nut in order to hold the spring away from the "pip" while the nut is being unscrewed.

Pressure Springs. Withdraw from the cups.

Pressure Plate. Remove complete with cups.

Clutch Operating Rod. Take this out of the gearbox mainshaft.

Fig. 29. REMOVAL OF CLUTCH NUTS.

DISMANTLING CLUTCH

Note.—When this stage has been reached, reconditioned clutch plates or new absorber rubbers can be fitted. Full instructions for fitting the shock absorber rubbers are contained in the shock absorber section, page 89. Fitting the new rubbers is just as easy with the shock absorber on or off the machine.

The instructions below cover complete dismantling but may be varied if it is not desired to remove the primary transmission completely.

Alternator Stator. Remove the three nuts and ease the stator off the adaptor, taking care not to damage the insulation. Disconnect the triple snap connector and pull the output cable clear off the inner chaincase. Remove the stator adaptor which is secured by three flange-headed bolts.

Engine Sprocket and Rotor. Remove sufficient plates from the clutch housing to insert the locking tool shown in Fig. 30. Bend back the locking tabs and place a well-fitting box spanner and tommy bar on the nut. In the majority of cases the nut can be unscrewed by jarring the tommy bar with a hammer against the inertia of the flywheel. If it is difficult to move, engage Top gear and apply the rear brake. Collect the tab washer, rotor, key and plain washer.

Clutch Sprocket and Shock Absorber. With the locking tool still in position, bend back the locking tabs and remove the clutch securing nut in the same way. Collect the tab washer and plain washer. Screw in the body of the extractor DA50/1 to the full depth of the thread in the clutch hub. Tighten the centre bolt to release the hub from the taper. The engine sprocket, chain and clutch can now be removed as an assembly. Collect the key from the gearbox mainshaft.

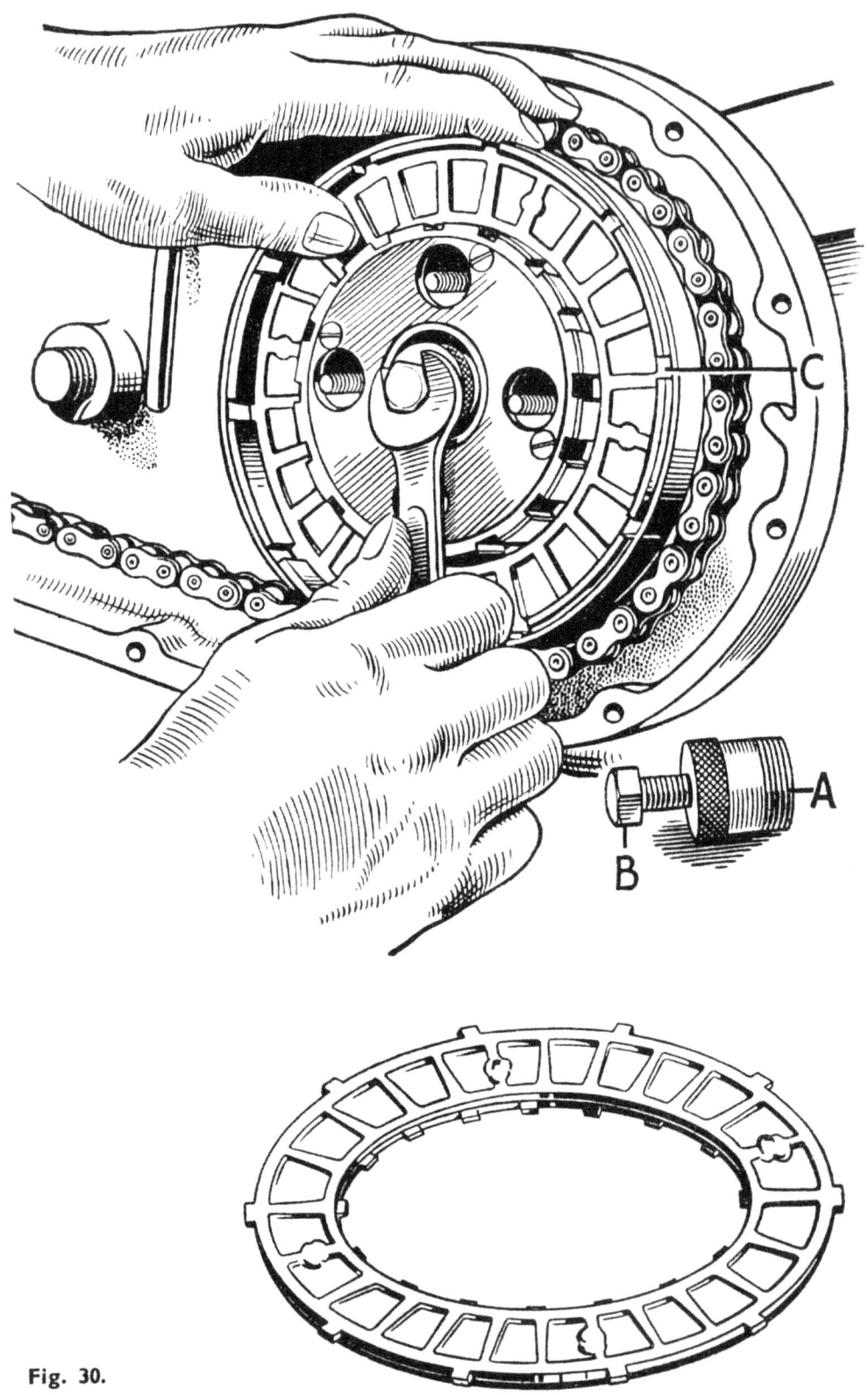

Fig. 30.

USE OF CLUTCH EXTRACTOR.

PREPARATION AND INSPECTION

Clutch Springs. The free length of new springs is 4 plate clutch, 1.5 in. (3.81 cm.) and 5 plate clutch, 1.969 in. (5.0 cm.). The Bonneville 120 clutch spring is the same length but is made of thicker wire. If a spring has shortened more than 0.1 in. (2.5 mm.) or is distorted, replace it with a new one, or preferably a complete set.

Friction Plates. Wash in paraffin and examine the segments for wear and general condition. The segments should protrude $\frac{1}{32}$ in. (0.8 mm.) on each side of the plate when new, and show no signs of burning. The driving tongues should be a good fit in the clutch housing.

Steel Plates. These must be perfectly flat and free from scoring. They have a bonderised finish and must NOT be polished.

Clutch Hub. Inspect the bearing surface for pitting and indentation. The splines should be a push fit into the shock absorber spider and not allow any radial movement.

Clutch Rollers. The diameter when new is 0.2500 to 0.2495 in. (6.350 to 6.337 mm.). If they are undersize fit a new set.

Clutch Sprocket and Housing. Inspect the condition of the sprocket teeth. If these are worn or damaged they will cause rapid chain wear. Next examine the bearing surface for pitting or indentation. Finally check that the outer strengthening band is secure and that the driving slots are not worn or stepped.

Shock Absorber. Remove the four screws and outer cover plate and press out the spider from the back. The spider should be a good working fit in the holes in the plates and also the inner faces of the plates adjacent to the arms of the spider should not be worn or damaged. If in doubt, check these points by assembling the parts without the rubbers. To obtain satisfactory results, check the fit between the splines on the spider and hub before assembly.

To replace the rubbers, insert the four large (drive) rubbers and use a broad-bladed screwdriver, as in the illustration, to hold the spider while inserting three of the small (rebound) rubbers. Use a slight smear of thin oil to replace the last rubber. Replace the cover plate and tighten the screws securely.

Assembling Clutch

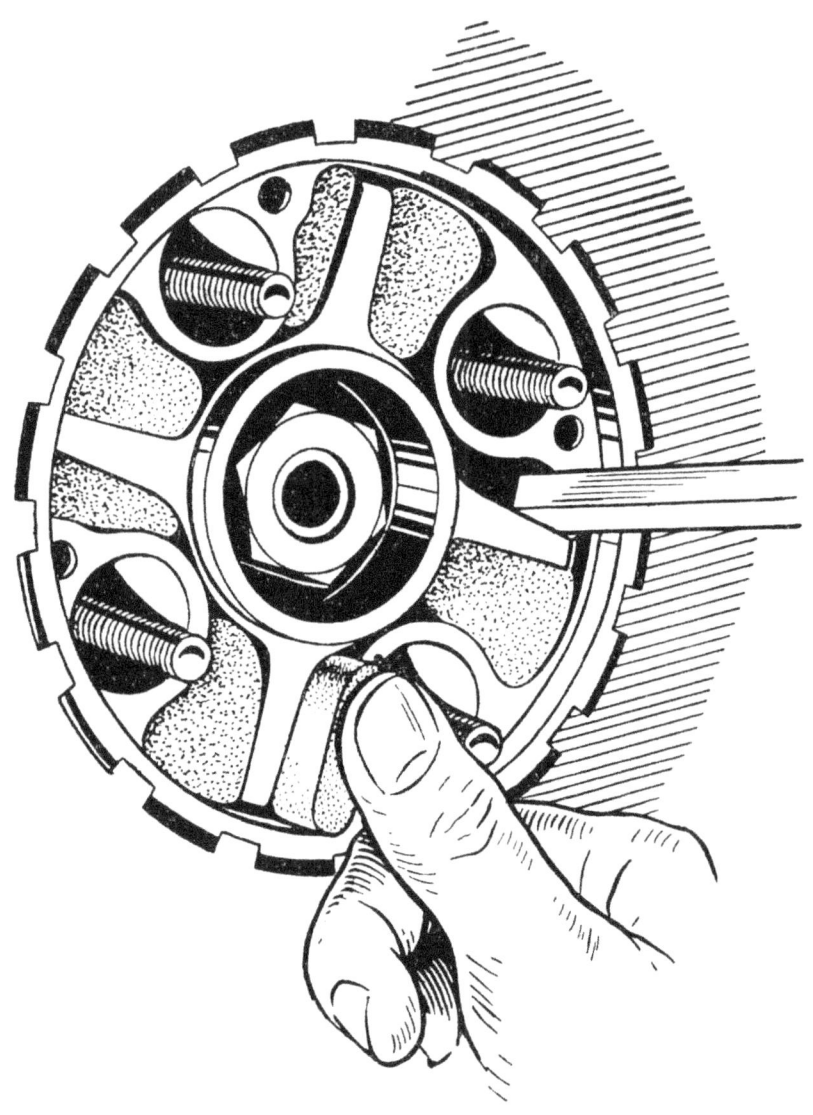

Fig. 31. REPLACING SHOCK ABSORBER RUBBERS.

ASSEMBLING THE CLUTCH

Clutch Sprocket and Shock Absorber. Apply a smear of grease to the hub and place the twenty rollers in position. Place the sprocket over the rollers. Insert the four square headed pins into the shock absorber and press it onto the hub. Make sure the pins are correctly located up against the flange on the shock absorber or it will be impossible to press it fully home. Check that sprocket spins freely with up to $\frac{1}{16}$ in. (1.6 mm.) lateral play at the teeth to allow a self-aligning action.

Assembling Clutch

Engine Sprocket and Primary Chain. Place the key in the gearbox mainshaft. Assemble the engine sprocket, primary chain and clutch to the shafts. (N.B.—The ground boss on the engine sprocket must be towards the crankcase and the connecting link on the chain outwards). Next secure the clutch with the flat washer (cupped side out), tab washer and nut. Replace the locking plate (Fig. 30) and tighten the nut, which must be secured by the tab washer.

Alternator. Fit the plain washer, key, rotor, tab washer and nut. Tighten the nut and secure it with the tab washer. Remove the locking plate from the clutch. Replace the adaptor ring and secure it with three bolts. Fit the stator and secure it with the three nuts. Check that there is clearance between rotor and stator at each pole. Pull the output cable through the inner cover so that there is no loop which can be cut by the chain. See page 158.

Clutch Plates. The friction plates are best assembled dry, commencing with a plain steel plate and fitting each alternately. Insert the clutch operating rod in the mainshaft with the chamfered end at the operating lever. Fit the pressure plate complete with cups and then the springs and nuts. Screw down the nuts so that about $\frac{1}{8}$ in. (3.2 mm.) of the pin shows through. Now hold the clutch lever and operate the kickstarter so that the pressure plate revolves. If the adjustment is correct it will lift by an equal amount all round. In most cases it will be necessary to increase the loading slightly on one or two springs until it does lift evenly. This operation is most important to secure a smooth clutch operation.

Clutch Cable Adjustment. Slacken off or disconnect the cable and adjust the screw inside the inspection cover (see page 82) until there is $\frac{1}{16}$ in. (1.6 mm.) free movement at the end of the operating lever. Now connect the cable and adjust it to allow $\frac{1}{8}$ in. (3.2 mm.) free movement at the handlebar lever.

Outer Cover. Adjust the primary chain as described on page 92. Grease the paper joint washer and place it on the inner cover. Fit the outer cover and insert the screws. Tighten the screws working outwards alternately from the centre. Pour $\frac{1}{4}$ pint (150 c.c.) of S.A.E. 20 grade oil into the case.

Footrest and Brake Pedal. Replace the footrest and tighten the securing nut. Connect up the brake pedal, test the free movement and adjust as necessary.

Exhaust Pipe and Silencer. Fit the assembly to the machine and tighten the fixings.

SPEEDOMETER DRIVE

The drive on all models is taken from the gearbox layshaft and is situated in the gearbox inner cover. To disconnect the drive it is only necessary to unscrew the cable nut at the gearbox end and withdraw the cable.

If an oil leak occurs at the drive bush in the outer cover, this indicates that the bush oil seal has broken down. To remedy this fault, remove the outer cover (See page 76) when the bush can be removed to enable the fitting of a new oil seal (See page 79).

TACHOMETER DRIVE (with Dynamo in position)

A tachometer can be installed to indicate the engine R.P.M. The standard timing cover is replaced by a special cover, in which the drive is taken from the exhaust camshaft by a special nut. The tachometer and speedometer heads are mounted in a special dual bracket on the fork top lug.

CHAINS

Slack or badly adjusted chains are a prolific cause of harsh running and excessive wear. It is therefore of the greatest importance that the adjustments are made correctly, both front and rear chains are adequately lubricated and all clamping nuts are securely tightened.

PRIMARY CHAIN ADJUSTMENT
Vertical Play. Primary chain $\frac{1}{2}''$.

Gearbox Pivot Bolt. This bolt locates the gearbox to the lower frame and must be slackened off before making an adjustment.

Gearbox Clamping Bolt. Slacken the securing nut which also positions the adjuster.

Adjuster. On current models there is a duplicate adjuster on the left side of the gearbox. The easiest method is to slacken off both adjuster lock nuts on the left adjuster and carry out the adjustment with the right adjuster. It is advisable to adjust the chain a little too tightly and then slacken it to the correct figure. If the primary chain is to be TIGHTENED, slacken off the front locknut a few turns and then tighten up the REAR LOCKNUT until the chain tension is correct. To SLACKEN the chain, reverse the locknut procedure.

Securing Gearbox. Re-tighten the clamp nut, all adjuster locknuts and pivot bolt and ensure absolute security.

REAR CHAIN ADJUSTMENT
This adjustment may be made with the machine off the stand, $\frac{3}{4}''$ vertical play or on the stand, $1\frac{3}{4}''$ vertical play.

Wheel Nuts. Slacken off both nuts.

Chain Maintenance

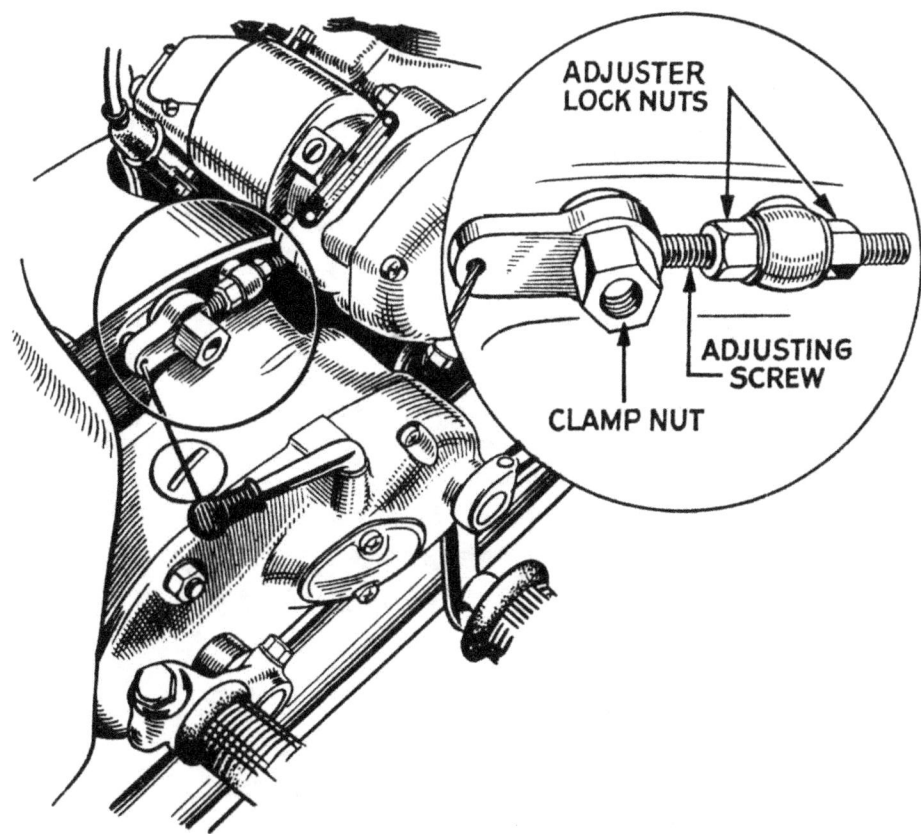

Fig. 32. GEARBOX IN POSITION showing adjustment points.

Adjusters. These are located on the wheel spindle and swinging fork end lugs. To TIGHTEN the chain, turn the adjuster nuts clockwise an equal number of turns until the chain tension is correct. To SLACKEN the chain tension, reverse the procedure and push the wheel forward against the adjuster end plates. Tighten the wheel spindle nuts.

Brake. Check adjustment.

CHAIN MAINTENANCE

Although both chains are lubricated, it is advisable to remove the rear chain at intervals and thoroughly clean and re-grease (See below).

Cleaning and Greasing the Rear Chain. Remove all external dirt by brushing vigorously with a wire brush. Soak the chain in a paraffin bath, moving it about until the joints are washed clean. Finally rinse in clean paraffin and leave to drain and dry. The chain after drying will then be ready for lubricating. Immerse the chain in a bath of grease which has been melted over a pan of boiling water. The chain should remain in the bath for five to ten minutes, being moved about freely to ensure penetration of the grease into the chain bearings. Allow the grease to cool to its normal state, then take the chain out of the bath, wipe off the surplus grease and

Chain Maintenance

replace the chain on the machine. When fitting the spring clip fastener on the connecting link, care must be taken to ensure correct fitting. The fastener is roughly the shape of a fish and, if it is remembered that a fish swims nose first and the fastener is fitted so that the nose (closed end) is always proceeding in the forward direction when the machine is running, the fitter will have an easy aid to memory. It is a good plan to carry out this cleaning and greasing service at the beginning of the winter, half-way through the winter and at the commencement of the summer.

ALTERATIONS AND REPAIRS

If the chains have been correctly serviced, very few repairs will be necessary. Should the occasion arise to repair, lengthen or shorten a chain, a rivet extractor and a few spare parts will cover all requirements.

To SHORTEN a chain containing an EVEN NUMBER OF PITCHES remove the dark parts shown in No. 1 and replace by cranked double link and single connecting link, No. 2.

No. 1

No. 2

To SHORTEN a chain containing an ODD NUMBER OF PITCHES remove the dark parts shown in No. 3 and replace by a single connecting link and inner link as No. 4.

No. 3

No. 4

To REPAIR a chain with a broken roller or inside link, remove the dark parts in No. 5 and replace by two single connecting links and one inner link as No. 6.

No. 5

No. 6

Fig. 33. CHAINS.

Chain Maintenance

RIVET EXTRACTOR

The rivet extractor can be used on all motorcycle chains up to ¾″ pitch, whether the chains are on or off the wheels.

When using the extractor:—

1. Turn screw anti-clockwise to permit the punch end to clear the chain rivet.

2. Open the jaws by pressing down the lever (See below).

3. Pass jaws over chain and release the lever. Jaws should rest on a chain roller free of chain link plates (See below).

4. Turn screw clockwise until punch contacts and pushes out rivet end through chain outer link plate. Unscrew punch, withdraw extractor and repeat complete operation on the adjacent rivet in the same chain outer link plate. The outer plate is then free and the two rivets can be withdrawn from opposite sides with the opposite plate in position. Do not use the removed part again.

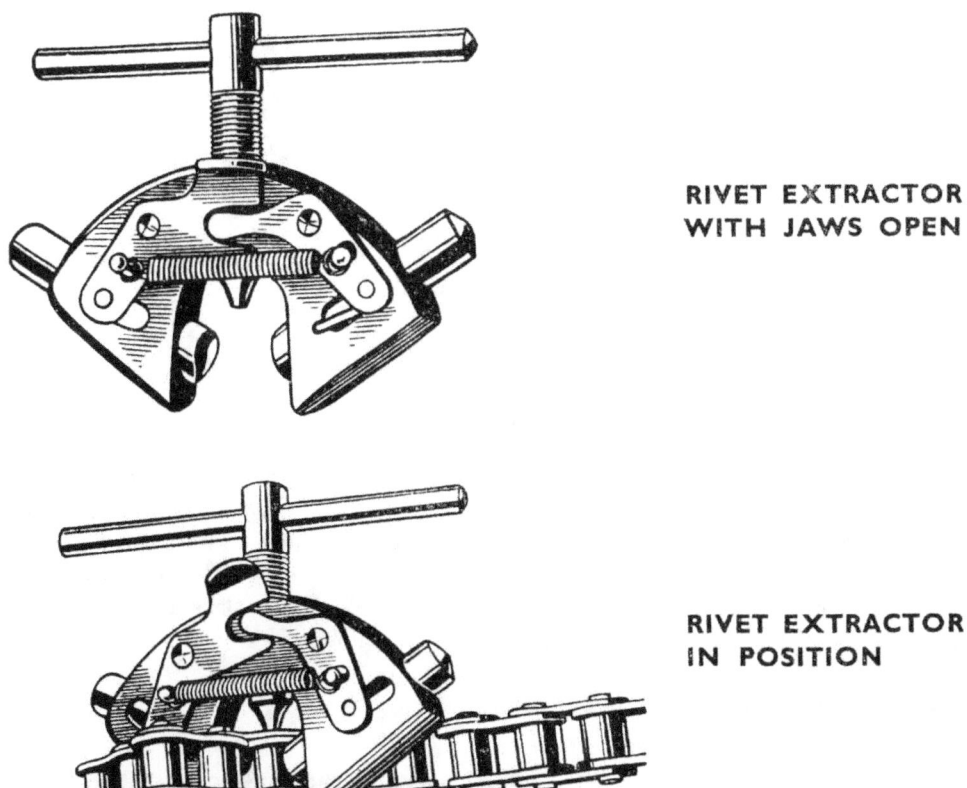

RIVET EXTRACTOR WITH JAWS OPEN

RIVET EXTRACTOR IN POSITION

Fig. 34. CHAIN RIVET EXTRACTOR.

TRIUMPH TELESCOPIC FORK

(CURRENT TYPE)

MAINTENANCE

The Triumph telescopic hydraulically controlled fork will require little attention other than an occasional check of the external nuts, screws and washers. At no time during normal service will the forks need topping up with oil; slight leakage that may have taken place will not affect the fork action.

The following instructions refer to the type of fork shown in Fig. 36. For the earlier type of fork see the instructions on pages 106 to 113.

Periodic draining and re-filling every 5,000 miles (8,000 kms.) or Spring and Autumn, should be carried out, and if the leakage has become excessive it will be necessary to drain and re-fill the forks before this distance.

Draining. To drain the oil from the fork, remove the two drain plugs at the base of the bottom cover tubes and compress the fork two or three times. This causes the oil to be expelled at a greater rate.

Re-filling. Replace the drain plugs. Remove the headlamp rim assembly from the nacelle, exposing the upper part of the stanchions. Unscrew the two screwed oil plugs in the stanchion and pump $\frac{1}{4}$ pint (150 c.c.) oil (see Lubrication Chart, page 180) into each fork leg by means of a pressure can or gun. Machines with longer sidecar fork legs require $\frac{3}{8}$ pint (225 c.c.) in each leg. For best results the recommendations for summer and winter grades should be strictly adhered to.

The TR6 and Bonneville 120 fork is re-filled simply by removing the stanchion cap nuts.

TO ADJUST THE STEERING HEAD RACES

Lower the central stand and raise the front wheel clear of the ground by placing a box of suitable height under the crankcase. To test the play in the steering head, slacken off the damper and stand to the left of the machine. Rest the fingers of the right hand on the top steering race dust cover and with the left hand raise and lower the nose of the front mudguard (see Fig. 35). Any slackness means that adjustment is necessary, which is carried out as follows :—

Top Lug Pinch Bolt. Slacken off the nut.

Fork Stem Sleeve Nut. By swinging the fork to the left and right alternately, a tommy bar can be inserted. The nut should be turned clockwise to eliminate play, *but only two finger pressure should be applied.* Now ease the pressure off by lightly turning the nut in the opposite direction and then test.

Telescopic Fork

Fig. 35. TO TEST THE ADJUSTMENT OF THE STEERING HEAD RACES.

Testing. The fork should move to the full lock position in both directions under its own weight. If the movement is sluggish, slacken off the adjuster nut slightly more and test again. When the adjustment is correct, tighten the top lug pinch bolt.

If it is not possible to adjust the bearings so that the fork moves freely from lock to lock without any fore and aft play, the balls and races are worn or damaged and must be replaced with a complete new set.

Telescopic Fork

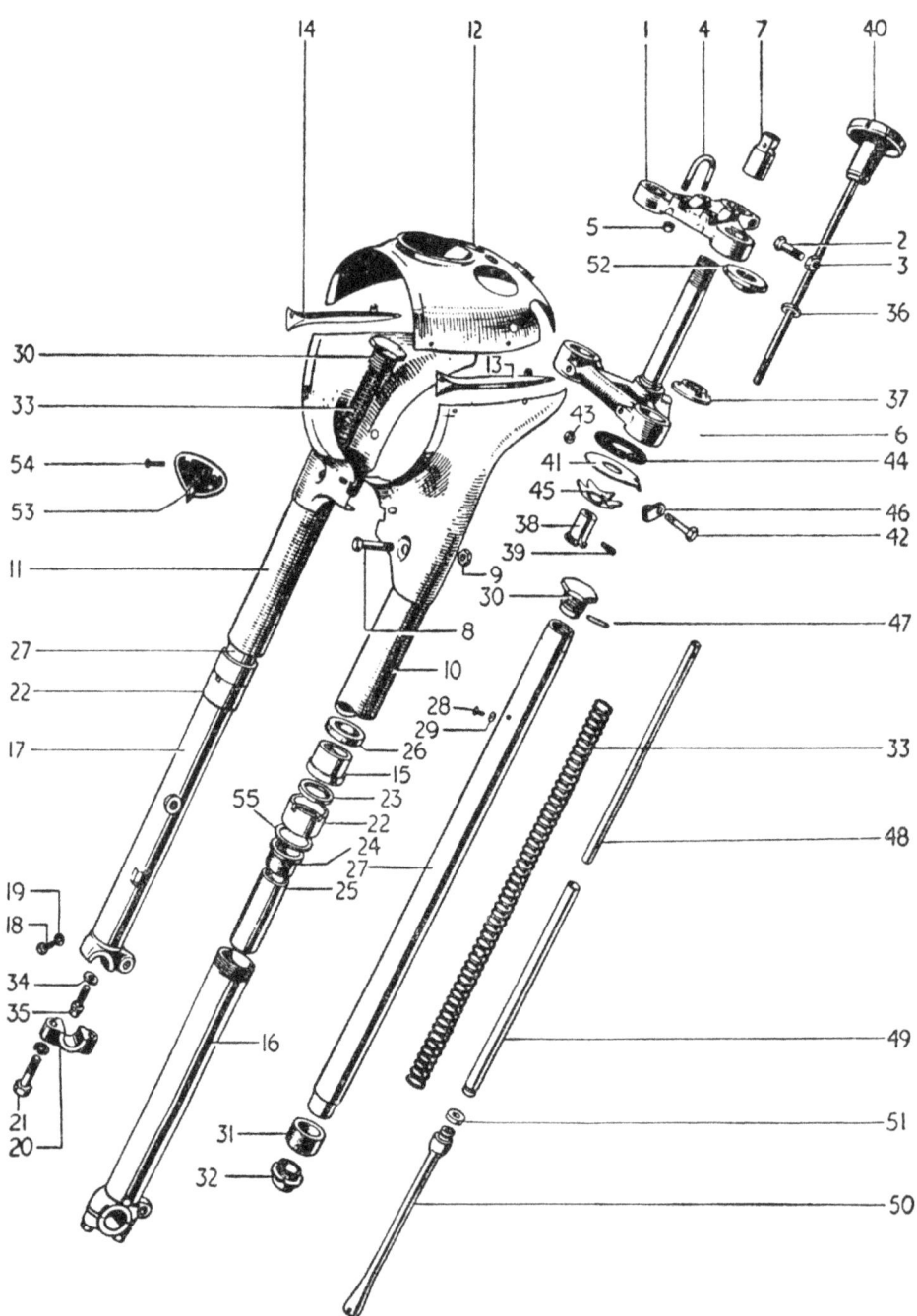

Fig. 36. TELESCOPIC FORK (CURRENT TYPE).

Telescopic Fork

INDEX TO FIG. 36

TELESCOPIC FORK

Index No.	Description.	Index No.	Description.
1	Lug, fork top.	29	Washer, fibre.
2	Bolt, pinch.	30	Nut, cap.
3	Nut.	31	Bearing, lower.
4	"U" Bolt.	32	Nut, retaining.
5	Nut.	33	Spring.
6	Lug, middle and stem.	34	Washer, aluminium.
7	Nut, fork stem.	35	Bolt, flanged.
8	Bolt, pinch.	36	Washer, steel.
9	Nut.	37	Cone, bottom.
10	Cover, nacelle L.H.	38	Sleeve, damper.
11	Cover, nacelle R.H.	39	Bolt, locating.
12	Top, nacelle.	40	Knob, steering damper.
13	Motif, L.H.	41	Plate, damper anchor.
14	Motif, R.H.	42	Bolt.
15	Sleeve, oil seal.	43	Nut.
16	Member, bottom L.H.	44	Disc, friction.
17	Member, bottom R.H.	45	Washer, star.
18	Plug, drain.	46	Clip, speedo cable.
19	Washer, fibre.	47	Pin, tube guide.
20	Cap, spindle.	48	Tube, guide upper.
21	Bolt.	49	Tube, guide lower.
22	Nut, dust excluder.	50	Rod, restrictor.
23	Seal, oil.	51	Washer, spring support.
24	Bearing, upper.	52	Cone and dust cover.
25	Sleeve, damping.	53	Horn grille.
26	Washer, rubber.	54	Screw.
27	Stanchion.	55	Washer.
28	Plug, filler.		

TO REMOVE THE FORK FROM THE FRAME

First remove the front wheel, mudguard and nacelle top unit as described on pages 115 and 168 and then proceed as follows:—

Handlebar. Detach control levers and loosen the twistgrip retaining screw. Unscrew four nuts from the handlebar retaining 'U' bolts. Disconnect the cables and lift off the horn. Slide the handlebar out of the twistgrip sleeve and the rubber grommets.

Stanchion Cap Nuts. Using a ring spanner to avoid damage to the nut heads, unscrew the two large stanchion cap nuts. A suitable spanner is available under Part No. D220. Lift out the nuts complete with inner guide tubes.

Top Lug. Undo the top lug pinch bolt and strike the top lug a sharp blow from underneath, with a soft metal drift, to free the lug from the stanchion tapers. Support the fork assembly whilst unscrewing the fork stem sleeve nut. Lower the fork assembly and collect the ball from the top and bottom steering races.

Alternatively, if it is wished to remove the fork legs and leave the steering column undisturbed, unscrew the stanchion cap nuts only a few turns and remove the two oil filler plugs from the stanchions and the two middle lug pinch bolts, then give the cap nuts a sharp blow with a hide mallet to release the stanchions. The fork leg assemblies can now be pulled downwards out of the middle lug. Remove the rubber washers from the nacelle bottom cover tubes.

TO DISMANTLE THE FORK

Middle Lug. Invert the fork and pour the oil into an oil tray. Hold the stem horizontally in a vice and remove the middle lug pinch bolts. Pull out the fork leg assemblies. Remove one of the screws securing the horn grille and pull off the nacelle bottom cover sideways. Remove the rubber washers from the nacelle bottom covers.

Fork Leg Assemblies. Hold the assembly in a vice by means of the wheel spindle lug and unscrew the restrictor rod bolts, also remove the drain plugs. Invert the leg and collect the restrictor rod assembly. Replace the leg in the vice and unscrew the dust excluder sleeve nut. Special tool No. Z.127 may be needed to extract the stanchion, which will come out carrying with it the sleeve nut, steel washer, top bearing, damping sleeve and bottom bearing. Undo the hydraulic stop nut and pull off the various parts.

TO DISMANTLE, PREPARE AND ASSEMBLE THE UNITS

First thoroughly degrease all parts and lay them out for inspection. If the mileage covered is more than 20,000 miles (30,000 kms.) it is recommended that all bushes and seals are changed.

Stanchions. Check that the stanchion is true by rotating it between centres or by rolling it on a flat surface, preferably a surface plate. If the stanchion is to be used again after straightening, the bow should not exceed $\frac{3}{16}$ in. (4.8 mm.). The owner is not advised to undertake the servicing of a fork in this condition; it should be returned to a Triumph dealer for a service replacement assembly.

Top Lug and Middle Lug. If the machine has been involved in an accident these lugs will require expert attention. No attempt should be made to carry out this work without the necessary jigs.

Bottom Cover Tubes. Examine the tubes for distortion or indentations and scrap them if defective. Check that all threads are in good condition.

Springs. The free length of the spring is: 6T, T110, $18\frac{5}{16}$ in. (46.5 cm.), TR6, T120, $19\frac{1}{16}$ in. (48.4 cm.) when new, and provided that the springs are within $\frac{1}{2}$ in. (1.2 cm.) of this length and are not otherwise damaged, they are fit for further use.

Steering Races. The cups, cones and balls should be examined for pitting or wear, and if any are found to be defective the complete set should be changed.

Top and Bottom Race: 20 $\frac{1}{4}$ in. (6.35 mm.) diameter balls each.

Friction Damper. Examine the friction damper assembly for traces of oil, grease, rust, etc. Renew the friction disc if at all worn and the spring plate if weak or broken.

Assembling Fork

Sleeve Nut. Press out the oil seal and dust shroud. The oil seal will be damaged and a new one must be fitted with the spring-loaded side downwards. Replace the dust shroud.

Inner Guide Tubes. Check that the inner guide tubes telescope freely and are securely, but not rigidly, attached to their respective fixings.

TO ASSEMBLE AND INSTALL THE FORK

Fork Leg Assemblies. Insert the spigoted drain plug in the bottom cover tube and tighten securely. Place the restrictor rod assembly in position and engage the slot in the base with the drain plug spigot. Fit a new aluminium washer to the bolt and tighten securely. Now place the dust excluder sleeve nut on the stanchion from the bottom, followed by the steel washer, top bush, damping sleeve, bottom bush and finally the hydraulic stop nut which must be tightened securely. Smear the stanchion with clean oil and press the assembly into the bottom cover, tighten the sleeve nut and check that the stanchion moves freely to the limit of its travel in both directions.

Middle Lug. Grease the steering cups in the frame and insert 20 $\frac{1}{4}$ in. (6.35 mm.) diameter balls in each. Place the top cone and dust cover in position and insert the middle lug and stem complete with bottom cone. Take care not to disturb either race and when the middle lug is fully home, screw down the fork stem sleeve nut until the fork stem turns freely with only the bare minimum of play in the bearing. Place the fork top lug in position and tighten the pinch bolt medium hard. Place the nacelle bottom covers in position and insert the pinch bolt. Place the rubber washer over the top of the stanchion and insert the fork leg assembly into the appropriate hole. Push the bottom cover upwards until the stanchion taper enters the top lug, and then sufficiently tighten the middle lug pinch bolt to retain the stanchion. Follow the same procedure with the other leg and pour $\frac{1}{4}$ pint (150 c.c.) of oil into each fork leg (see page 180). Replace the springs and insert the cap nuts, so that the guide tubes engage with each other, and screw the cap nuts down finger tight.

Aligning Fork

To Align the Forks. If an alignment jig is available, proceed as follows:—

A suitable jig is available from the Triumph Spares Department, through your Dealer, under Part No. Z103 (see page 104).

Fit the wheel spindle in position and place the jig on the lower fork members as indicated in the illustration. To avoid scratching the enamel finish on the fork members, apply a smear of grease at the four points. Hold it firmly and if the alignment is correct, contact will be made at all four points marked "X". If the jig does not make contact at "A" or "B", it will be necessary to make an adjustment. Slacken off the top lug and middle lug pinch bolts. If the jig can be rocked at "A" this indicates that "D" is too far forward. To remedy, strike the top lug at point "D" a sharp blow with a hide mallet and then make a further check with the jig; if the error is at "B" the application is the same, only at point "C". When the adjustment is satisfactory, tighten the pinch bolts and make another check.

If no jig is available, continue to assemble the forks, and after fitting the mudguard, wheel and handlebars, tighten the top lug pinch bolt but leave the middle lug pinch bolts loose. Now grasp the handlebars and pump the fork up and down until it moves freely without binding or sticking. Tighten the middle lug pinch bolts.

Stanchion Cap Nuts. After aligning the fork, tighten the stanchion cap nuts. Make sure that the nacelle bottom cover tubes are central and are not fouling the sliding members. To rectify, slacken the middle lug pinch bolts and hold the cover tube central while re-tightening. *To ensure satisfactory fork operation, the cap nuts and pinch bolts must be tightened securely.* Replace the remaining horn grille screw and nut.

Handlebar. Fit the handlebars, with the horn under the two front "U" bolt nuts, and tighten the "U" bolts evenly.

Mudguard. Replace the front stand and front mudguard.

Front Wheel. Replace as instructed on page 121.

Nacelle Top Unit. Replace and connect the wires and speedometer cable as instructed on page 169.

Aligning Fork

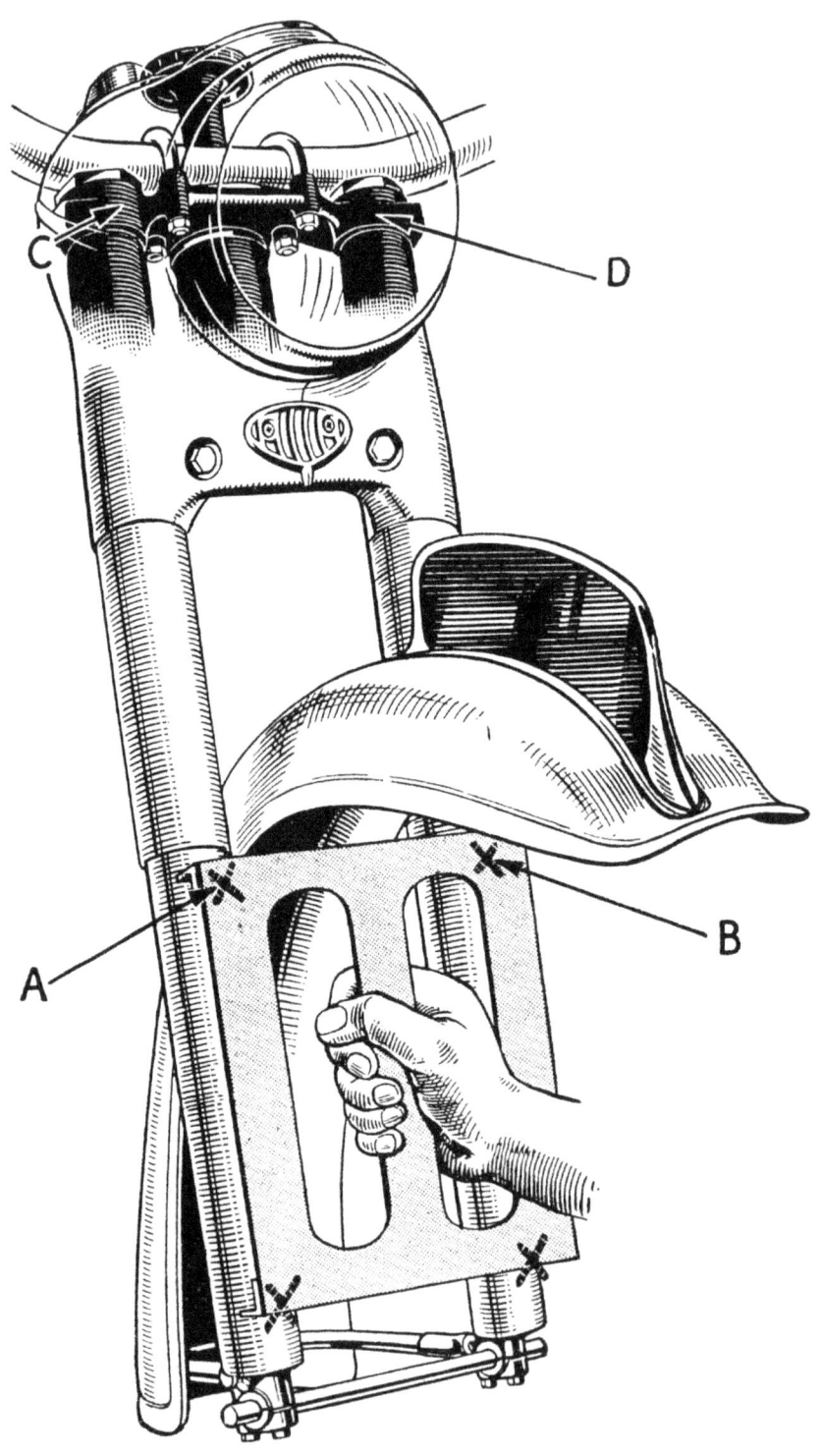

Fig. 37. ALIGNING THE FRONT FORK.

To Change Fork Springs

Headlamp. Replace as instructed on page 169.

TO CHANGE THE MAIN SPRINGS

Rest the crankcase on a suitable box so that the front wheel is clear of the ground. Lift the nacelle top unit as described on page 168, the slack in the electrical cables will be sufficient, but it will be necessary to disconnect the speedometer cable. Undo the handlebar "U" bolts and raise the handlebar sufficiently to unscrew the cap nuts. Lift out the old springs and insert the new. Insert the cap nuts carefully so that the guide tubes engage with each other and tighten. Replace the handlebars and nacelle top.

FORK SPRING IDENTIFICATION

		Free Length (New)	*Colour*
6T/T110	SOLO	$18\frac{5}{16}$ in. (46.5 cm.)	Black
6T/T110	SIDECAR	$18\frac{5}{16}$ in. (46.5 cm.)	Red/White
TR6/T120	SOLO	$19\frac{1}{16}$ in. (48.4 cm.)	Black/White
TR6/T120	SIDECAR	$19\frac{1}{16}$ in. (48.4 cm.)	Black/Red

TRIUMPH TELESCOPIC FORKS
(EARLIER TYPE)

MAINTENANCE

The Triumph telescopic hydraulically controlled fork will require little attention other than an occasional check of the external nuts, screws and washers. At no time during normal service will the forks need topping up with oil; slight leakage that may have taken place will not affect the fork action.

Periodic draining and re-filling every 5,000 miles (8,000 kms.) should be carried out and if the leakage has become excessive, it will be necessary to drain and re-fill the forks before this distance.

Draining. To drain the oil from the fork, remove the two drain plugs at the base of the bottom cover tubes and compress the forks two or three times. This causes the oil to be expelled at a greater rate.

Re-filling. Replace the drain plugs. Remove the headlamp rim assembly from the nacelle, exposing the upper part of the stanchions. Unscrew the two screwed oil plugs in the stanchion and pump 1/6 Pint (100c.c.) oil (See Lubrication Chart, page 180) into each fork leg by means of a pressure can or gun.

Re-filling the Trophy Forks. To re-fill the forks on the Trophy, unscrew the two large cap nuts, securing the stanchions to the fork head lug and pour in the oil past the springs.

It is estimated that, under normal conditions, the time between fork overhauls should be about 20,000 miles (30,000 kms.). This work should be carried out by a dealer or by the Triumph Service Department.

ADJUSTING THE STEERING HEAD RACES

Lower the central stand and raise the front wheel clear of the ground by placing a box of suitable height under the crankcase. To test the play in the steering head, slacken off the damper and grip the fork lower tubes; rock the fork in a fore and aft direction. Care must be taken however, to observe that the play felt is in the steering head and not in the fork bushes. By watching the lower portion of the fork crown, any movement in the races will be easily seen. If play is detected, adjust the races in the following manner.

Top Lug Clip Bolt. Slacken off the nut.

Fork Stem Sleeve Nut. By swinging the fork to the left or right a spanner can be placed on the nut hexagon. The spanner should be turned clockwise to eliminate play, but only two finger pressure should be applied. Now ease the pressure off by lightly turning the spanner in the opposite direction and then test.

Testing. The fork should move to the full lock position in both directions under its own weight. If the movement is sluggish slacken off the adjuster nut slightly more and test again. Finally, check the steering when riding the machine on the road.

Telescopic Fork

REMOVING THE FORK FROM THE FRAME

The following refers to all models with the exception of the Trophy. For these models, the operator should disconnect the lighting plug at the headlamp, remove the headlamp, handlebars and steering damper knob and proceed from "Stanchion Cap Nuts". First remove the front wheel, mudguard, headlamp assembly and nacelle top unit as described on pages 115, 166 and 168 and proceed as follows:-

Handlebar. Detach control levers and loosen the twistgrip retaining screw. Unscrew four nuts from the handlebar retaining "U" bolts. Slide the handlebar out of the twistgrip sleeve and through the rubber grommets.

Stanchion Cap Nuts. Using a ring spanner to avoid damage to the nut heads, unscrew the two large stanchion cap nuts. A suitable spanner is available under Part Number D.220.

Top Lug. Remove the crown and stem sleeve nut, undo the top lug pinch bolt, and, using a soft metal drift, give the top lug a sharp blow from underneath to loosen it from the taper of the stanchions. Remove the damper anchor plate bolt and raise the top lug lifting with it the two stanchion nuts which in turn carry the pressure tube and spring assembly, and the lower fork crown is eased downwards from the frame. The complete fork assembly can be withdrawn from the frame as there is sufficient clearance between the top of the fork crown stem and the underside of the top lug. If care is taken, the top ball race can be left undisturbed and the balls collected from the lower race as the clearance becomes sufficient.

If the mechanic does not wish to disturb the steering column, carry out the first two operations and proceed as follows:—

Middle Lug Pinch Bolts. Remove both bolts.

Trophy Models. Slacken the gaiter clips.

Top Lug. Undo the top lug pinch bolt and loosen the top lug with a sharp blow as described.

Oil. Remove the drain plugs at the bottom tube covers and let the oil drain out.

Pressure Tube Body Bolt. Remove these bolts from the base of the bottom cover tube.

Pressure Tube Assembly and Spring. Withdraw from the forks by lifting the stanchion cap nuts.

Fork Legs. Remove from the middle lug by pulling downwards.

Telescopic Fork

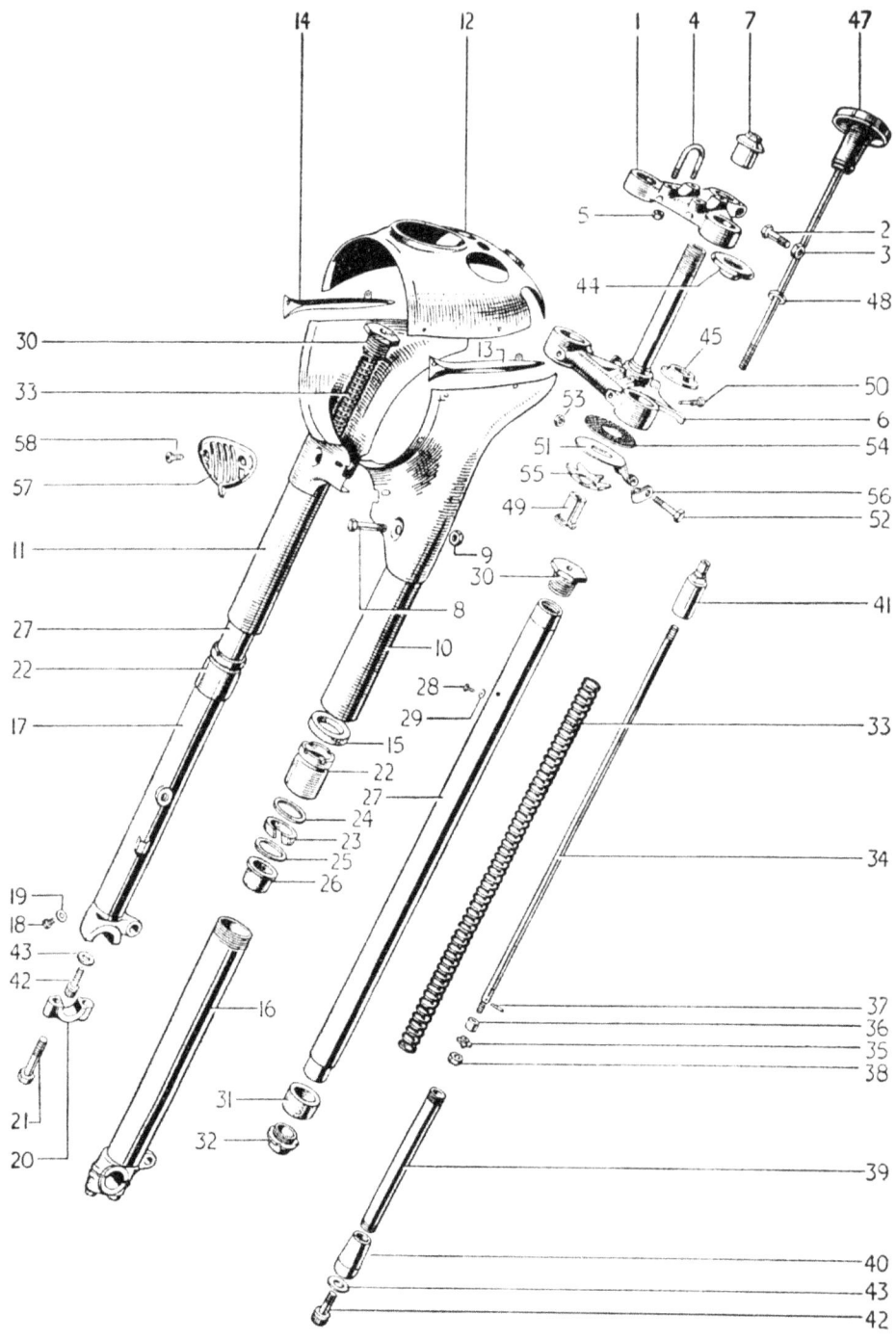

Fig. 38. TELESCOPIC FORK (Earlier Type)

INDEX TO FIG. 38.   TELESCOPIC FORK.

Index No.	Description.	Index No.	Description.
1	Lug, fork head.	30	Nut, cap.
2	Bolt, pinch.	31	Bearing, stanchion, lower.
3	Nut.	32	Nut, hydraulic stop.
4	"U" bolt.	33	Spring, fork.
5	Nut.	34	Rod, oil restrictor.
6	Crown and stem.	35	Restrictor, oil.
7	Nut, sleeve.	36	Cup.
8	Bolt, pinch.	37	Pin, cup.
9	Nut, stop.	38	Nut.
10	Cover, nacelle, N.S.	39	Tube, pressure.
11	Cover, nacelle, O.S.	40	Body, pressure tube.
12	Nacelle, top.	41	Sleeve, pressure tube.
13	Motif, N.S.	42	Socket, screw.
14	Motif, O.S.	43	Washer, aluminium.
15	Washer, rubber.	44	Cone and dust cover.
16	Cover, bottom tube, N.S.	45	Cone.
17	Cover, bottom tube, O.S.	47	Knob, damper assy.
18	Plug, drain.	48	Washer, damper.
19	Washer.	49	Sleeve.
20	Cap, wheel spindle.	50	Pin, securing.
21	Bolt, spindle cap.	51	Plate, damper anchor.
22	Sleeve, dust excluder.	52	Bolt, anchor plate.
23	Washer, felt.	53	Nut.
24	Washer.	54	Disc, friction.
25	Washer.	55	Plate, friction.
26	Bearing, upper.	56	Clip, speedometer cable.
27	Stanchion.	57	Horn grille.
28	Plug, oil filler.	58	Screw.
29	Washer.		

Dismantling Telescopic Fork

DISMANTLING THE FORK

Pressure Tube Assembly. Unscrew the two pressure tube securing screws and withdraw the pressure tube assemblies and top lug.

Trophy Models. Slacken the gaiter clips.

Lower Nacelle Covers. Remove the two middle lug pinch bolts and take off the lower nacelle covers.

Bottom Cover Tubes. Unscrew the dust excluder sleeves from the bottom cover tubes and pull the cover tubes downwards sharply, this will remove the bushes at the same time.

Dust Excluder Sleeves. Remove the two steel rings and the felt strip.

Stanchion Lower Bearing. Grip the stanchion above the bearing surface and remove the hydraulic stop nut and the stanchion lower bearing.

DISMANTLING THE PRESSURE TUBE ASSEMBLY

Main Spring. Compress the main spring and grip the oil restrictor rod in a pair of pliers. Remove the large cap nut and release the spring.

Pressure Tube Sleeve. Grip the pressure tube and unscrew the pressure tube sleeves.

Restrictor Rod Assembly. Remove the restrictor rod from the pressure tube, unscrew the oil restrictor nut and remove the restrictor, restrictor cup and pin.

DISMANTLING, PREPARATION AND ASSEMBLY OF UNITS

First thoroughly degrease all parts and lay out for inspection. If the mileage covered is more than 20,000 (30,000 kms.) it is recommended that all bushes and seals are changed.

Stanchions. Check that the stanchion is true by laying a straight edge along it to find out if there is any distortion. If the stanchion is to be used again after straightening, the bow should not exceed $\frac{3}{16}$ in. (4.8 mm.). The owner is not advised to undertake the servicing of a fork in this condition; it should be returned to a Triumph Dealer for an exchange service replacement.

Head Lugs and Middle Lug. If the motorcycle has been involved in an accident the lug will require expert attention. No attempt should be made to carry out the work without jigs.

Bottom Cover Tubes. Examine for indentation and scrap if defective.

Springs. If the coils are not unduly compressed, the springs are fit for further service. The free length of the spring should be within $\frac{1}{2}$ in. (12.7 mm.) of the original length which is 20 in. (51 cm.).

Assembling Telescopic Fork

Ball Races. Cups, cones and balls should be examined for indentation and pitting and changed if necessary.

All Models ... 20   ¼ in. (6.35 mm.) diam. balls.   Top and Bottom.

Friction Damper. Examine the friction damper assembly for traces of oil, grease rust, etc. Renew the friction disc if at all worn and the spring plate if weak or broken.

PRESSURE TUBE ASSEMBLY

Restrictor Rod. Fit the pin to the restrictor rod, then the cup, restrictor, and finally the locking nut.

Pressure Tube. Screw the lower valve body to the pressure tube and insert the restrictor rod assembly. Slide the top support sleeve over the restrictor rod and screw onto the pressure tube.

Checking. To ensure correct operation of the valve, place the assembly in a tin of oil and pump the rod up and down. When the pressure tube is filled, the upward movement of the rod should be restricted and the downward movement unrestricted.

Spring and Cap Nut. Fit the spring over the restrictor rod and compress until the rod can be gripped with a pair of pliers. Screw the cap nut into position and release the spring.

ASSEMBLING AND INSTALLING THE FORK (NACELLE TYPE)

Before commencing to assemble the fork, lubricate all parts.

Stanchion Bearing. Fit the bearings to the stanchions and lock with the hydraulic stop nut. Check the bearings for freedom of movement.

Drain Plugs. Screw the drain plugs into the bottom cover tube, ensuring tightness.

Dust Excluder. Fit a new felt washer to each dust excluder cap making sure that the two thin metal washers are on either side of the felt.

Bottom Cover Tube Assembly. Assemble the stanchion to the bottom cover tube and fit the top bearing. Screw on the dust excluder and check the movement of the stanchions which should be free and smooth.

Steering Races. If the steering column assembly has been dismantled, grease the cups in the frame and press the balls onto them.

Fork Crown and Stem and Top Lug. Assemble the fork crown and stem and top lug to the steering column and tighten down the sleeve nut until the steering moves freely from side to side with no up and down movement. Fit and tighten the pinch bolts and lower damper parts.

Assembling Telescopic Fork

Horn. Fit the horn to the fork crown and stem.

Lower Nacelle Covers. Assemble the lower nacelle covers and position the pinch bolts and nuts, but do not tighten.

Stanchion and Bottom Cover Tube Assembly. Fit the felt washers into the nacelle covers and slide the stanchions through the fork crown lug into the tapers of the top lug. Lightly tighten the fork crown pinch bolts.

Pressure Tube Assembly. Make sure the drain plugs are in position. There is a slot in the pressure tube valve body, which must be engaged with the spigot on the drain plug by turning the pressure tube assembly until the parts are felt to engage. Fit the socket screw with a new aluminium washer and tighten securely.

Lubrication. Push the bottom cover tube into the upper cover and pour 100 c.c. ($\frac{1}{6}$ pint) oil past the springs and into the top of each stanchion.

Cap Nut. Force the bottom cover tubes down and screw the cap nut into the stanchion, ensuring that it is well tightened. If this precaution is not taken, the stanchion taper will not be drawn into the top lug and excessive strain will be put on the crown and stem.

Fork Crown Pinch Bolts. Tighten up the pinch bolts. (See Fig. 37 and text describing fork alignment).

Handlebars. Fit the handlebars to the top lug and connect the horn together with all controls and cables.

Nacelle Top Unit. Replace the top unit and connect all wires, speedometer cables, etc., as described on page 169.

Steering Damper Knob. Replace the damper knob, making sure that the steel thrust washer is in position.

Headlamp Assembly. Replace as described on page 169.

Mudguard. Replace to the fork and secure all fastenings.

Front Wheel. Replace the front wheel (see page 121).

ASSEMBLING THE FORK (TROPHY)
When fitting the Trophy, the operator should complete the first six operations listed in the previous paragraph and proceed as follows:—

Fork Top Covers. Fit in the same way as the lower nacelle covers.

Stanchion and Bottom Cover Tube Assembly. Place the gaiters in position and proceed as above.

Pressure Tube Assembly. Assemble as described.

Lubrication. Fill the forks as described.

Cap Nut. Tighten the cap nuts as described.

Fork Crown Pinch Bolt. Tighten the bolts.

Gaiter Clips. Fit and tighten.

Handlebars. Fit the handlebars to the top lug and connect all levers and cables.

Headlamp. Fit the headlamp to the forks and connect the lighting plug.

Speedometer. Re-fit speedometer and cable.

Steering Damper. Re-fit the steering damper knob making sure that the steel thrust washer is in position.

Mudguard. Replace to the fork and secure all fastenings.

Wheel. Replace as described.

CHANGING THE MAIN SPRINGS

In order to change the main springs, or to fit stronger ones for sidecar purposes, the operator should remove the headlamp and nacelle cover as described on page 168 and the handlebars as described on page 107 and proceed as follows:—

Cap Nuts. Unscrew the two cap nuts in the top lug.

Spring. Grip the spring which should now be showing, and force it down until the restrictor rod can be gripped with a pair of pliers.

Restrictor Rod. Unscrew the cap nuts from the restrictor rod and secure a piece of soft wire to the rod before releasing the spring. This enables the operator to retain control of the restrictor rod during removal and replacement of the spring. Repeat the operation on the other fork leg and re-assemble the forks in exactly the reverse procedure. The fork springs have a colour identification as follows:—

Solo	Red
Sidecar	Blue
Extra-Heavy Sidecar	Purple

WHEELS

ADJUSTING THE BRAKES

Before attempting to make an adjustment, the wheels must be raised clear of the ground by placing the machine on its stand or stands as the case may be.

Front Brake. To adjust the brake shoes closer to the brake drum, turn the knurled thumb nut (See Fig. 39) in a clockwise direction. The brake should be set so that when it is fully applied the lever is just clear of the handlebar. By this adjustment, the rider will be able to exert the maximum amount of grip on the lever. After making an adjustment, spin the wheel to ensure that the brake shoes are not binding on the brake drum.

Rear Brake. The adjustment is made by turning the knurled thumb nut (See Fig. 39) at the rear end of the brake operating rod in a clockwise direction. After adjusting, spin the wheel to ensure that the brake is not binding.

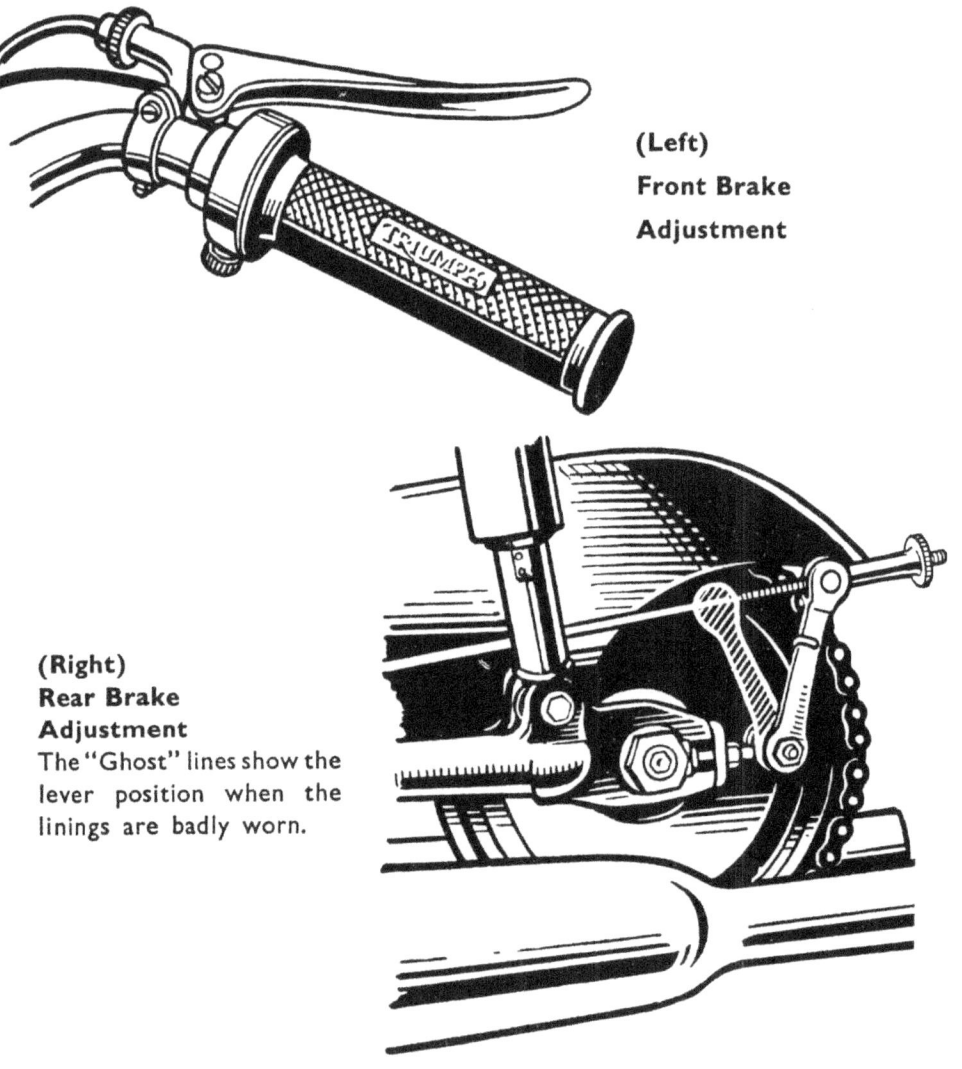

(Left)
Front Brake
Adjustment

(Right)
Rear Brake
Adjustment
The "Ghost" lines show the lever position when the linings are badly worn.

Fig. 39. ADJUSTING THE BRAKES.

FRONT WHEEL

The front wheel as fitted to all models requires very little maintenance beyond re-packing the hub with clean grease every 10,000 miles (15,000 kms.). The wheel bearings are of the ball journal type and therefore require no adjustment. The rim is 19 in. diam. (WM2-19) fitted with a 3.25 × 19 in tyre. The 5T, 6T and TR5 models have a full width hub containing a 7 in. (17.78 cm.) diam. brake. The hub is built into the rim with 40 identical, straight-pull spokes. The TR6, T100 and T110 models have an 8 in. (20.32 cm.) diam. brake drum bolted to the hub, and two lengths of spoke are used each with two different head angles. Later TR6, T100, T110 and all T120 Models have a full width hub containing an 8 in. (20.32 cm.) diameter brake. Except for its greater diameter it is identical to the full width hub fitted to the 5T, 6T and TR5.

TO REMOVE THE FRONT WHEEL FROM THE FORKS

Brake Cable. Remove the split pin and pivot pin from the lower end of cable.

Anchor Plate Bolt (Earlier TR6, T100 & T110 only). Unscrew the nut and remove the bolt securing the anchor plate to the fork leg.

Spindle Cap Bolts. Unscrew the spindle cap bolts (two on each fork leg).

Front Stand. Lower the front stand by loosening the retaining nut at the rear of the mudguard and swing the stand forward. The front wheel can now be withdrawn from the forks.

TO DISMANTLE THE FRONT WHEEL

Anchor Plate Nut. Hold the spindle in a vice with soft jaws, or alternatively hold the spindle by clamping it in one fork leg with the wheel outwards, and unscrew the anchor plate retaining nut.

Anchor Plate. Hold the brake lever slightly on and lift out the anchor plate assembly.

Left Wheel Bearing. Remove the circlip and drive out the bearing and dust cover by means of a hide mallet on the wheel spindle.

Bearing Retaining Ring. Remove the right wheel bearing retaining ring with a peg spanner. **N.B.**—This ring has a L.H. thread.

Right Wheel Bearing. Use the wheel spindle and hide mallet to drive out the remaining wheel bearing. There is a backing ring fitted only in the full width hub.

TO DISMANTLE THE FRONT BRAKE ANCHOR PLATE

Brake Shoes. Remove the return springs and the brake shoes will be released from the anchor plate.

Brake Operating Lever and Cam Spindle. Unscrew the retaining nut and take off the brake operating lever. Withdraw the cam spindle from the anchor plate. It is unnecessary to remove the brake shoe fulcrum pin.

Front Wheel

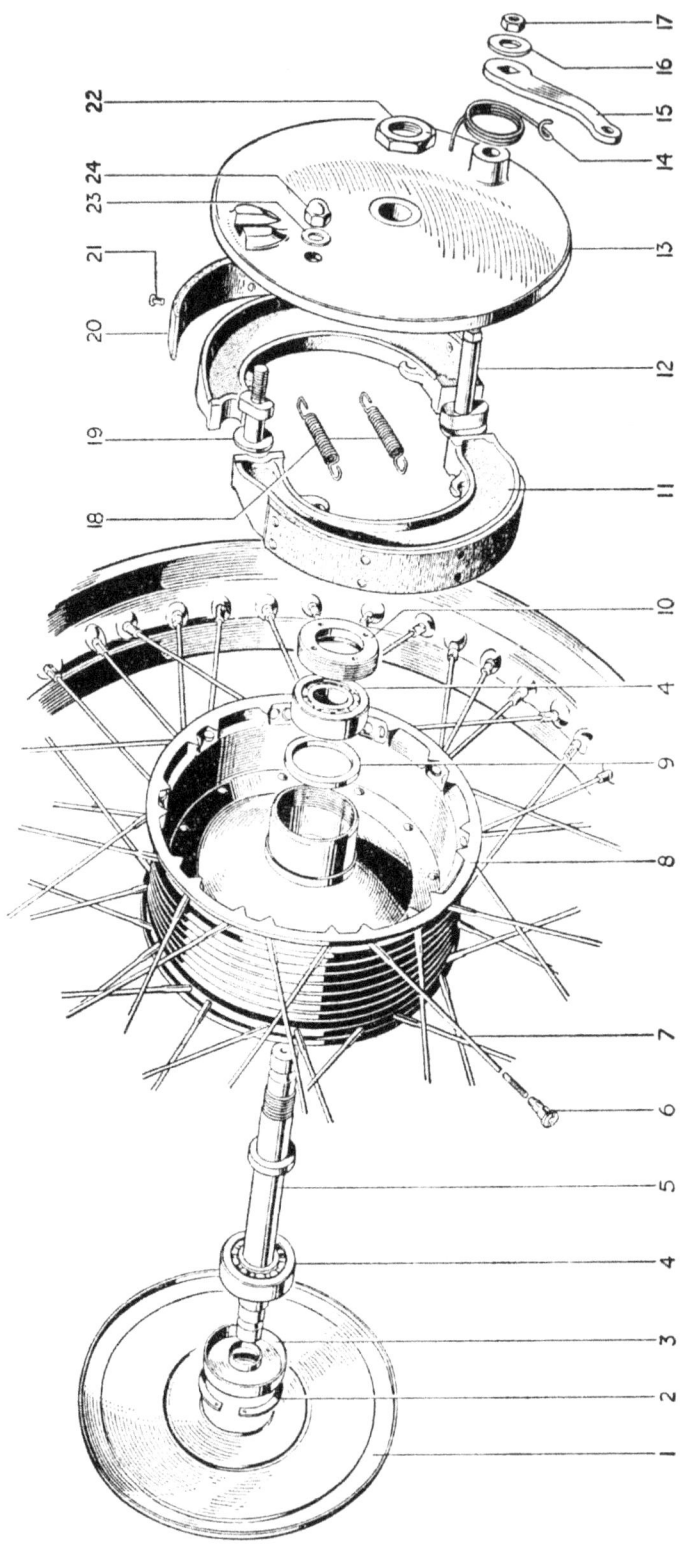

Fig. 40. FRONT WHEEL WITH FULL WIDTH HUB.

INDEX TO FIG. 40. FRONT WHEEL

Index No.	Description.	Index No.	Description.
1	Cover plate.	13	Plate, brake anchor.
2	Circlip, L.H. bearing.	14	Spring, lever return.
3	Dust cover.	15	Lever, brake operating.
4	Bearing, ball journal.	16	Washer.
5	Spindle.	17	Nut, brake lever.
6	Nipple, spoke.	18	Spring, shoe return.
7	Spoke.	19	Pin, shoe fulcrum.
8	Hub and brake drum.	20	Lining, brake.
9	Backing ring.	21	Rivet, brake lining.
10	Ring, bearing securing.	22	Nut, anchor plate.
11	Brake shoe c/w lining.	23	Washer.
12	Cam, brake operating.	24	Nut, fulcrum pin.

INSPECTION AND REPLACEMENT OF WORN PARTS

Washing. All parts with the exception of the brake shoes, should be thoroughly washed with petrol or paraffin.

Anchor Plate. This should be examined for cracks and distortion and excessive wear in the brake cam housing.

Brake Cam. Clean out the greaseways and remove any rust. Re-fill the greaseways with clean grease.

Ball Bearings. Clean and dry the bearings thoroughly. Compressed air should be used for drying out if possible. Test the end float and inspect the balls for any signs of indentation or pitting. Change the bearings if they are not up to the required standard. Pack the bearing with grease before replacing in the hub.

Return Springs. Inspect for signs of fatigue and renew if necessary.

Brake Drum. Inspect the brake drum for wear, ovality or scoring. If there is ovality or score marks, the drum will have to be detached from the wheel and skimmed. If it is necessary to skim more than .010 in. (0.254 mm.) from the drum it should be scrapped. After skimming the brake drum, the wheel will have to be re-built and trued up.

Brake Shoes. If the brake adjuster has been fully taken up, the brake shoe linings must be changed. Do not pack the heel of the shoe in an endeavour to make an adjustment. New linings and rivets can be purchased from a Triumph Dealer, but if the owner wishes, he can exchange the brake shoes for a re-conditioned set at very little extra cost. If the old brake shoes are to be used for further service, inspect the rivet heads as these must be below the surface of the lining. Rivets which show signs of contact with the brake drum can be lowered by using a suitable round punch. Support the shoe at the point where the rivet is to be knocked down.

Front Wheel

Fig. 41. FRONT WHEEL (Earlier TR6, T100 & T110).

INDEX TO FIG. 41.   FRONT WHEEL (Earlier TR6, T100 & T110)

Index No.	Description.	Index No.	Description.
1	Bearing, ball journal.	18	Circlip, L.H. bearing.
2	Spindle.	19	Dust cover.
3	Spoke, 90° head.	20	Bolt, drum to hub.
4	Nipple, spoke.	21	Spoke, short 95° head.
5	Spoke, 88° head.	22	Spoke, short 80° head.
6	Hub.	23	Drum, brake.
7	Lockplate.	24	Cam, brake operating.
8	Nut.	25	Bearing, ball journal.
9	Pin, shoe fulcrum.	26	Ring, bearing securing.
10	Shoe, brake trailing.	27	Shoe, brake leading.
11	Lining, brake shoe.	28	Spring, shoe return.
12	Rivet, brake lining.	29	Plate, brake anchor.
13	Washer.	30	Spring, lever return.
14	Nut, fulcrum pin.	31	Lever, brake operating.
15	Cover plate (alternative).	32	Washer.
16	Gauze, anchor plate.	33	Nut, brake lever.
17	Screw, gauze securing.	34	Nut, anchor plate.

TO ASSEMBLE THE FRONT BRAKE ANCHOR PLATE

Brake Cam. Grease the spindle of the brake cam and insert it into the housing on the brake anchor plate. Fit the return spring over the spindle (long end away from the anchor plate) and tap the lever arm on to the square shoulder with the lever arm in the same line as the cam. Fit the washer and nut and tighten.

Brake Shoes. Place the two shoes on the bench in their relative positions. Fit the return springs to the retaining hooks, then, taking a shoe in each hand and at the same time holding the springs in tension, position the shoes to the anchor plate. By turning the top of the shoes inwards the assembly can be placed over the cam and fulcrum pin and snapped down into position by pressing on the outsides of the shoes. Floating brake shoes must have the steel thrust pads next to the fulcrum pin and the linings at the trailing end of the shoe relative to the direction of rotation (See page 120).

ASSEMBLING THE FRONT WHEEL

Preparation. Thoroughly clean the inside of the hub and brake drum. **Pack the ball races with grease.**

Right Wheel Bearing. A backing ring must first be placed in the full width hub. Press the bearing into the hub and secure it with the L.H. threaded bearing retaining ring.

Spindle. Turn over the wheel and insert the spindle and pack about one eggcup-full of clean grease into the hub.

Left Wheel Bearing. Press the remaining bearing in position, followed by the dust cap and circlip. Lightly tap the wheel spindle from the right side, to press the bearing close up against the dust cap and circlip.

Replacing Front Wheel

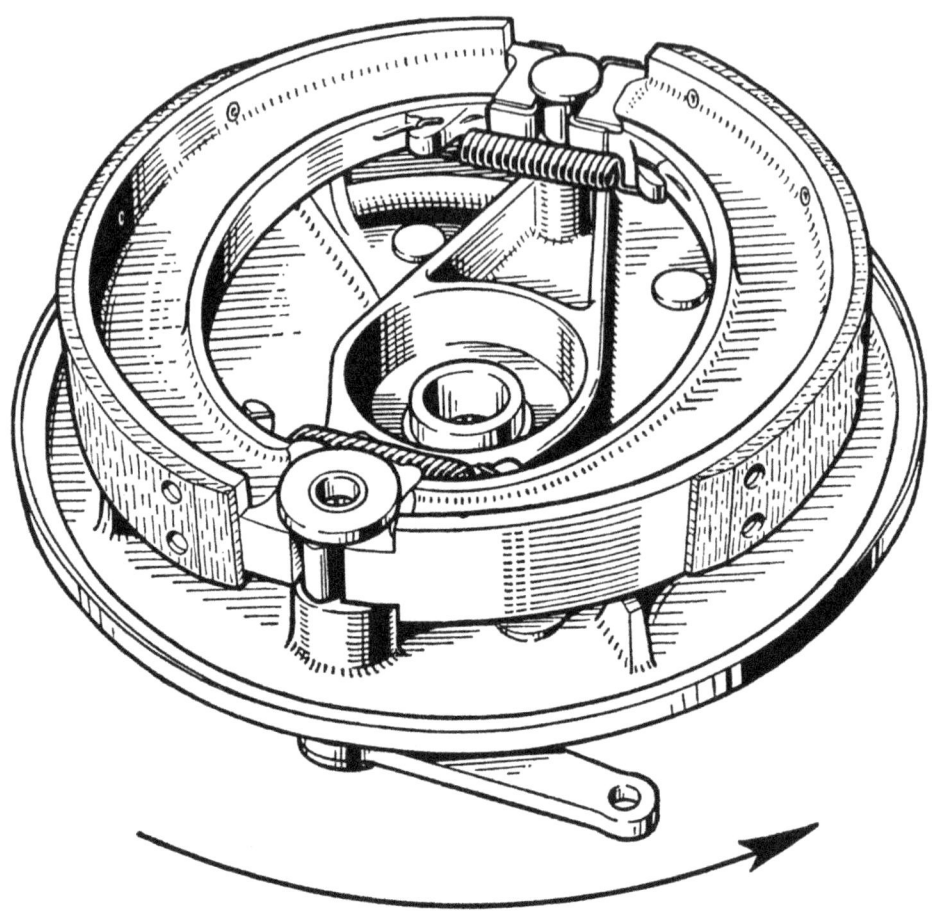

Fig. 42. REPLACING FLOATING BRAKE SHOES.
(Arrow shows direction of rotation of wheel)

Brake Anchor Plate. Hold the left end of the wheel spindle in a vice and then holding the brake lever slightly on, place the anchor plate assembly in position and secure with the retaining nut.

TO REPLACE THE FRONT WHEEL

Place the wheel in position in the forks and swing the front stand backward. If available add a small weight in front of the parcel grid so that the fork legs rest on the wheel spindle.

Spindle Caps. Hold the spindle caps in position and screw the bolts a few turns into the fork legs. The spindle is recessed at the bolt positions and it may be necessary to move the wheel a little from side to side before the bolts can be inserted. Do not tighten the bolts yet.

Brake Anchorage. On the full width hub models make sure the anchor peg on the fork leg engages with the channel on the anchor plate. On the earlier TR6, T100 and T110 models insert the brake anchor bolt and tighten it securely.

Spindle Cap Bolts. Tighten the bolt evenly, keeping the space between the cap and fork leg equal, in front of, and behind the wheel spindle.

Brake Cable. Refit the brake cable to the abutment and insert the pivot pin and split pin. Check the cable adjustment.

Front Stand. Tighten the front stand securing nut.

IMPORTANT: ALL MODELS

SLACKEN THE BRAKE SHOE FULCRUM PIN NUT AND APPLY THE BRAKE HARD, KEEPING THE PRESSURE ON THE LEVER WHILE THE NUT IS RE-TIGHTENED, IN ORDER TO CENTRALISE THE BRAKE SHOES.

REAR CHAINGUARD

The rear chainguard extends round the rear sprocket and to remove the complete rear wheel it is necessary to slacken the securing nut and bolt near the bottom of the left suspension unit and swing the chainguard upwards. There is one additional bolt on the TR5 and TR6 models which must be removed, securing the guard to a clip on the brake torque stay.

The Quickly Detachable rear wheel may be removed from all models without disturbing the chainguard, leaving the brake drum and sprocket in position.

Rear Wheel

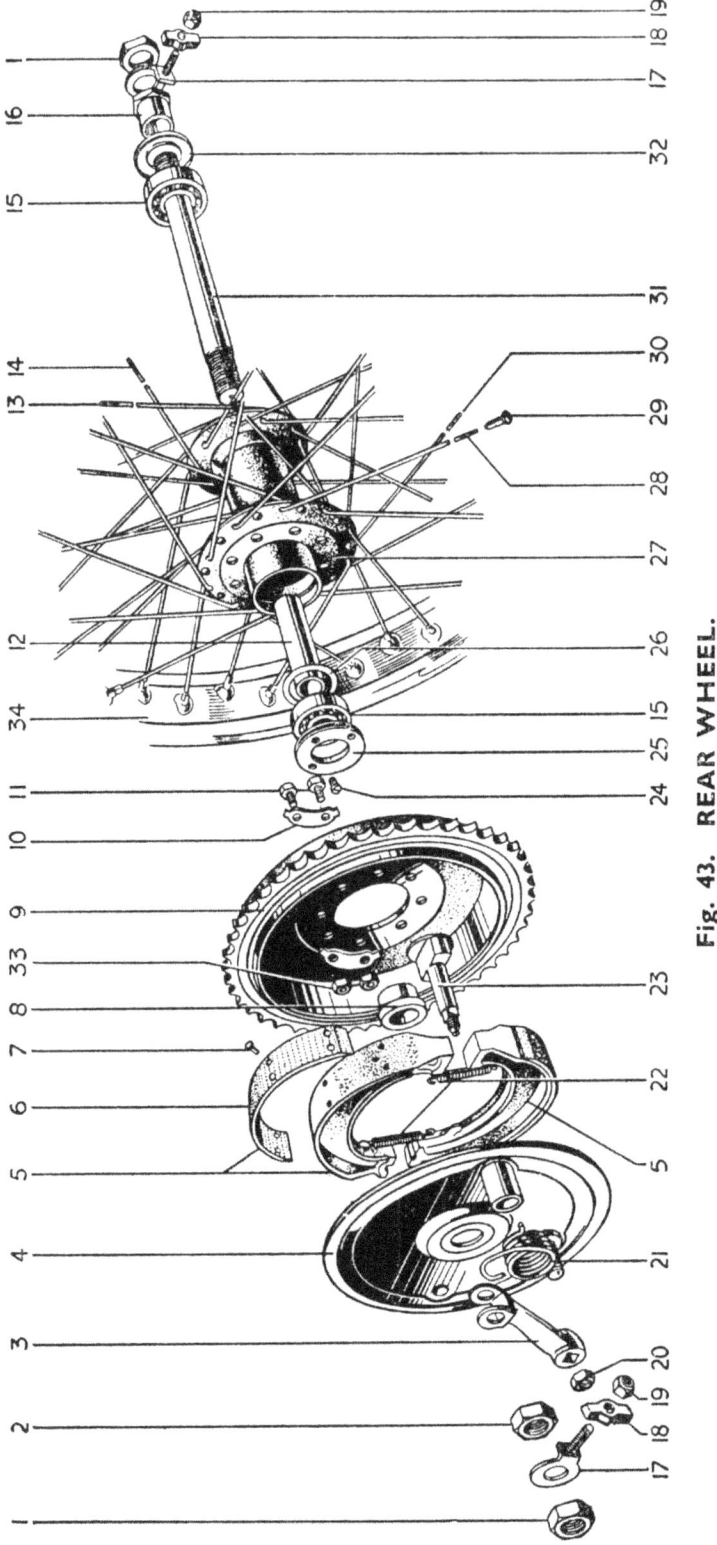

Fig. 43. REAR WHEEL.

REAR WHEEL

This wheel is mounted on journal ball bearings and therefore requires no adjustment. Slackness in the bearing can be checked by first placing the machine on the central stand and then testing the lateral movement which should be hardly perceptible if the bearings are in good condition.

REMOVING THE REAR WHEEL FROM THE FRAME

Rear Chain. Depress the gear lever to make sure that the gearbox is not in neutral. This prevents the chain rotating on the gearbox sprocket and falling off when the spring link is removed. Remove the spring link and clear the chain from the sprocket.

Brake Torque Stay. Remove the rear nut and loosen the front nut and bolt.

Brake Adjusting Nut. Unscrew this nut and remove the brake rod from the lever arm.

Spindle Nuts. Unscrew the two spindle nuts and remove from the spindle.

Chain Adjuster Assembly. Pull the wheel back in the frame a short distance and disconnect the adjuster assembly from the spindle.

DISMANTLING THE REAR WHEEL

Brake Anchor Plate. Unscrew the anchor plate nut and hold the brake lever against the spring tension just sufficiently to permit the removal of the anchor plate.

Spindle. Remove the anchor plate distance piece and knock out the spindles, taking care not to damage the thread.

INDEX TO FIG. 43.   REAR WHEEL

Index No.	Description.	Index No.	Description.
1	Nut, spindle.	18	End plate, adjuster.
2	Locknut, anchor plate.	19	Nut.
3	Lever, cam operating.	20	Nut, cam lever.
4	Plate, anchor.	21	Spring, cam lever return.
5	Shoe, c/w lining.	22	Spring, shoe return.
6	Lining, shoe.	23	Cam, operating.
7	Rivet, lining.	24	Locking screw, bearing retaining ring.
8	Distance piece, L.H. bearing.	25	Ring, bearing retaining.
9	Brake drum and sprocket.	26	Ring, L.H. bearing backing.
10	Lockplate.	27	Hub.
11	Bolt, drum to hub.	28	Spoke, 76° head.
12	Distance piece.	29	Nipple, spoke.
13	Spoke, 80° head.	30	Spoke, 100° head.
14	Spoke, 97° head.	31	Spindle.
15	Bearing.	32	Cap, dust.
16	Nut, R.H. bearing retaining.	33	Distance piece.
17	Adjuster, chain.	34	Rim, wheel.

Dismantling Rear Wheel

Bearing Retaining Ring Nut. Slacken off the ring nut grub screw and unscrew the ring nut. If a suitable peg spanner is not available, the nut can be tapped round with a pin punch.

Bearings and Backing Rings. Remove both bearings by knocking out of the hub from opposite sides with a suitable metal drift. The bearing distance tube and backing rings will now be released.

Brake Drum and Sprocket. This part need not be detached from the hub if the drum does not require attention and the sprocket teeth are not hooked or worn. If removal is necessary, bend back the locking tabs and remove the eight bolts and nuts when the drum can be released.

DISMANTLING THE REAR BRAKE ANCHOR PLATE

Brake Shoes. Take off both brake shoe return springs and remove the brake shoes.

Brake Shoe Cam. Remove the nut and washer securing the lever arm to the cam spindle and take off the lever arm. Withdraw the cam from the plate.

INSPECTION AND REPLACEMENT OF WORN PARTS

Cleaning. All parts with the exception of the brake shoes, should be thoroughly washed in petrol or paraffin.

Anchor Plate. Examine the anchor plate for distortion and wear, particularly in the brake cam housing. Check that the locating stud is secure.

Brake Cam. Clean out the greaseways and remove any rust with a fine emery cloth. Re-fill the greaseways with clean grease.

Bearings. Clean and dry the bearings thoroughly. Test the end float and inspect the balls for any signs of indentation or pitting. Change the bearings if they are not up to the required standard. Pack the bearings with grease before replacing to the hub.

Bearing Backing Rings. These rings should be examined carefully as they are very liable to damage when the bearings are withdrawn from the hub and will probably require replacing.

Anchor Plate and Bearing Locking Nuts. Examine these nuts for damage to the threads and hexagons.

Spindle. The rear wheel spindle should be checked for bends and signs of the wheel nuts having been overtightened. Do not replace a wheel spindle which shows any sign of damage or distortion.

Return Springs. Inspect for signs of fatigue and renew if necessary.

ASSEMBLING THE REAR BRAKE ANCHOR PLATE

Brake Shoe Cam. Grease the spindle of the cam and insert it into the housing from the inside of the brake anchor plate. Place the return spring in position (long end away from the anchor plate) and tap the lever arm onto the square shoulder at right angles to the flat side of the cam. Fit the lever nut and tighten.

Brake Shoes. Place the two shoes side by side in the positions which they will occupy in the drum. Fit the return springs to the retaining hooks, then, taking a shoe in each hand and at the same time holding the springs in tension, position the shoes to the anchor plate. With floating brake shoes see page 120. By turning the top of the shoes inwards, the assembly can be placed over the cam and the fulcrum pin and snapped down into position by pressing on the outside of the shoes.

ASSEMBLING THE REAR WHEEL

Brake Drum. If the brake drum and sprocket has been removed for rectification, it should be secured in position with the eight locking nuts. Ensure that four locking washers are used both on the inside and the outside of the brake drum. Tap the locking tabs up the sides of the bolts to lock them.

Bearing, Brake Drum Side. Place the locking ring into the hub from the brake drum side until it contacts the small shoulder inside the hub. Press the bearing in, up to the backing ring, and secure in position by tightening the ring nut. Lock the nut with the grub screw.

Bearing, R.H. Side. Turn the wheel brake drum downwards and insert the bearing distance piece into the hub until it contacts the brake drum side bearing. Press the R.H. side bearing into the hub, followed by the dust cover.

Spindle. Insert the spindle through the bearings and secure the spindle (opposite brake drum) in the vice. Do not forget to protect the spindle threads against damage by fitting soft clamps over the vice jaws.

Anchor Plate Assembly. Fit the distance piece (shouldered end towards the operator) and, holding the brake lever slightly towards the "ON" position to overcome the tension of the return spring, fit the anchor plate over the spindle and to the brake drum. Replace the anchor plate securing nut to the spindle and securely tighten.

Shouldered Spindle Nut. Remove the wheel from the vice and replace with the brake anchor plate downwards, this time holding the spindle nut. Fit and screw down the shouldered nut until it is hard against the bearing.
The wheel is now ready for assembly to the frame.

Rear Wheel (Quickly Detachable)

FITTING THE REAR WHEEL TO THE FRAME

Wheel. Tilt the machine to the left as in dismantling and position the wheel between the swinging fork. Ensure that the anchor plate stud is correctly located in the brake torque stay hole.

Brake Rod. Re-position to the brake lever.

Chain Adjusters. Fit the adjusters to the spindle and position the end plates.

Chain. Re-fit the chain to the sprocket and replace the connecting link. Check the chain tension and adjust if necessary.

Spindle Nuts. Screw the nuts onto the spindle and securely tighten.

Brake Torque Stay. Fit the rear nut and securely tighten both nuts.

Brake Adjustment. Spin the wheel and check the operation of the brake pedal. Adjust if necessary.

REAR WHEEL (QUICKLY DETACHABLE)

This wheel is mounted on three bearings, two roller bearings being situated in the hub and one journal ball bearing in the brake drum centre. The wheel is made quickly detachable by the simple method of splining the hub into the brake drum thus eliminating the necessity of removing the rear chain and disconnecting the rear brake. All other details are as the rigid frame rear wheel.

REMOVING THE Q.D. REAR WHEEL FROM THE FRAME

Spindle. Fit a spanner on, or insert a suitable bar through the hexagon shaped spindle end (right hand side) and unscrew until the spindle can be withdrawn.

Distance Piece. Remove from between the right hand fork end and the wheel.

Wheel. Ease the wheel to the right hand side until the hub splines are clear of the brake drum splines. Tilt the machine to the left (if a prop. stand is fitted, pull out and use as a steady) when the wheel can be removed from the right hand side.

DISMANTLING THE Q.D. REAR WHEEL

Spindle Sleeve. Unscrew the two locknuts on the right hand side of the spindle sleeve and push the sleeve out of the hub from the right hand side.

Bearings. Extract the inner roller races and dust cover. The outer races are a press fit in the hub and should be tapped out from the opposite side with a soft drift. Care should be taken not to damage the bearing backing rings if there are no replacement rings available.

REMOVAL OF BRAKE DRUM AND SPROCKET

Chain. Engage a gear and remove the spring link; clear the chain from the sprocket.

Brake Adjusting Nut. Unscrew this nut and remove the brake rod from the lever arm.

Dismantling Rear Wheel (Quickly Detachable)

Brake Torque Stay. Remove the rear nut.

Spindle Sleeve Nut. Unscrew this nut and remove the brake drum assembly from the frame.

DISMANTLING THE BRAKE DRUM AND SPROCKET ASSEMBLY

Anchor Plate Assembly. Hold the lever arm against the tension of the spring to prevent the brake shoes from binding and lift the anchor plate assembly away from the brake drum.

Brake Drum Spindle Sleeve. Push this sleeve out of the brake drum, applying pressure on the threaded end.

Bearing. Remove the bearing retaining circlip with a pair of thin nosed circlip pliers and tap out the bearing, dust cap and felt washer.

DISMANTLING THE ANCHOR PLATE ASSEMBLY

Brake Shoes. Take off both brake shoe return springs and remove the brake shoes.

Brake Shoe Cam. Remove the nut and washer securing the lever arm to the cam spindle and take off the lever arm. Withdraw the cam from the plate.

INSPECTION AND REPLACEMENT OF WORN PARTS

The examination of the wheel parts is exactly as described on page 124, for the non Q.D. standard rear wheel, except for the following differences:-

Brake Drum and Hub Splines. These should be a push fit into one another.

Brake Drum Bearing. Wash in petrol and when dry, check for pitting and indentation of the balls or race tracks and end float. Scrap if this is in evidence.

Sleeves. Examine the threads and the cone fittings on both. Also check the fit of the bearings as any slackness would cause a certain amount of wheel shake.

Felt Washer and Hub to Brake Drum Rubber Seal. When overhauling the wheel, the washers and seal should be replaced to ensure against loss of grease and grease penetration into the brake drum.

ASSEMBLING THE REAR BRAKE ANCHOR PLATE

Brake Shoe Cam. Grease the spindle of the cam and insert it into the housing from the inside of the brake anchor plate. Place the return spring in position (long end away from the anchor plate) and tap the lever arm onto the square shoulder at right angles to the flat side of the cam. Fit the lower nut and tighten.

Brake Shoes. Place the two shoes side by side in the positions which they will occupy in the drum. Fit the return springs to the retaining hooks, then, taking a shoe in each hand and at the same time holding the springs in tension, position the shoes to the anchor plate. By turning the top of the shoe inwards the assembly

Rear Wheel (Quickly Detachable)

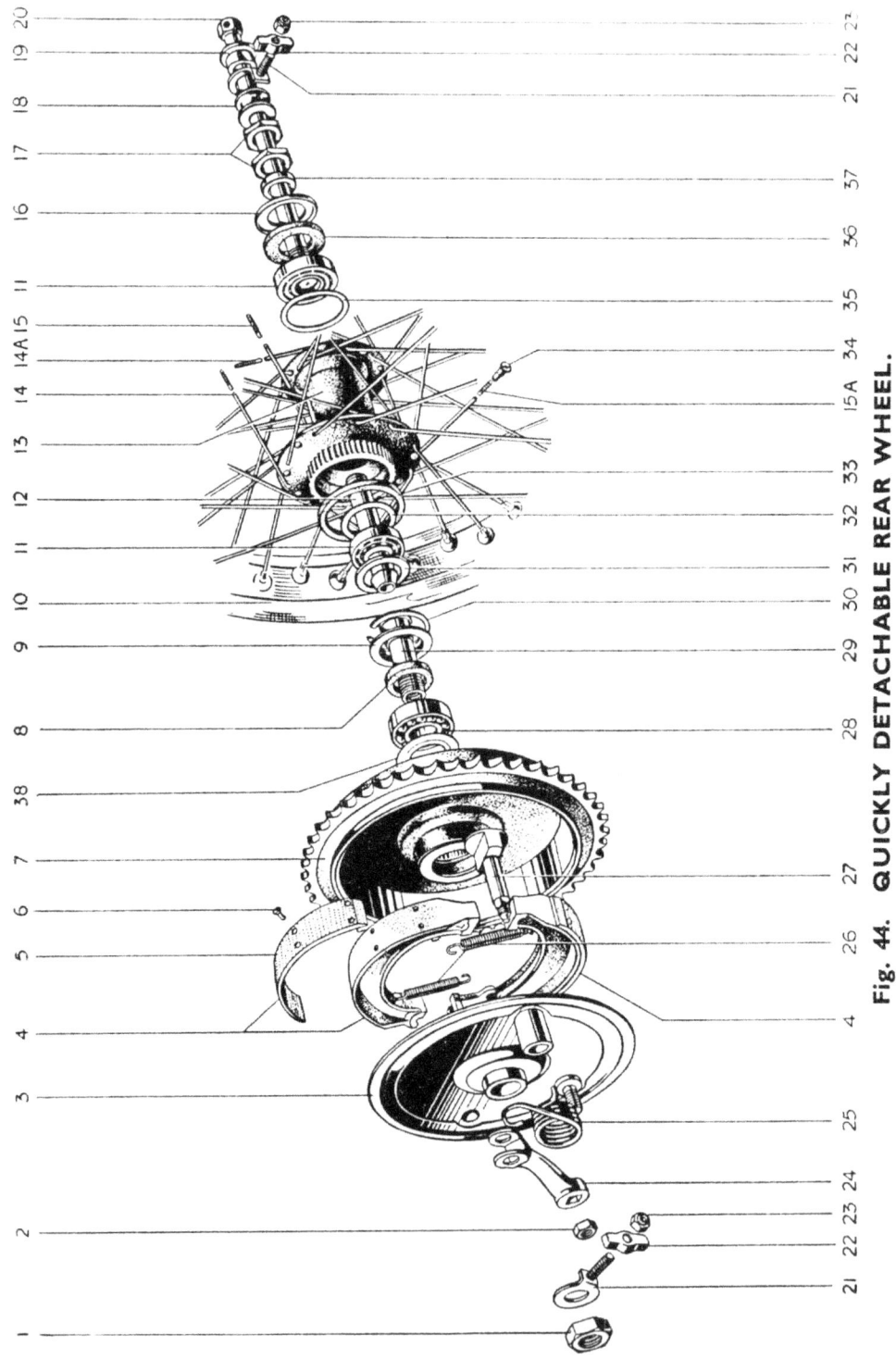

Fig. 44. QUICKLY DETACHABLE REAR WHEEL.

Assembling Rear Wheel (Quickly Detachable)

can be placed over the cam and the fulcrum pin and snapped down into position by pressing on the outside of the shoe. With floating shoes see Page 120. Wind the brake lever arm anti-clockwise to engage the return spring.

ASSEMBLING THE BRAKE DRUM AND SPROCKET ASSEMBLY

Bearing. Insert the shim steel grease retainer. Pack the bearing with High Melting Point Grease (see page 180). Press the bearing into the brake drum and fit the felt dust excluder and washer on top. Secure in position with the circlip.

Spindle Sleeve (Short). Slide the spindle sleeve, threaded end first, through the dust cover, bearing and brake drum.

Anchor Plate Assembly. Hold the brake lever arm towards the "ON" position and slide the anchor plate assembly over the spindle sleeve and into the brake drum.

REPLACING THE BRAKE DRUM AND SPROCKET IN THE FRAME

Brake Drum and Sprocket. Position to the swinging fork and ensure that the stud on the anchor plate is located in the brake torque stay hole and screw the nut in position.

Rear Brake Rod. Engage the rod in the lever trunnion and screw on the adjuster nut.

Chain Adjuster. Fit over the sleeve and engage the end plate to the fork end. Screw on the adjuster nut to hold the adjuster in position.

INDEX TO FIG. 44.   QUICKLY DETACHABLE REAR WHEEL

Index No.	Description.	Index No.	Description.
1	Nut, L.H. side sleeve.	20	Spindle.
2	Nut, cam lever.	21	Adjuster, chain.
3	Plate, anchor.	22	End plate, adjuster.
4	Shoe c/w lining.	23	Nut.
5	Lining, shoe.	24	Lever, brake cam.
6	Rivet, lining.	25	Spring, cam lever return.
7	Brake drum and sprocket.	26	Spring, shoe return.
8	Felt washer.	27	Cam, brake operating.
9	Retainer, brake drum bearing.	28	Bearing, brake drum.
10	Rim, wheel.	29	Sleeve, brake drum.
11	Bearing, taper roller.	30	Circlip, bearing retaining.
12	Sleeve, bearing.	31	Cap, dust.
13	Hub.	32	Ring, bearing backing.
14	Spoke, 14A. Spoke.	33	Seal, hub to drum dust.
15	Spoke, 15A. Spoke.	34	Nipple, spoke.
16	Cap, dust.	35	Ring, bearing backing.
17	Locknut, bearing.	36	Felt washer.
18	Collar, spindle distance.	37	Distance piece, R.H. bearing.
19	Collar, spindle.	38	Grease retainer.

Fitting Rear Wheel (Quickly Detachable)

Sleeve Nut. Screw onto the spindle sleeve and lightly tighten.

Chain. Fit the chain to the sprocket and fit the connecting link.
Do not make any adjustments or tighten the wheel nut until the wheel is fitted.

ASSEMBLING THE Q.D. REAR WHEEL

Bearings. Press the backing rings into the hub up to the small shoulder and press in the outer races up to them. Smear the bearings with grease and place the inner roller races in position.

Spindle Sleeve. Enter the threaded end of the spindle sleeve into the hub at the splined side and press the sleeve through both bearings.

Dust Covers. The brake drum side dust cover is a press fit and should be pushed in up to the bearing. The dust cover on the opposite side has a felt washer insert which should be fitted before the cover is pressed into the hub.

Locking Nuts. Place the small spacing washer over the threaded end of the spindle sleeve and press it into the space between the dust cover and the spindle sleeve. Screw one of the locknuts onto the sleeve until a "nip" is felt, and then slacken back a $\frac{1}{4}$ of a turn so that the sleeve will rotate freely. Tighten the other nut up to it and lock into position. Again test the rotation of the sleeve.

FITTING THE WHEEL TO THE FRAME AND BRAKE DRUM

Hub Rubber Seal. Fit the new rubber seal over the hub splines.

Wheel. Tilt the machine over as in dismantling and enter the wheel between the forks. Right the machine and then locate the hub splines into the brake drum splines.

Spindle. To the spindle, first fit the collar with the cone shaped end towards the hexagon, then the chain adjuster with the stud inwards. Fit the distance piece between the fork and wheel and insert the spindle through the wheel; screw into the hub sleeve.

Chain Adjuster End Plate. Fit to the R.H. adjuster stud and fork end and secure with the nut.

Adjustments. Check the chain and brake adjustments, and finally the wheel alignment. When correct, tighten the L.H. wheel nut and then place a bar or spanner to the spindle hexagon and turn until the spindle is tight. Check the brake torque stay nuts for tightness.

TYRES

The Dunlop Motorcycle Tyres as fitted to all models, are of the wire bead type and are fitted into a well-base rim. The wire bead ensures that there will be no stretch in the tyre and in combination with the well-base rim, provides for easy fitting and removal of the tyres and the safe use of air pressures.

TYRE PRESSURE

Tyre pressure should always be carefully maintained as an insufficiently inflated tyre is a prevalent cause of failure of the tyre walls. The actual pressure at which the tyres should be maintained, is a matter for experiment and depends on the rider's weight and also the weight of a passenger and luggage if carried.

DUNLOP RECOMMENDED TYRE PRESSURES (SOLO)

MODEL.		TYRE SIZE.	INFLATION. P.S.I.	PRESSURE. Kgms/sq.cm.
5T, 6T, T110 & T120	... ...	FRONT	3.25	20	1.4
		REAR	3.50	20	1.4
T100	... ...	FRONT	3.25	20	1.4
		REAR	3.50	20	1.4
TR5 & TR6	... ...	FRONT	3.25	20	1.4
		REAR	4.00	18	1.3

These inflation pressures are based on a rider's weight of 170 lb.

When additional weight is added, reference should be made to the Dunlop Booklet which advises the necessary increased inflation pressure.

EXAMINATION

Especially during the period when the roads are being tarred and gritted, the tyres should be examined periodically and any sharp pieces of stone removed from the treads. If they are allowed to remain, no immediate damage may be done, but they will later work right through the cover and puncture the tube.

REMOVING THE TYRE

Valve Cap and Core. Unscrew the valve cap and use the specially shaped end to unscrew the valve core and deflate the tyre. Unscrew the knurled nut and with the valve cap and core, place the parts where they will be free from dirt and grit.

Preparation of Tyre and Levers. It is advisable to lubricate the cover beads with a little soapy water before commencing to remove the tyre. Levers should be dipped in this solution before each insertion.

Removing Tyres

Removing the First Bead. Insert a lever AT THE VALVE POSITION and while pulling on this lever, press the bead into the well of the rim diametrically opposite the valve position. Insert a second lever close to the first and prise the bead over the rim flange. Remove the first lever and insert a little further away from the second lever. Continue round the bead in steps of 2-3 inches (5 to 8 cm.) until the bead is away from the rim.

Inner Tube. Push the valve out of the rim and remove the inner tube.

Removing the Second Bead. Stand the wheel upright and insert a lever between the remaining bead and the rim. Pull the cover away from the rim.

FITTING THE TYRE
Rim Band. Make sure that the rough side of the rubber rim band is fitted against the rim and that the band is central in the well.

Fig. 45. ILLUSTRATION SHOWING THE POSITION OF THE VALVE IF THE TYRE HAS CREPT ROUND ON THE RIM

Inner Tube. Inflate the inner tube just sufficiently to round it out without stretch, dust it with french chalk and insert it into the cover, leaving it protruding beyond the beads for about 4 inches either side of the valve.

Lubrication. Here again it is a wise precaution to lubricate the beads and levers with soapy water.

First Bead. Squeeze the beads together at the valve position to prevent the tube from slipping back inside the cover and push the cover towards the rim, threading the valve through the valve holes in the rim band and rim. Allow the first bead to enter the well of the rim and the other bead to lie above the level of the rim flange. Working from the valve, press the first bead over the rim flange by hand, moving forward in small steps and making sure that the part of the bead already dealt with lies in the well of the rim. If necessary, use a tyre lever for the last few inches.

Second Bead. Press the second bead into the well of the rim diametrically opposite the valve. Insert a lever as close as possible to the point where the bead passes over the flange and lever the bead into the flange, at the same time pressing the fitted part of the bead into the well of the rim. Repeat until the bead is completely over the flange, finishing at the valve position.

Valve. Push the valve inwards to make sure that the tube near the valve is not trapped under the bead. Pull the valve back and inflate the tyre. Check that the fitting line on the cover is concentric with the top of the rim flange and that the valve protrudes squarely through the valve hole. Fit the knurled rim nut and valve cap.

SECURITY BOLT

The rear tyre is fitted with a security bolt and although the basic procedure for fitting and removing the tyre is the same, the following additional instructions should be followed:-

REMOVING THE TYRE

Valve Cap and Core. Remove as described and deflate the tyre.

Security Bolt and Nut. Unscrew the nut and push the bolt through the inside of the cover.

First Bead. Remove as described.

Security Bolt. Remove from rim.

Inner Tube. Remove as described.

Second Bead. Remove as described.

FITTING THE TYRE

Rim Band. Fit as described.

First Bead. Fit as described but without the inner tube inside.

Security Bolt. Fit to the rim.

Inner Tube. Inflate as described and fit into the cover.

Second Bead. Fit as described but as the security bolt and valve position is reached, push the security bolt well into the cover and make sure that the inner tube is resting on the canvas flap of the security bolt and not overlapping the sides.

Valve. Fit the valve and inflate the tyre. Bounce the wheel at the point where the security bolt is fitted and tighten the security bolt nut.

FRAME

SWINGING FORK

The swinging fork is pivoted to the main frame by a ground, hollow spindle. Two phosphor bronze bushes are pressed into the fork bridge lug to provide a bearing surface for the fork to swing on. The spindle is a drive fit into the frame lug and a working fit in the fork bushes. To retain the spindle in position, a rod is passed through the hollow in the spindle and at each end a retainer cap is made captive, by a nut screwed on the rod end. Between the bridge lug and frame lug on the R.H. side, a spacing washer is fitted in order to control the clearance which may be up to 0.015 in. (0.375 mm.) when new. Shims of 0.003 in. (0.075 mm.) and 0.005 in. (0.125 mm.) thickness are available to reduce the clearance, which may increase after a large mileage. A grease nipple is fitted to the frame to provide access for grease to the bearing by means of a grease gun.
(See Routine Maintenance).

Under average conditions the life of the bearing bushes is approximately 20,000 miles (30,000 kms.). The operation required to replace the bushes is of a major type which calls for the removal of the primary chaincase assembly, gearbox covers, rear wheel and mudguard assembly. If the private owner attempts this work, he should ensure that he has sufficient tools available to complete the work. Details of removing the above mentioned parts will be found by referring to the index on page 189.

GIRLING SUSPENSION UNITS

The Girling suspension units, type SB4, are sealed on assembly and cannot be adjusted. All servicing arrangements are carried out through Girling service agents. The address of the nearest agent may be obtained from Messrs. Girling Ltd., or your local Triumph dealer.

Girling Suspension Unit

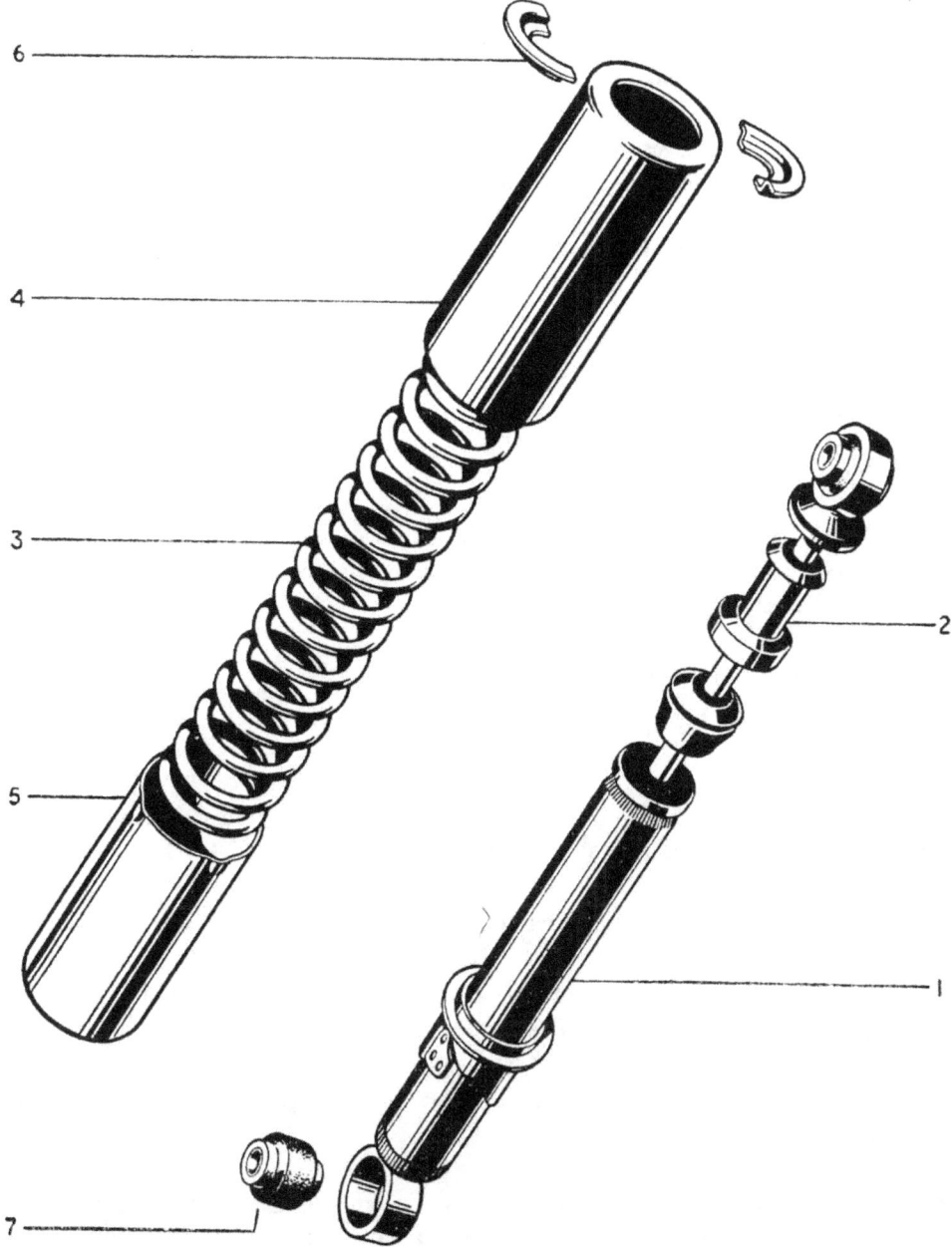

Fig. 46. GIRLING HYDRAULIC SUSPENSION UNIT

INDEX TO FIG. 46. GIRLING HYDRAULIC SUSPENSION UNIT.

Index No.	Description.	Index No.	Description.
1	Damper unit.	5	Dust cover, inner.
2	Bump stop.	6	Spring retainer.
3	Main spring.		
4	Dust cover, outer.	7	Bonded bush and sleeve.

Changing Girling Spring Units

TO INCREASE THE STATIC SPRING RATE

If additional weight is added to the rear of the machine such as a heavy pillion passenger and pannier equipment with luggage, the swinging fork member will position itself above the horizontal. This condition will reduce the springing effect and to overcome it, the main spring poundage in the damper unit can be increased by turning the spring abutment cam (see Fig. 46) with the 'C' spanner (supplied in the toolkit) to engage the second position, or, if necessary the third position. This operation is more easily carried out with the machine on the stand.

CHANGING THE MAIN SPRINGS
DISMANTLING

Unit Fixing Bolts. Remove top and bottom bolts when the unit can be detached.

Dust Cover. Secure the bottom eye between vice jaws on the side faces (protect the jaws with aluminium clamps). Grip and depress the cover sufficiently to enable the removal of the split spring retainer collars.

Spring. Remove the dust cover and spring.

ASSEMBLY

The assembly is carried out in exactly the reverse order to the dismantling sequence but the following observations should be carefully noted.

Springs. Before replacing, lubricate with high melting point grease.

Dust Covers. Ensure that these are not damaged and are completely free from any foreign matter. Either would cause noisy operation of the unit.

Unit Piston Rod. Do not lubricate with either oil or grease but ensure that the rod is perfectly clean.

Checking the Damper Unit Operation. If the handling of the machine is suspect or at least every 2,000 miles (3,000 kms.) check the damping of the movement. If the rear of the machine is depressed several times in quick succession, the units should not extend immediately but should return slowly. If in doubt, remove the units from the machine and take off the main springs. Hold the units vertically, when it should be possible to depress the piston rods quickly but distinct resistance should be felt when lifting the piston rods. The units should be carefully compared, as one faulty unit will cause "rolling" or "weaving".

MAXIMUM MOVEMENT

The stroke of the units is $2\frac{1}{2}$in. (6.35 cm.), Trophy $3\frac{1}{2}$in. (8.89 cm.), and this allows for approximately $\frac{5}{16}$in. (8.0 mm.) compression of the bump rubber.

TWISTGRIP CONTROL

A quick-action twistgrip throttle control is fitted. The damping of the rotor is controlled by a knurled adjuster nut fitted in the twistgrip. To increase the damping, screw in the adjuster until the friction is sufficient to hold the rotor sleeve in any position. Remember that the twistgrip will close immediately the hand is removed to give a road signal if the damping device is not sufficiently adjusted. Maintenance of the twistgrip calls only for light grease lubrication when assembled.

DISMANTLING

Cable Thimble. Unscrew the thimble from the twistgrip head. This is usually made easier by pulling on the cable adjacent to the twistgrip. When unscrewed, the cable simply pulls out of the twistgrip.

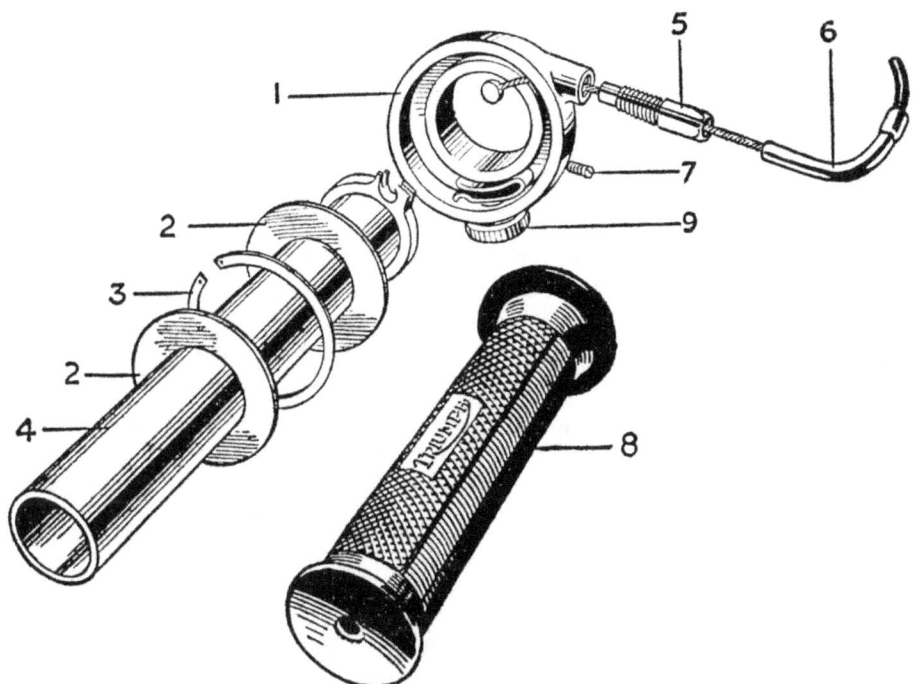

Fig. 47. TWISTGRIP.

Index No.	Description.	Index No.	Description.
1	Head assembly.	6	Guide tube.
2	Plate, retaining.	7	Grub screw.
3	Circlip.	8	Grip, rubber.
4	Sleeve assembly.	9	Screw, friction adjuster.
5	Thimble, cable.		

Petrol Tap

Rotor Sleeve. Pull back the twistgrip rubber and insert a thin blade behind the first retaining plate. Remove the circlip, when the rotor sleeve assembly can be withdrawn.

Head. Slacken the grub screw which secures the head to the handlebar and withdraw the head.

ASSEMBLING

Rotor Sleeve to Head. These can be replaced before assembling to the handlebar. Lightly grease rotor end ring and fit the rotor sleeve into the head with the nipple housing adjacent to the cable hole.

Slide the retaining plate into position and assemble the circlip to the head. Fit the second retaining plate. Roll back the rubber grip. If a new rubber is to be fitted, first wet the inside with petrol and then push it smartly over the sleeve. This job is done better after the twistgrip has been fitted to the handlebar.

Twistgrip to Handlebar. Grease the swaged portion of the handlebar and slide on the twistgrip; lock in the desired position with the grub screw.

Throttle Cable. Holding the outer casing, pull the inner wire, gripping it close to the cable ferrule with a pair of soft nosed pliers. With the other hand rotate the twistgrip sleeve to the closed position, thread the nipple end of the wire into the head and slowly rotate the sleeve when the nipple housing will locate the nipple. When located, replace the cable thimble over the wire and screw into the head.

PETROL TAP ADJUSTMENT

To make an adjustment, replacement or repair to either type of petrol tap the petrol must be drained from the tank.

Push-pull Type. To adjust a leaking tap, first remove the grub screw locking the plunger to the body, when the plunger assembly can be removed. Grip the plunger end in a suitable tool and turn the plunger knob in a clockwise direction; this expands the cork washer and will make a petrol tight fit when replaced in the petrol tap body. If the cork has deteriorated to any degree, a new cork can be fitted at a very low cost.

Taper Type. Remove the faulty tap and dismantle; take out the split pin, remove the washer, spring back plate and withdraw the spindle and lever assembly. Clean the body and spindle and then apply a smear of rouge to the spindle; add a little oil and rotate the spindle in the tap body using the same motion as when grinding-in the valves. When a true surface is obtained, wash the parts thoroughly in petrol and apply tallow fat to the spindle before assembly. Check the tension of the spring and if insufficient stretch slightly.

FITTING A SIDECAR

First prepare the motorcycle. Fit an engine sprocket having 2 or 3 teeth less than the solo sprocket. Replace the springs in the rear suspension units with 150 lb. rate springs. The appropriate front fork springs (see pages 105 and 113) should be fitted and additionally if a machine with rear panels is being converted, fit longer fork legs available under part number CP.183.

There are fixing points on the frame of the motorcycle at the top and bottom of the seat tube. For frames with the single front down tube a lug is also available for fixing to the front engine plates. Any other connections are provided by the sidecar manufacturers. Fittings on the front down tube should be fitted as high as possible with the smaller part projecting in front of the tubes.

THE CONNECTION MUST BE CLEAR OF THE MUDGUARD WHEN THE FORKS ARE FULLY COMPRESSED, OR THE STEERING MAY JAM WHEN BRAKING HEAVILY.

The following settings give good results although many experienced sidecar drivers may have their own preferences. The sidecar wheel should be 6 in. ahead of the rear wheel and toe-in $\frac{3}{8}$ in. measured at the front wheel. The motorcycle should be upright when the outfit is carrying its normal load, that is it will probably lean towards the sidecar when unladen.

With most makes of sidecar it is necessary to remove the centre stand to allow for the bottom connection, but a light jack and bracket are available for 1954-59 models under part number CP.153.

THE AMAL MONOBLOC CARBURETTER

HOW IT OPERATES

When the engine is idling, mixture is supplied from the pilot jet system, then as the throttle slide is raised, via the pilot by-pass. The mixture is then controlled by the tapered needle working in the needle jet and finally by the size of the main jet. The pilot system is supplied by a pilot jet, which is detachable, for cleaning purposes and which when assembled into the carburetter body is sealed by a cover. The main jet does not spray directly into the mixing chamber, but discharges through the needle jet into the primary air chamber, and the fuel goes from there as a rich petrol-air mixture through the primary air choke into the main air choke.

This primary air choke has a compensating action in conjunction with bleed holes in the needle jet, which serve the double purpose of air-compensating the mixture from the needle jet and allowing the fuel to provide a well, outside and around the needle jet, which is available for snap acceleration.

The carburetter is provided with an air control lever for use when starting from cold or experimenting. At all other times the control should be kept fully opened.

OPERATION OF CARBURETTER PARTS

Throttle Stop Screw. This screw should be set to open the throttle sufficiently to keep the engine running at a low tick over when the twistgrip is shut off.

Pilot Air Screw. To set the idling mixture, this screw should be set in or out to enrich or weaken, normal number of turns out is about $2\frac{1}{2}$. The screw controls the suction on the pilot petrol jet by metering the amount of air which mixes with the petrol.

Needle and Needle Jet. A tapered needle is attached to the throttle and allows more or less petrol to pass through the needle jet as the throttle is opened or closed throughout the range, except when idling or nearly full throttle.

The taper needle position in relation to the throttle opening can be set according to the mixture required by fixing it to the throttle with the needle clip spring in a certain groove, thus either raising or lowering it. Raising the needle enriches the mixture; lowering it weakens the mixture at throttle openings from a quarter to three quarters open. Machines are delivered from the factory with the needle in the fourth notch from the top, and the needle should be lowered to the middle notch after 1,000 miles (1,500 kms.).

Throttle Valve Cut-Away. The atmospheric side of the throttle is cut away to influence the depression on the main fuel supply and thus gives a means of tuning between the pilot and needle jet range of throttle opening. The amount of cut-away is recorded by a number marked on the throttle, viz. 376/3 means throttle type 376 with No. 3 cut-away; larger cut aways, say 4 and 5 give weaker mixture and 2 and 1 richer mixtures.

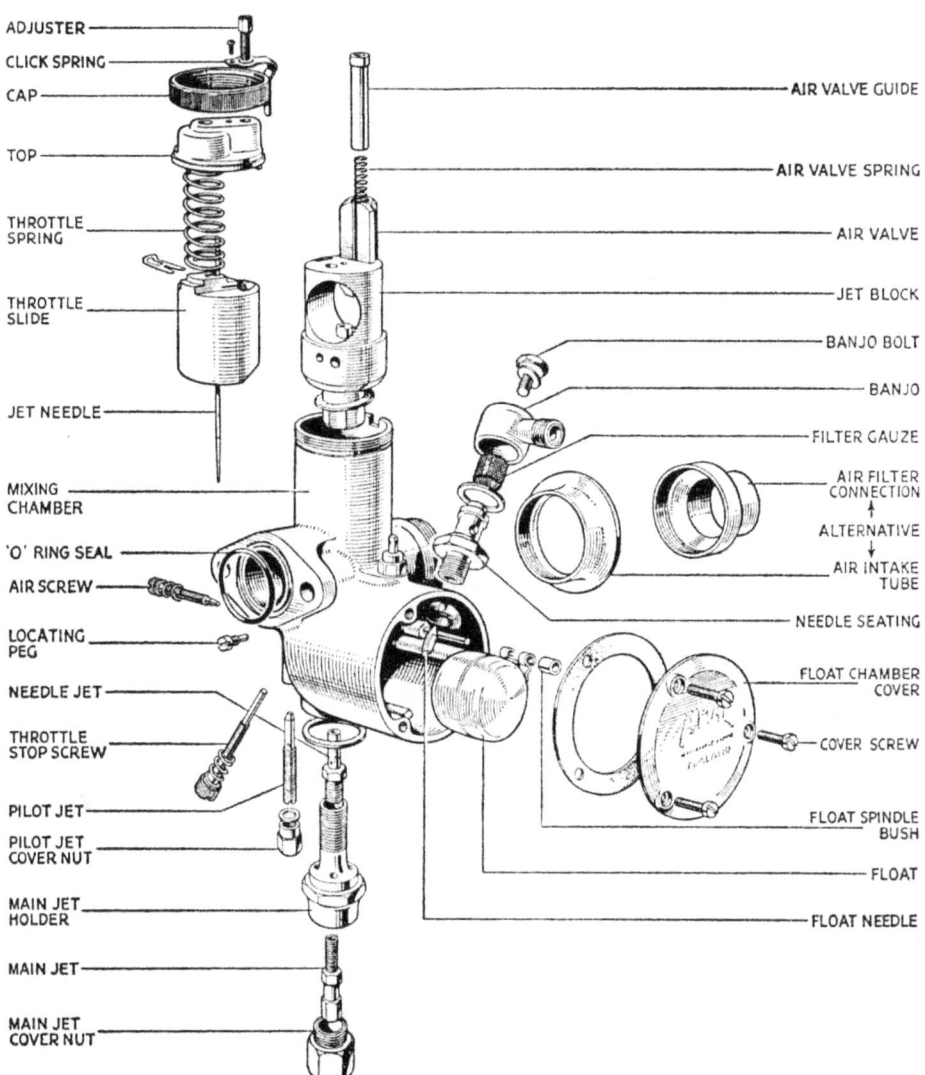

Fig. 48. AMAL MONOBLOC CARBURETTER.

Amal Monobloc Carburetter

Air Valve. Is only used for starting and running when cold, and for experimenting with, otherwise, run with it wide open.

Tickler. A small plunger spring loaded in the float chamber lid. When pressed down on the float, the needle valve is dislodged from its seat and so "flooding" is achieved. Flooding temporarily enriches the mixture until the level of the petrol subsides to normal.

FAULT FINDING AND MAINTENANCE

Occasionally remove and clean the petrol filter gauze from inside the banjo connection. If flooding occurs check this gauze to see that it is in good condition and then remove the float chamber cover, float and float needle. Examine for dirt or damage on the needle and the needle seating. When replacing the float see that the narrow hinge leg is uppermost, as this operates the needle, and do not forget to replace the float spindle bush. Make sure that the cover plate and washer are clean and in good condition before re-assembling.

GENERAL

Erratic running at low speeds can be due to distortion of the carburetter flange; this fault is generally caused by uneven tightening of the flange nuts. To rectify, first place a straight edge across the flange face to ascertain the amount of bow; if the bow is only slight, rub the flange surfaces over with a piece of emery cloth which has been tacked to a flat surface. If the flange cannot be trued up in this way it should be filed with a 6 in. (15 cm.) flat smooth file, and then finished off as stated above. Always use a new "O" ring seal, Part No. 244/765 when refitting the carburetter.

For more detailed instructions on tuning see the Amal leaflet number 502.

BONNEVILLE 120

The twin carburetters fitted to the Bonneville 120 may require synchronisation and a simple method is as follows:—First adjust the cables from the junction box so that they have the minimum of free play. Now start the motor and take off one plug lead and then adjust the pilot air screw and throttle stop screw in the OPPOSITE carburetter until the motor runs regularly. Replace the plug lead and repeat the process similarly for the other carburetter. With both plug leads replaced the tickover will be too fast and the stop screws should be lowered simultaneously until correct. It is most important the throttle slides lift simultaneously or the motor will run roughly, particularly when accelerating.

The initial setting height of the Bonneville float chamber is with the top face of the float chamber $1\frac{5}{16}$ in. (3.34 cm.) above the central "pip" on the carburetter side covers. This figure may require adjustment on individual machines and should be altered $\frac{1}{16}$ in. (1.6 mm.) at a time and the result tested before further adjustment. A low setting will cause starvation and loss of power and a high setting will cause "lumpy" running with an erratic tickover.

AIR FILTER

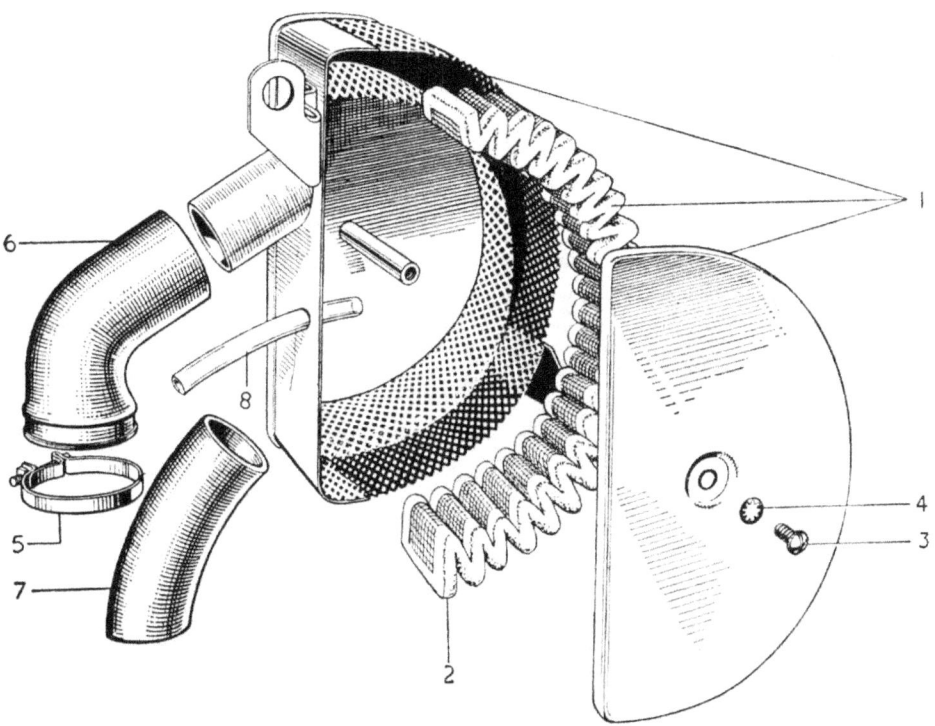

Fig. 49. AIR FILTER.

INDEX TO FIG. 49.   AIR FILTER

Index No.	Description.
1	Filter assembly.
2	Element, filter.
3	Screw, cover.
4	Washer, shakeproof.
5	Clip, connection to carburetter.
6	Connection, Amal carburetter to filter (rubber).
7	Connection, S.U. carburetter to filter (rubber) 6T.
8	Vent pipe, carburetter to filter, 6T.

SERVICING THE FILTER

To service the filter, the oil tank must first be detached. This operation necessitates the removal of the three fixing bolts and disconnection of the oil pipes. Disconnect the rubber sleeve and remove the air filter.

To remove the filter element, unscrew the screw securing the cover, when the latter can be removed and the element extracted.

Air Filter

The air filter on the 6T and T110 models with rear panels is detached by first removing the battery and battery carrier. In this type of filter the element is sealed in and must be cleaned in situ as detailed below.

Every 2,000 miles (3,000 kms.), the filter element should be removed and washed in petrol until all road dust is extracted. Put the element in a convenient place to dry off. In extreme conditions (dust, sand, etc.) this servicing should be at more frequent intervals. When dry, re-oil the element with "Vokes Trifiltrene" filter oil. If this is unobtainable SAE.20 grade oil may be used.

The filter element should be changed every 10,000 miles (15,000 kms.) and in countries where dusty conditions prevail the change should be made at more frequent intervals. This procedure is most important as a choked filter will cause loss of performance and heavy petrol consumption.

The maximum power output with the air filter attached, is very little affected, but if the absolute maximum is required, remove the rubber sleeve and increase the main jet size by 20 c.c. and fit air intake tube, Part No. 376/066.

PETROL TANK MOUNTING

The following instructions refer to earlier models only; for the current strap fixing see page 63.

The petrol tank rear bracket is rubber-mounted to the frame and the assembly procedure is as follows:—

1. Place the petrol tank on the machine and insert two thick rubber washers under the front. Secure with a rubber washer, steel washer and bolt each side. Fully tighten the bolts and wire them together.

2. Fit the rear bracket to the frame with the spigoted washers in the lower cups and the thin rubbers in the upper cups. Adjust the bolts until one of the thick rubber washers will just slide between the bracket and tank each side. Now wire the bolts together.

3. Secure the tank to the rear bracket with a flat rubber washer between the bracket and the tank and a spigoted rubber washer, cup and fixing bolt below the bracket. Tighten the bolts up to the shoulder and finally wire them together.

THE S.U. M.C.2 CARBURETTER*

ADJUSTMENT AND TUNING

The S.U. Carburetter is of the automatically expanding type in which the cross sectional area of the air passage, and the effective orifice of the jet are variable. The choice of the needle which governs the effective orifice of the jet is settled for a particular engine after considerable testing, both on the engine test bed and afterwards on Road Test, with Premium Grade Petrols, and it is not, therefore, a common requirement that the needle type should be changed from the maker's original specification. Low grade and alcohol blended petrols may require the substitution of a richer than standard needle.

The standard needle is M9, but sidecar machines are sometimes improved by fitting M7. If any doubt arises as to the correctness of the type fitted, this can be checked by first removing the suction chamber and then slackening the side needle screw when the needle can be pulled out and its markings by numbers or letters checked. These identifying letters and numbers may be rolled round the shank, or stamped on the flat end of it. If, therefore, an alteration to mixture strength is required this needle alone should be changed, as all jets are of standard size and as THE JET ADJUSTING NUT IS FOR SETTING THE IDLING ONLY.

It is most important that the needle is fitted with its shoulder FLUSH WITH THE FACE OF THE PISTON, as shown in the diagram.

When detaching the suction chamber and piston assembly from the main carburetter body (necessary when checking or changing the needle) it will be necessary to remove the OIL CAP. After the two side screws have been removed lift the assembly off the carburetter body. This will call for a certain amount of manual dexterity, as the suction chamber can only be lifted a limited amount. One hand is required to lift the suction piston upwards inside the chamber against the piston spring, whilst the other steadies the suction chamber. The complete unit can then be moved sideways, clear of the main instrument, but great care must be taken to see that the JET NEEDLE IS NOT BENT.

When re-fitting the suction chamber and piston the procedure is, of course, reversed, and the piston should be held as high up as possible inside the suction chamber whilst the assembly is guided carefully into the piston bore and jet in the main body. A slot in the small piston diameter registers with a riveted brass guide in the body.

Tuning the carburetter, which should only be carried out after the engine has reached its normal running temperature, is confined to correct idling adjustment by means of the throttle stop screw, which governs the amount of throttle opening for IDLING SPEED, and the jet adjusting nut (18) which controls the IDLING MIXTURE. Screwing this nut up weakens the mixture and down enriches it.

NOTE. This nut must not be forced, as this may set the jet off centre.

*All references to numbers in the script apply to Fig. 51 only.

S.U. Carburetter

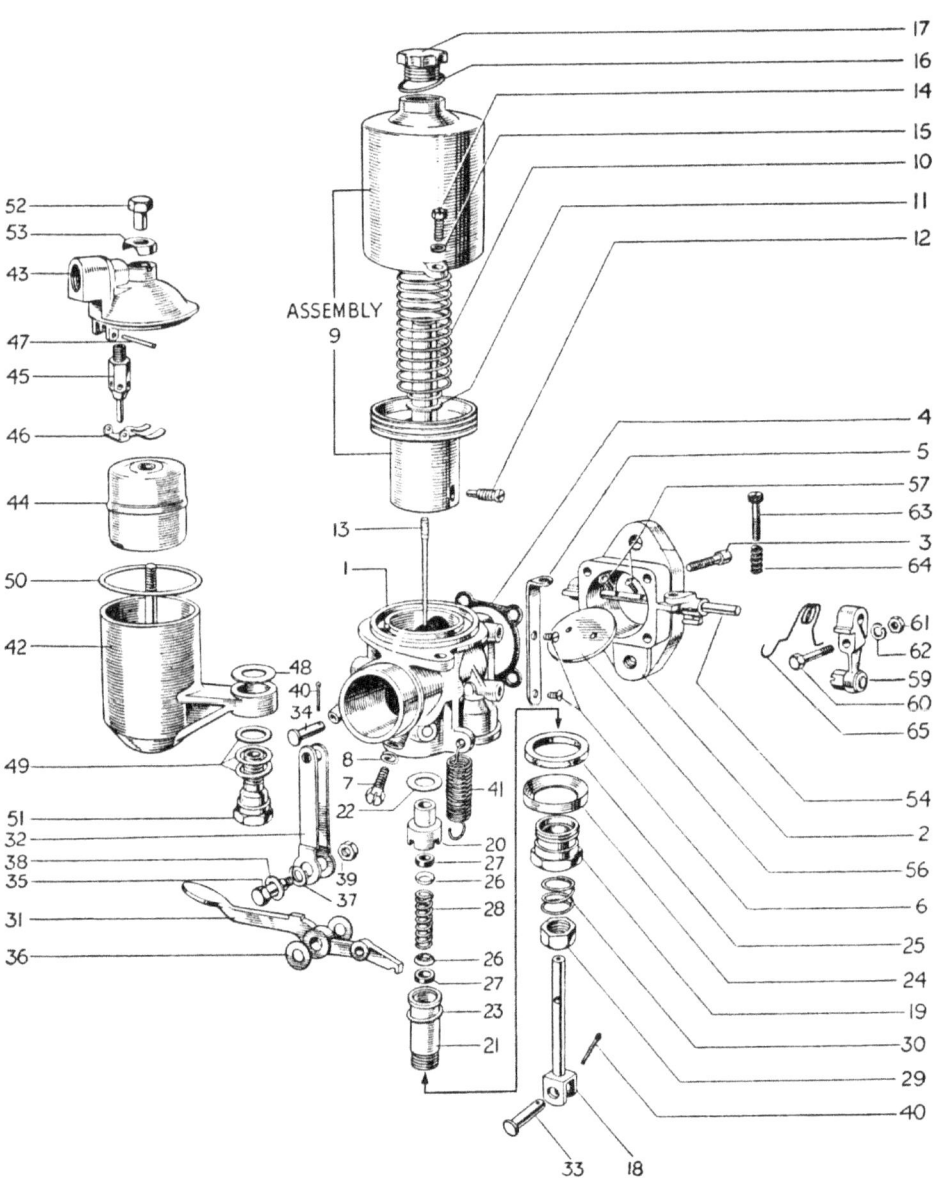

Fig. 50. S.U. CARBURETTER (COMPONENT PARTS).

S.U. Carburetter

INDEX TO FIG. 50. S.U. CARBURETTER (COMPONENT PARTS)

Index No.	Description.	Index No.	Description.
1	Body.	33	Pivot pin, long.
2	Adaptor, throttle barrel.	34	Pivot pin, short.
3	Screw, adaptor to body.	35	Bolt.
4	Gasket, adaptor to body.	36	Washer, fibre.
5	Abutment, throttle cable.	37	Washer, spring.
6	Screw.	38	Washer.
7	Screw, plug 2 B.A.	39	Nut.
8	Washer.	40	Split pin.
9	Chamber, suction complete.	41	Spring, return.
10	Spring, piston.	42	Chamber, float.
11	Washer, thrust.	43	Lid, float chamber.
12	Screw, needle.	44	Float.
13	Needle, jet.	45	Needle and seat.
14	Screw.	46	Lever, hinged.
15	Washer, spring.	47	Pin, hinge.
16	Washer, oil cap.	48	Washer, fibre.
17	Oil cap, octagonal.	49	Washers, 2-fibre, 1-brass.
18	Jet.	50	Washer, float chamber lid.
19	Screw, jet.	51	Bolt, holding.
20	Bearing, jet top half.	52	Nut, float chamber lid.
21	Bearing, jet bottom half.	53	Cap, brass.
22	Washer, copper.	54	Throttle spindle.
23	Washer, copper.	56	Disc throttle.
24	Ring, sealing (Brass).	57	Screw.
25	Ring, sealing (Cork).	59	Lever, throttle.
26	Washer, gland (Brass).	60	Bolt.
27	Washer, gland (Cork).	61	Nut.
28	Spring.	62	Washer.
29	Nut, adjusting.	63	Screw, adjusting.
30	Spring.	64	Spring, adjusting screw lock.
31	Lever, jet.	65	Spring, lever return.
32	Link, jet.		

WARNING. Move one "flat" of the nut round at a time and remember to apply slight downward pressure on the jet lever to ensure that the jet follows the adjusting nut, as the jet lever spring (Pt. No. 4872/1) is not strong enough to do this of itself (as in car practice), its sole purpose being to retain the jet against vibration in the position set by the rider. Three "flats" in either direction should be sufficient to identify progress; excess movement would indicate an air leak in the induction system or an ignition fault. A correct idling mixture gives an even beat with a colourless exhaust—too rich a mixture gives a trace of black in the exhaust with a rhythmical or regular misfire—too weak a mixture gives a splashy irregular type of misfire with a marked tendence to stop. To test remove the plug (29) and lift the piston $\frac{1}{16}$ in. (1.5 mm.) with a thin rod. If the mixture is correct the engine will stop, but if it is too rich the engine will speed up.

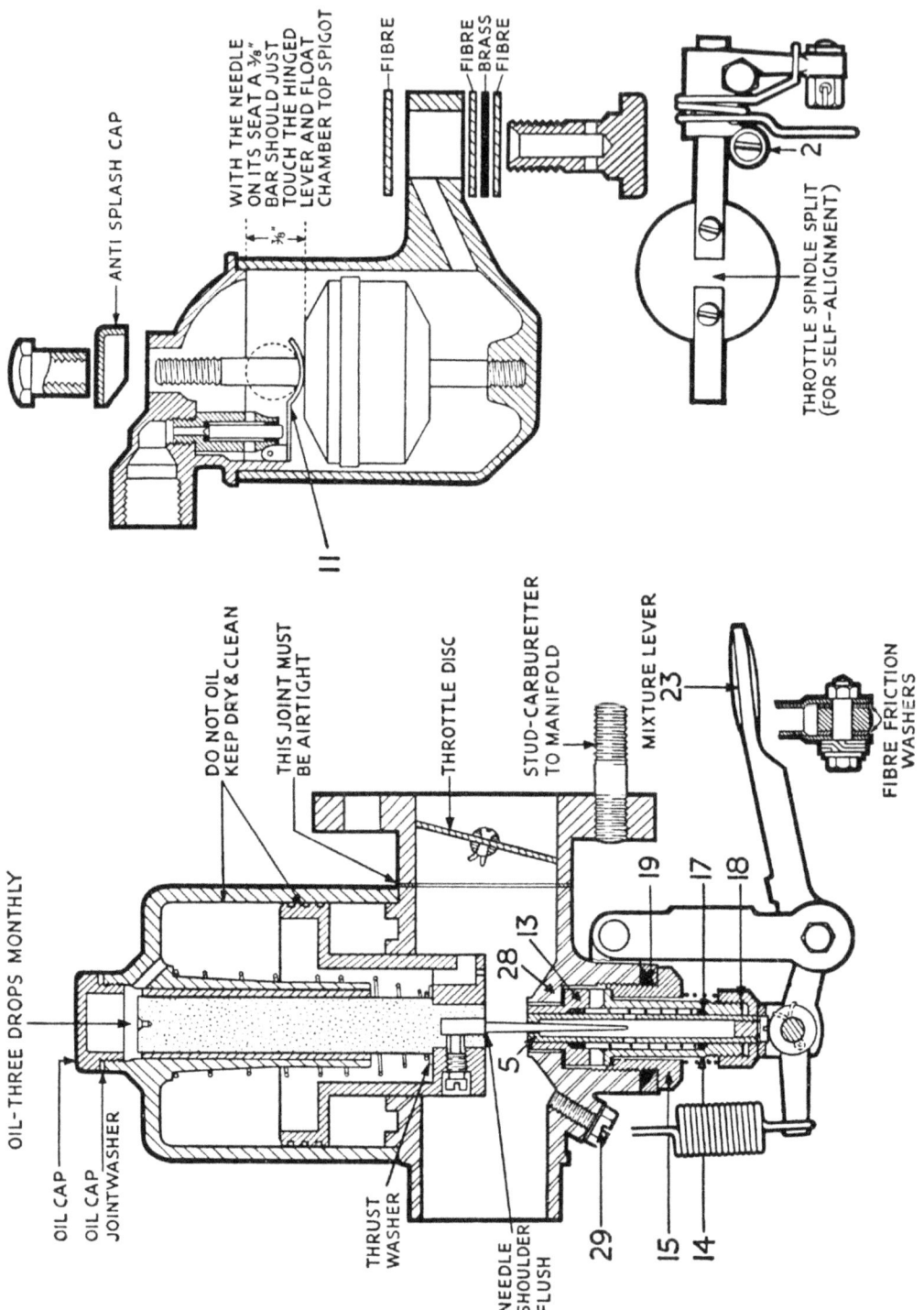

Fig. 51. S.U. CARBURETTER (DIAGRAM).

Maintenance S.U. Carburetter

DEFECTS IN OPERATION

When an engine runs erratically, faults other than carburation can be contributory causes. Before interfering with the carburetter, the following possibilities should be considered:—

(a) Compression—Equal pressure in both cylinders; check tappet clearances.
(b) Moisture condensation (water)—Examine float chamber and H.T. cables.
(c) Ignition System—Inspect the distributor points, clean and adjust if necessary.

Contact breaker and condenser condition is most important. Sparking plugs should be cleaned and re-gapped (See Technical Data) and pressure tested. Correct timing is vital to good idling, in particular excessive advance and faulty operation of the automatic mechanism must be rectified.

(d) Check for air leaks:—
    (i) Between the MANIFOLD and CYLINDER HEAD.
    (ii) Between the MANIFOLD and CARBURETTER.
    (iii) Between the TWO HALVES of the CARBURETTER.
    (iv) at the SUCTION CHAMBER CAP.

If, however, the engine and ignition are found to be faultless the following points should be checked on the carburetter:—

STICKING OF PISTON

The symptoms here are either stalling and a refusal of the engine to run slowly or, alternatively, lack of power accompanied by excessive fuel consumption. This defect is easily detectable. When the engine is not running the piston should rest upon the bridge (28). When raised by the hand through the air intake, the piston should drop freely and strike the bridge sharply and distinctly. To do this the filter rubber connection must first be removed.

If it becomes prematurely arrested in its downward movement, or appears unduly reluctant to break away from its position of rest on the bridge when an attempt is made to raise it from this position, the jet should be lowered by means of its lever, and the test repeated.

If the symptoms persist, it can be assumed that either the large diameter of the piston is making contact with the bore of the suction chamber, or the small diameter with the carburetter body, or that the piston rod is not sliding freely within its bush.

When, on the other hand, sticking has been eliminated by the act of lowering the jet, the indication is that the needle is binding on the jet either due to its being bent or to the latter being out of centre. Normally the needle should never touch the jet orifice when correctly assembled.

(If visual evidence clearly indicates needle wear and jet ovality, both should be renewed).

Rectification should be conducted as follows according to the diagnosis:—
Dirt or contact between the piston and suction chamber, or sticking of the piston rod in its bush.

If dirt or corrosion of the suction chamber, piston or piston rod is responsible then the parts should be cleaned with a solvent such as petrol, thinners, degreasing fluid or alcohol, but no abrasive material should be used. They should be re-assembled dry and clean with OIL ON THE PISTON ROD ONLY. If, on the other hand, there is metallic contact the high spot may be removed with a scraper PROVIDED THAT THE GREATEST CARE IS TAKEN; INDISCRIMINATE SCRAPING WILL RENDER THE PARTS SCRAP.

Bent Needle or incorrectly centred Jet

A bent needle should be replaced as straightening is seldom satisfactory, and an incorrectly centred jet should be re-centred according to the instructions given below. In either case contact between these two parts is likely to have caused wear and both may have to be replaced.

LUBRICATION

EVERY MONTH, or as frequently as may be found necessary, remove the plastic oil cap from the top of the suction chamber and thoroughly oil the piston rod and guide bush assembly with thin machine oil.

When the oil cap and joint washer have been replaced, ensure that the cap is FIRMLY SCREWED DOWN. An air leak at this point would upset the automatic operation of the piston in the suction chamber, causing a rich setting and loss of speed.

ECCENTRICITY

Re-centring of the jet in relation to the needle will be necessary should the jet have become laterally displaced in service due to inadequate tightening of the locking screw (15), or any other cause. This operation will of course, also be necessary if the jet and its associated parts have been removed for any reason. Before proceeding as described in the next paragraph, first try turning the jet round 180° as, if the jet head has been connected to the mixture lever in a different place to that at which it was originally "centred" the action of the piston will be restricted.

The procedure for re-centring the jet is as follows:—

The jet adjusting nut (18) should first be screwed upwards to its fullest extent. THE JET HEAD THEN BEING RAISED TO CONTACT IT so that the jet assumes its highest possible position. The locking screw (15) should now be loosened sufficiently to release the jet and the jet bush assembly (5), (13), (14), etc., and permit this to be moved laterally.

A moderate side loading applied to the lower protruding part of the lower jet bush (14) will indicate whether or not the assembly has been sufficiently freed. The piston should now be raised and, maintaining the jet in its highest position, allowed to drop. This will cause the needle to move the jet gradually but positively into position, and thus bring about the required centralisation.

The locking screw should now be tightened and the jet returned to its former position. Should any indication of contact between the needle and the jet persist, which may sometimes occur due to further displacement of the assembly on finally tightening the locking screw, this must again be slackened off and the operation repeated.

S.U. Carburetter

FLOODING FROM FLOAT CHAMBER OR MOUTH OF JET

Flooding may occur due to a punctured float, or to dirt between the float chamber needle valve and its seating. To remedy either defect, the float chamber lid should be removed and the necessary cleaning, float replacement or repair effected. The needle and seating unit number is T2, to identify which two ring grooves are machined around the seating.

Flooding may also occur if the original manufacturer's setting of the hinged fork lever (11) in the top of the float chamber has been disturbed, possibly causing the petrol level to be higher than normal, this higher level giving a slow petrol bleed over the jet bridge. The setting figure for this fork is that with the fork pressing the needle home on its seating, a $\frac{3}{8}$in. (9.5 mm.) diameter test bar should just slide easily between the curve of the fork and the circular facing of the float lid casting.

Flooding may also be caused by a bad seal between the float needle and its seating, and which may sometimes be restored by giving the needle a few light taps with a delicate instrument such as the handle of a screwdriver:

ROUGH HANDLING WILL RENDER THE PARTS SCRAP.

Leakage from bottom of Jet

If persistent slow leakage is observed in the neighbourhood of the jet head, it is probable that the jet gland washer (7) and its lower counterpart, together with the locking screw washer (19) require replacement. The jet lever (23) should first be detached from the jet head, the locking screw (15) removed, and the entire jet and jet bush assembly withdrawn. On re-assembly, great care should be taken to replace all parts in their correct situations, as shown in the diagram. Re-centring of the jet, as previously described, will of course be necessary after this operation.

HINTS AND TIPS

These are a few of the points to which the Owner should pay particular attention in order to maintain minimum fuel consumption and maximum power.

1. The Float Chamber. If rough running and poor idling are suddenly experienced, the internal float chamber condition is usually responsible. To overcome this trouble remove the float chamber every two months and thoroughly clean. When replacing, do not overtighten the lid sleeve nut as this will cause distortion and leakage of fuel at the joint between lid and float chamber.

2. Air Leaks. Leakage at the manifold to engine and carburetter to manifold will completely upset the smooth performance of the engine.

3. Sticking Piston. Dirt, corrosion or malalignment of the jet will cause the piston to stick. Make sure that the suction chamber and piston are perfectly dry and clean, and that the PISTON ROD, which must move freely in its bush, IS OILED. Before attempting to re-centre the jet try the effect of turning it through 180°. It may have been replaced in the opposite position, in the mixture lever.

4. Throttle Spindle. Overstressing the throttle spindle torsion return spring is a common fault. This causes the coils to bind before full throttle is attained, and may disturb the whole mechanism. Incorrect positioning of the movable throttle lever may do the same.

S.U. Carburetter

LUBRICATE THROTTLE CABLE TO ENSURE SMOOTH AND POSITIVE THROTTLE OPERATION.

5. Plastic Cap. Do not forget to fit the washer, as the spindle can foul the cap before full lift occurs, resulting in restricted power. Always use the correct part, a car type (with a hole in) will **NOT** do.

6. Piston Spring. Do not mutilate the spring by stretching, otherwise the performance and fuel consumption of the motorcycle will be adversely affected. If in doubt regarding the spring pressure a new one of the correct type should be fitted.

Make sure that the ignition control is working properly, that the timing is correct and, in particular, that it is not advanced—**especially** at idling.

AIR FILTER

THE AIR FILTER SHOULD NOT BE DISCONNECTED IN AN ATTEMPT TO INCREASE THE MAXIMUM SPEED OF THE MACHINE. THE CARBURETTER AND AIR FILTER ARE DESIGNED TO GIVE MAXIMUM EFFICIENCY AND, IN FACT, THE REMOVAL OF THE FILTER WILL IMPAIR GENERAL PERFORMANCE AS THE CARBURETTER IS EXPOSED TO ROAD DUST AND OTHER FOREIGN MATTER. IF THE AIR FILTER IS NOT CONNECTED THERE IS A LIKELIHOOD THAT THE FREEDOM OF THE PISTON IN THE SUCTION CHAMBER WILL BE RESTRICTED. **ITS FREE MOVEMENT IS VITAL TO THE SATISFACTORY OPERATION OF THE CARBURETTER, OF THE ENGINE AND, THEREFORE, OF THE WHOLE MOTORCYCLE.**

LUCAS ELECTRICAL EQUIPMENT
DYNAMO LIGHTING AND MAGNETO IGNITION

DYNAMO

Output Control. The dynamo works in conjunction with a regulator unit to give compensated voltage control. Although combined structurally, the regulator and cut-out are electrically separate. Both are accurately adjusted during manufacture and should not be tampered with.

The regulator provides a completely automatic control. It causes the dynamo to give an output which varies according to the load on the battery and its state of charge. When the battery is discharged, the dynamo gives a high output, but if the battery is fully charged then the dynamo gives only a trickle charge so as to keep the battery in good condition. In addition to controlling the output of the dynamo according to the condition of the battery, the regulator provides for an increase of output to balance the current taken by the lamps when in use.

The cut-out is an automatic switch which connects the dynamo to the battery only when the dynamo voltage exceeds the battery voltage, or conversely, which disconnects to prevent the battery discharging through the dynamo windings.

The dynamo output is accurately set to suit the requirements of the motorcycle and in normal service the battery will be kept in a good condition. If due to special running conditions it is found that the battery is not kept in a charged condition or is being overcharged, the regulator should be re-set by a Lucas Service Depot or Agent. Accurate measuring equipment is required to set the regulator correctly.

Ammeter Readings. Normally, during day time running when the battery is in good condition, the dynamo gives only a trickle charge so that the ammeter needle should show only a small deflection to the "+" side of the scale.

A discharge reading should be observed immediately after switching on the headlamp. This usually happens after a long run when the battery voltage is high. After a short time the battery voltage will drop and the regulator will respond, causing the dynamo output to balance the lamp load.

Lubrication. No lubrication is required to these models as ball bearings are fitted at both ends. These bearings are packed with grease during assembly and will last until the machine is taken down for a general overhaul.

Inspection of Brushgear and Commutator. Every six months, remove the commutator cover and inspect the brushgear and commutator. The brushes, which are held in boxes by means of springs, must make firm contact with the commutator. Move each brush to see that it is free to slide in its holder; if it sticks, remove it and clean with a cloth moistened with petrol. Care must be taken to replace the brushes in their original position, otherwise they will not "bed" properly on the commutator. If after long service the brushes have become worn to such an extent that they will not bear properly on the commutator they must be replaced. Always use genuine Lucas brushes, which should be fitted by a Service Agent so that they can be properly bedded to the commutator.

Dynamo Wiring Diagram

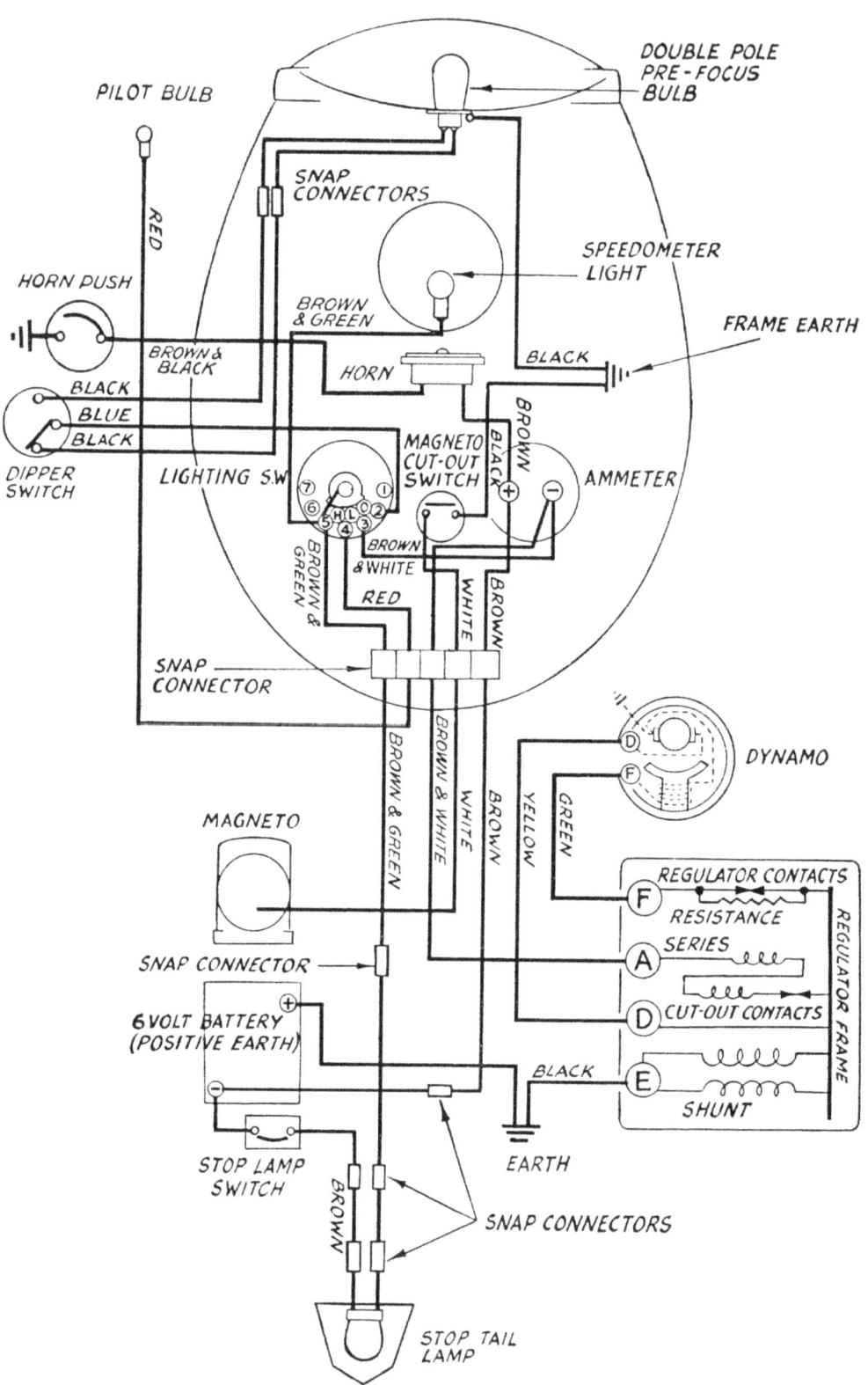

Fig. 52. **WIRING DIAGRAM (Models with Dynamo).**

Examine the commutator, which should be free from any trace of oil or dirt and should have a highly polished appearance. Clean a dirty or blackened commutator by pressing a clean dry cloth against it whilst the engine is slowly turned over by means of the kickstarter crank. (It is an advantage to remove the sparking plugs before doing this). If the commutator is very dirty, moisten the cloth with petrol.

MAGNETO

The magneto is of rotating armature pattern, having its magnet cast into the body, so eliminating joints and improving the weatherproof properties of the magneto. The ignition timing is controlled by a manual lever situated on the handlebar.

Lubrication—Every 3,000 miles (5,000 kms.). The cam is supplied with lubricant from a felt pad contained in a pocket in the contact breaker housing. A small hole in the cam fitted with a wick, enables the oil to find its way to the surface of the cam. Remove the contact breaker cover, turn the engine over until the hole in the cam can be clearly seen and then carefully add a few drops of thin machine oil. Do not allow any oil to get on or near the contacts. If the cam ring is removed, the wick should be taken out and soaked in thin machine oil. Wipe the wick to remove surplus oil, before replacing.

The contact breaker rocker arm pivot also requires lubrication and the complete contact breaker must be removed for this purpose. Take out the hexagon-headed screw from the centre of the contact breaker and carefully lever the contact breaker off the tapered shaft on which it fits. Push aside the rocker arm retaining spring, lift off the rocker arm and lightly smear the pivot with Mobilgrease No. 2 or an equivalent grease.

Remove the cam ring, which is a sliding fit in its housing, and lightly smear inside and outside surfaces with Mobilgrease No. 2. Removal and re-fitting of the cam can be made easier if the handlebar control lever is half retarded, thus taking the cam away from its stop pin. Allow one or two drops of thin machine oil to the felt cam lubricator in the housing. Re-fit the cam, taking care that the stop peg in the housing and the timing control plunger engage with their respective slots.

If an earthing brush is fitted at the back of the contact breaker base, see that it is clean and can move freely in its holder, before re-fitting to the contact breaker. When replacing the contact breaker, take care to ensure that the projecting key on the tapered portion of the contact breaker base engages with the keyway cut in the magneto spindle, otherwise the timing of the magneto will be affected. Replace the contact breaker securing screw and tighten with care.

The armature bearings are packed with grease during assembly, and will not need attention until the motorcycle is dismantled for general overhaul, when it is advisable to have the magneto inspected by a Lucas Service Depot or Agent.

Magneto Maintenance

Adjustment of Contact Breaker Setting. The setting of the contact breaker must be checked every 3,000 miles (5,000 kms.). To do this, remove the contact breaker cover and turn the engine until the contacts are seen to be fully open. Check the gap with a feeler gauge having a thickness of 0.012in.-0.015in. (0.30-0.40 mm.). A gauge for this purpose is provided on the spanner usually supplied with each magneto. If the setting is correct, the gauge should be a sliding fit, but if the gap width varies appreciably from the gauge thickness it must be adjusted. Keep the engine in the position giving maximum separation of the contacts, slacken the locknut and turn the contact screw by its hexagon head until the gap is set to the gauge.

Cleaning Contacts. Every 6,000 miles (10,000 kms.), take off the contact breaker cover and examine the contact breaker. Dirty or pitted contacts can be cleaned with a fine carborundum stone, or, if this is not available, very fine emery cloth can be used.

Wipe away any dirt or metal dust with a cloth moistened with petrol. Contact breaker springs should be examined and any rust removed. To render contacts accessible for cleaning, proceed as outlined below.

After cleaning, check the contact breaker setting.

Removal of Contacts for Cleaning. Unscrew the contact breaker securing screw. Carefully lever the contact breaker off the tapered shaft on which it fits. Push aside the locating spring and lift the rocker arm off its pivot, when it will be possible to clean the contacts. When replacing the contact breaker, check that the projecting key, on the tapered portion of the contact breaker base, engages with the keyway cut in the armature spindle, otherwise the timing of the magneto wil lbe affected. Replace the contact breaker securing screw and tighten with care.

High Tension Pick-up. About every 6,000 miles (10,000 kms.), remove the high tension pick-up. Wipe the moulding with a clean dry cloth. Check that the carbon brush moves freely in its holder, but take care not to stretch the brush spring unduly. If the brush is dirty, clean it with a cloth moistened with petrol. If the brush is worn to within $\frac{1}{8}$ in. (3.0 mm.) of the shoulder it must be renewed.

Before re-fitting the high tension pick-up, clean the slip ring track and flanges by pressing a soft dry cloth on the ring with a suitably shaped piece of wood, while the engine is slowly turned.

Renewing High Tension Cables. When high tension cables show signs of cracking or perishing, they must be replaced, using 7 mm. rubber covered ignition cable.

To replace a high tension cable proceed as follows:—

Remove the metal washer and moulded terminal from the defective cable. Thread the new cable through the moulded terminal and cut back the insulation for about $\frac{1}{4}$in. (6.0 mm.). Pass the exposed strands through the metal washer and bend them back radially. Screw the terminal into the pick-up moulding.

LUCAS RM 14, RM 13/15 AND RM 15

A.C./D.C. LIGHTING AND IGNITION

GENERAL DESCRIPTION

Under NORMAL running conditions, electrical energy in the form of rectified A.C. passes through the battery from the alternator—the rate of charge depending on the position of the lighting switch. When no lights are in use, the alternator output is sufficient only to supply the ignition coil and to trickle-charge the battery. When the lighting switch is turned to the "PILOT" or "HEAD" positions, the output increases proportionately.

Under EMERGENCY starting conditions, trickle-charging continues whilst an ignition performance similar to that from a magneto is obtained. AFTER THE ENGINE HAS BEEN STARTED, NORMAL RUNNING IS RESUMED BY TURNING THE IGNITION KEY FROM "EMG" to "IGN". IF THE BATTERY MUST BE REMOVED, THE ENGINE CAN BE RUN TEMPORARILY WITH THE IGNITION SWITCH IN THE "EMG" POSITION PROVIDING THAT THE BATTERY NEGATIVE INPUT CABLE (BROWN) IS EARTHED TO THE FRAME. UNDER THESE CONDITIONS NO LIGHTS ARE AVAILABLE.

CIRCUIT DETAILS

The alternator stator carries three pairs of series-connected coils, one pair being permanently connected across the rectifier bridge network. The purpose of this latter pair is to provide some degree of charging current for the battery whenever the engine is running.

Connections to the remaining coils vary according to the positions of the lighting and ignition switch controls. When no lights are in use, the alternator output from the battery charging coil is regulated to a minimum by interaction of the rotor flux set up by current flowing in the short circuited coils.

In the "PILOT" position these latter coils are disconnected and the regulating fluxes are consequently reduced. The alternator output therefore increases and compensates for the additional parking light load. In the "HEAD" position, the alternator output is further increased by the connection of all three pairs of coils in parallel.

EMERGENCY STARTING (IGNITION SWITCH AT EMG.)

With this circuit the contact breaker is arranged to open when the alternating current in the windings reaches a maximum. The ignition coil primary winding and the contact breaker are connected in series. When the contacts separate H.T. current is induced in the coil secondary windings, thus producing a spark at the plug.

A.C. Generator

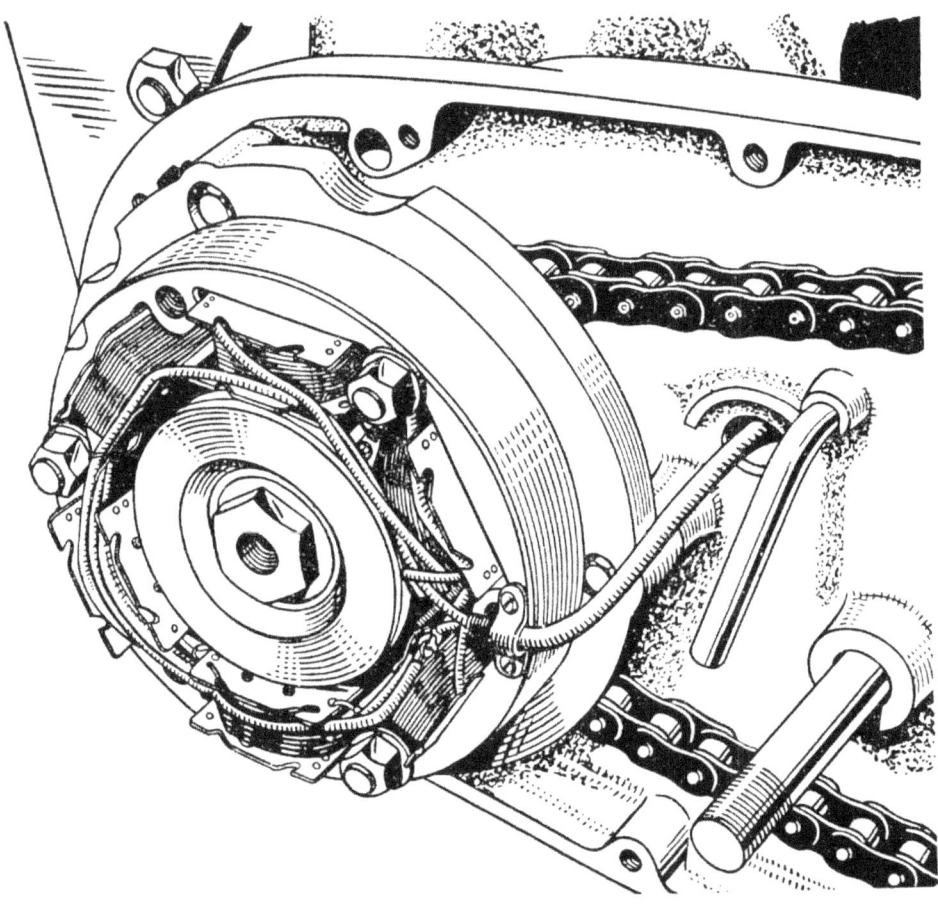

Fig. 53. PRIMARY CHAINCASE COVER REMOVED TO SHOW ROTOR AND STATOR.

A.C. Generator Wiring Diagram

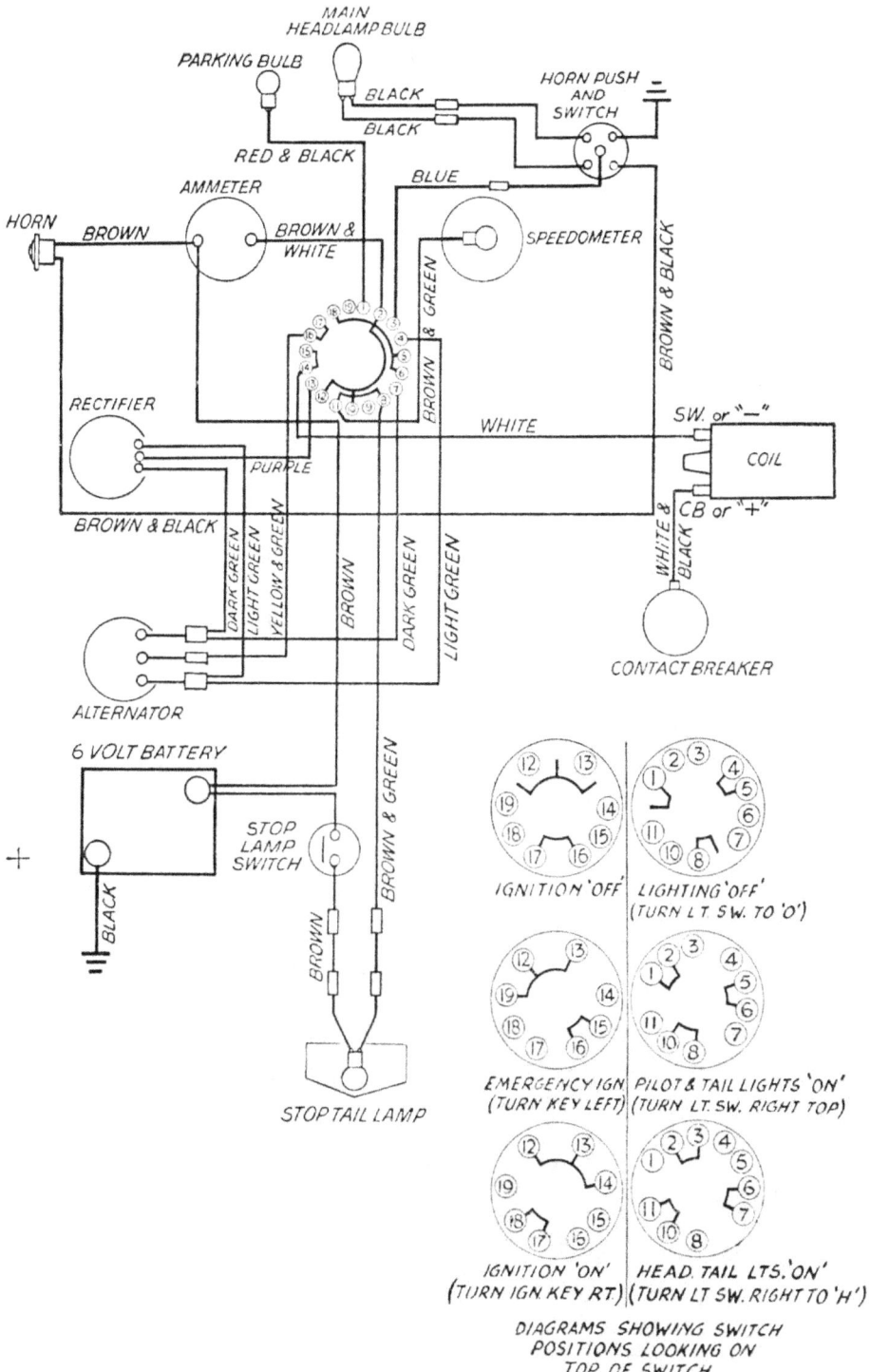

Fig. 54. WIRING DIAGRAM (5T & 6T).

A.C. Generator

Since, with the ignition switch at "EMG" and the engine running, the battery receives a charging current, the battery voltage soon begins to rise. The rising voltage opposes the alternator voltage, gradually effecting a reduction in the energy available for transfer to the coil. In the event of a rider omitting to return the ignition key from position "EMG" to position "IGN" this reduction in spark energy will cause misfiring to occur and will remind the rider to switch over to normal running.

As previously mentioned, continuous running without a battery is temporarily arranged by earthing the cable normally connected to the battery negative terminal.

CONSTRUCTION

The alternator consists essentially of a spigot-mounted and bolted 6-coil laminated stator with the centre-bored rotor carried on, and driven by, an extension to the crankshaft. The rotor has an hexagonal steel core, each face of which carries a high energy permanent magnet keyed to a laminated pole tip. The pole tips are riveted circumferentially to brass side plates, the assembly being cast in aluminium and machined to give a smooth external finish. The stator and rotor can be separated without any need to fit magnet keepers to the rotor poles.

RATING

The alternator is designed for use with headlamp bulbs not exceeding 30-watts rating (or equivalent Continental touring bulbs which, although of higher wattage rating, are yet suitable due to the generally higher average road speeds encountered abroad).

THE ALTERNATOR

Except for an occasional inspection of the snap-connectors in the three green output cables—these connectors must be clean and tight—the alternator requires no maintenance.

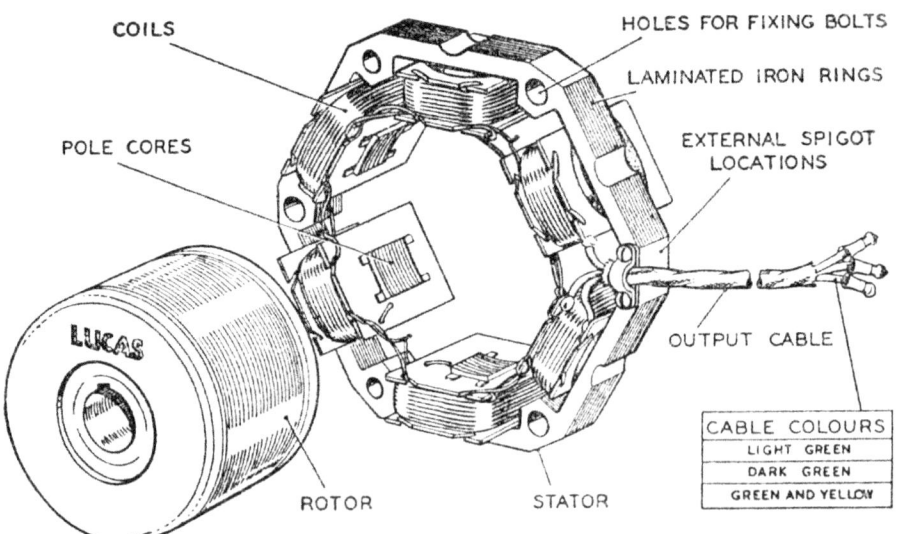

Fig. 55. ALTERNATOR (Model RM14).

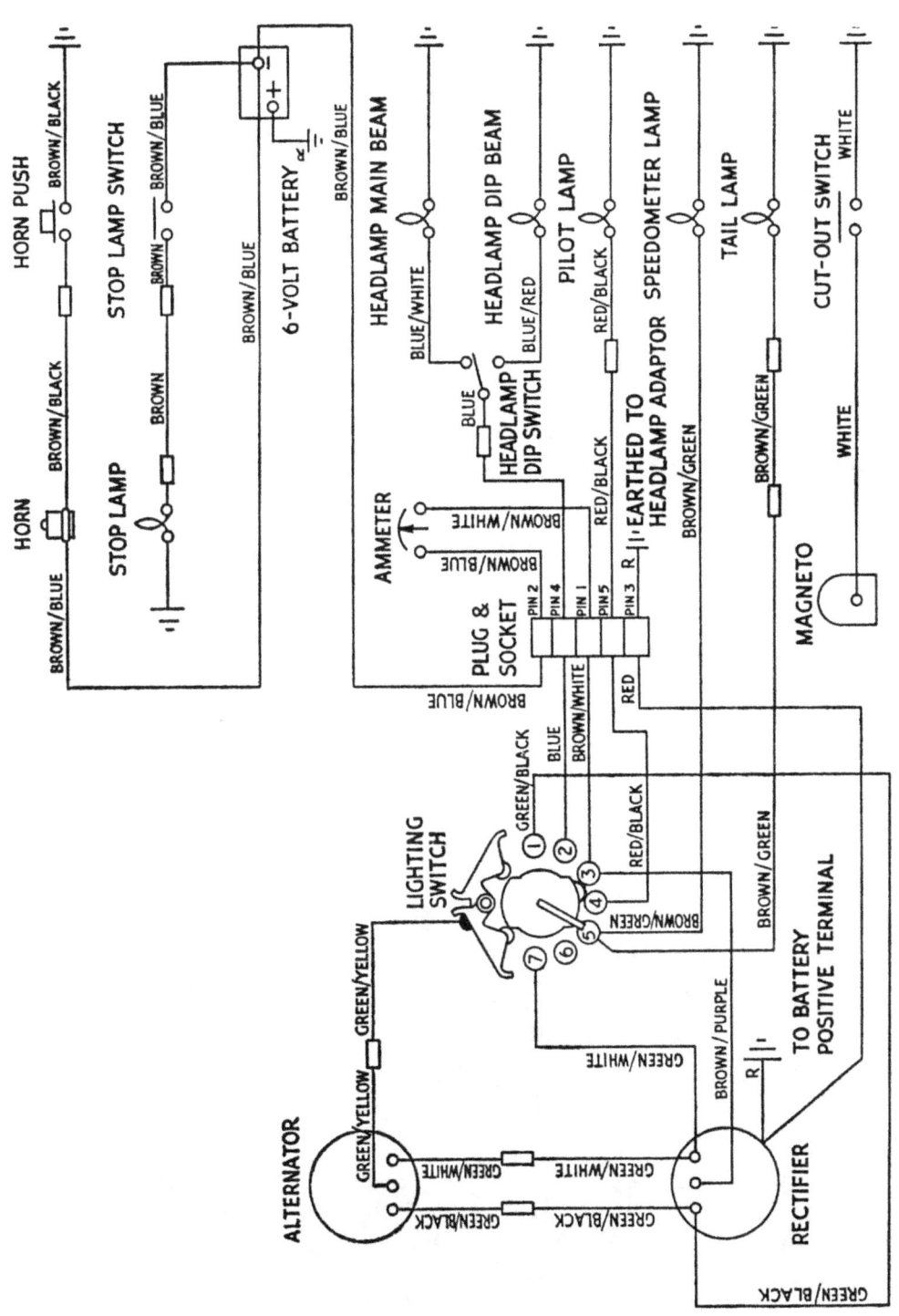

Fig. 56. WIRING DIAGRAM (LATER T110, TR6 & T120).

Distributor

CONTACT BREAKER UNIT

Lubrication every 3,000 miles (5,000 kms.)

(i) Remove the metal cover and lightly smear the face of the cam with one of the greases recommended for the grease gun use in the "Recommended Lubricants" chart in the Instruction book. If this is not available, clean engine oil may be used.

WARNING

When carrying out the above lubrication, no oil or grease must be allowed to get onto or near the contacts.

(ii) Lubricate the automatic timing control mechanism, using thin machine oil.

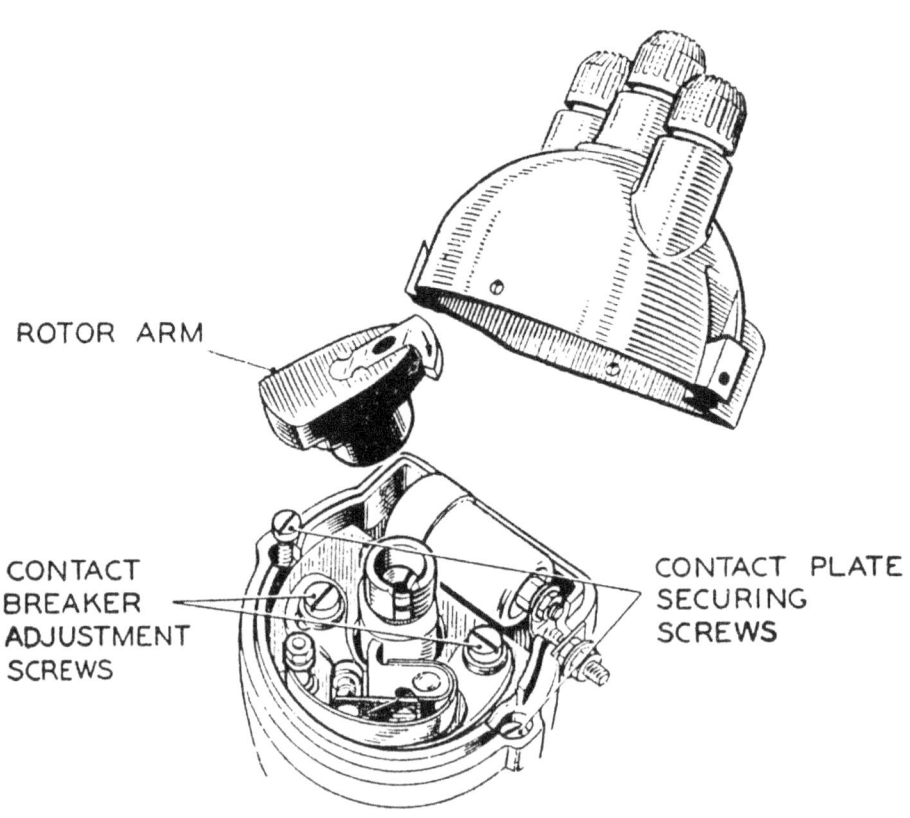

Fig. 57. **DISTRIBUTOR MODEL DKX2A**

Distributor

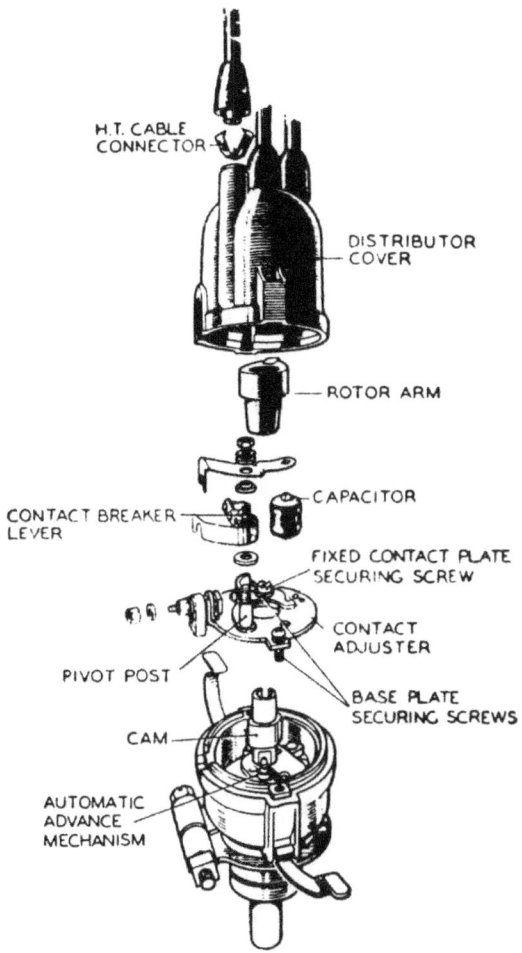

Fig. 58. DISTRIBUTOR, MODEL 18 D2.

Cleaning: Every 6,000 miles (10,000 kms.)

Remove the distributor cover and wipe it inside and outside with a clean, dry, fluffless cloth.

Examine the contact breaker. The contacts must be free from grease or oil. If they are burned or blackened, clean with fine carborundum stone or very fine emery cloth, afterwards wiping away any dirt or metal dust with a clean petrol-moistened cloth.

The easiest way to clean the contacts is to first take off the moving contact, by unscrewing the nut securing the end of the spring and lifting off the spring washer, spring and bush. Clean the pivot pin and smear it very lightly with clean engine oil before replacing the moving contact and spring.

Distributor

CONTACT BREAKER SETTING

The contact breaker setting should be checked after the first 500 miles (800 kms.) running and subsequently every 6,000 miles (10,000 kms.). To check the gap, turn the engine over slowly until the contacts are seen to be fully open and insert a 0.014 in.-0.016 in. (0.36-0.4 mm.) feeler gauge between the contacts.

If the gap width is correct, the gauge will be a sliding fit. If the gap width varies appreciably from the gauge thickness, the setting must be adjusted. To do this, keep the engine in the position giving the maximum contact opening and slacken the screw at the side of the unit body. Slide the fixed contact carrier into its slotted hole until the correct gap is obtained. Re-tighten the screw.

HIGH TENSION CABLES

If the high tension cables show signs of perishing or cracking, they should be replaced using a 7 mm. rubber covered ignition cable. To do this, remove the metal washer and moulded nut from the defective cable. Thread the new cable through the moulded nut and bare the conductor for about $\frac{1}{4}$ inch (6 mm.). Pass the exposed strands through the metal washer and bend back the strands radially. Re-fit the moulded nut into the H.T. terminal. The H.T. cable from the coil to distributor should also be treated in a similar manner.

The 18D2 distributor and also the latest type of coil use a clip-type connector on the H.T. cable. To replace a connector the end of the cable must be cut square and the centre prong of the connector pushed into the wires. The jaws can now be closed on rubber covered cable, but with hard plastic covers it is necessary to pierce the cover each side. The rubber grommets should be tight fitting and in good condition.

IGNITION COIL

The ignition coil should be kept clean, particularly between the terminals, and the terminal connections kept tight.

RECTIFIER

The connections at the rectifier must be clean and tight, including the central post which must be earthed to the frame.

A.C. Ignition Fault Finding

BEFORE SEARCHING FOR AN IGNITION FAULT, ALWAYS CHECK OVER ALL ELECTRICAL CONNECTIONS; CLEAN AND TIGHTEN IF NECESSARY.

ENGINE WILL NOT START.   NO SPARK AT PLUGS.

Note. To check, remove the plugs and place them on the cylinder head after re-fitting the connector. Turn the ignition switch to "IGN" (clockwise) and kick over the engine. The plugs should fire with a blue spark. If there is no spark, turn switch to "EMG" (anti-clockwise) and test again.

Plug Oily, Fouled or Faulty. Clean thoroughly, preferably in a plug cleaning machine, re-set the points gap to 0.020 in. (0.50 mm.) and re-fit. Replace with correct grade plug if faulty.

Distributor, Coil or Condenser Faulty

Distributor. See that the cover is properly fitted and the clips secure. Check the gap of the contact breaker points and clean and adjust if necessary (see page 162).

Coil. First clean the coil, particularly between the cable connections. To check the low tension circuit, connect a voltmeter between the coil terminal marked "SW" or "—" and earth. If there is no reading with the ignition switched on there is a fault in the switch or the lead to the coil. Next connect the voltmeter between the coil terminal marked "C.B." or "+" and earth. No reading here with the ignition switched on indicates a fault in the coil primary winding. If these tests show that the low tension primary circuit is in order, remove the coil H.T. lead from the distributor cover. Remove the cover and rotate the engine until the contact points are closed. Switch on the ignition and hold the end of the coil H.T. lead about $\frac{1}{4}$ in. (6 mm.) from the cylinder block. Flick the contact points open with the finger and a spark should pass to the cylinder block. No spark indicates a fault in the coil H.T. winding. Any fault in a coil can only be corrected by fitting a new unit.

Condenser. To test the condenser, switch on the ignition and connect a volt meter across the open contacts. If there is no reading, remove the condenser and re-test. If a reading on the meter is then obtained, the condenser is faulty and should be changed.

ENGINE WILL NOT START WITH SWITCH ON "IGN" BUT STARTS ON "EMG".

Battery discharged due to short circuit, poor condition due to age or damage, prolonged use for parking or low rate or charge from alternator. Have battery charged from external source and equipment checked by an authorised Lucas Agent or Triumph Dealer as soon as possible.

Lamps

ENGINE RUNS WITH SWITCH ON "IGN" BUT NOT ON "EMG"

Examine leads and connections from ignition switch to coil, and from coil to distributor. Check distributor contacts and ignition timing (See pages 70 and 162). If the machine will still not run in "EMG" switch position, have the equipment checked by an authorised Lucas Agent or Triumph Dealer.

ROUGH RUNNING AND MISFIRING WITH SWITCH AT "IGN".

Check earth connection for battery and rectifier and wiring of switch and rectifier.

LAMPS

HEADLAMPS FITTED TO MACHINES INTENDED FOR THE HOME MARKET AND FOR EXPORT, EXCLUDING EUROPE

These lamps have a double filament pre-focus Left Hand Dipping 6 volt 30/24 watt Lucas No. 373 main bulb and 6 volt 3 watt Lucas No. 988 pilot bulb.

HEADLAMPS FITTED TO MACHINES INTENDED FOR EXPORT TO EUROPE

These lamps have a double filament pre-focus 6 volt 35/35 watt Lucas No. 403 bulb.

HEADLAMPS FITTED TO MACHINES INTENDED FOR EXPORT TO FRANCE ONLY

These lamps have a double filament pre-focus 6 volt 36/36 watt bulb (yellow) with a three point connection to the lamp.

Basically the above lamps are identical, the difference occurring only with the method of attachment of the bulb in the French type headlamp and in the power of the bulbs.

HEADLAMPS FITTED TO THE TROPHY MODELS

These lamps have a double filament pre-focus 6 volt 30/24 watt Lucas No. 312 bulb and a pilot bulb 6 volt 3 watt Lucas No. 988.

REPLACING THE HEADLAMP BULB

To gain access to the headlamp bulb, slacken the front rim retaining screw situated at the top of the lamp fixing ring. Disengage and withdraw the front rim and light unit assembly, removing the upper edge first. With the exception of the French headlamp, press the moulded adaptor inwards and turn it to the left. Lift off the adaptor and withdraw the defective bulb. When inserting a replacement bulb, locate the slot in the bulb flange with the projection in the bulb holder. Re-fit the adaptor, engaging its moulded recesses with corresponding projections on the bulb holder. Press inwards and secure by turning the adaptor to the right.

Lamps

On the French headlamp, release the two clips securing the adaptor and remove the adaptor. Take out the defective bulb by pressing it in and turning to the left. When replacing the bulb, engage the three points on the bulb in the slots of the adaptor, press in and turn to the right to secure. Replace the adaptor with the projection on the adaptor engaging in the slot on the headlamp and secure by re-fastening the clips. Re-fit the rim to the nacelle, locating the bottom of the rim first. Tighten the securing screw and check the beam setting.

SETTING THE HEADLAMP BEAM

To check the headlamp beam setting, place the motorcycle in front of a light coloured wall at a distance of about 25 feet (8 metres). The machine should be carrying its normal load during this check, since the weight of the rider (and pillion passenger) may affect the setting. Switch on the main beam. This should be directed straight ahead and parallel with the ground. The beam is adjusted on the Trophy models by slackening the two headlamp securing bolts and tilting the lamp to the correct angle. On the models with the nacelle headlamp, loosen the two small screws on either side of the lamp fixing ring, and raise or lower the beam by pulling out or pressing in, the bottom of the ring. When the required adjustment has been obtained, re-tighten the two screws.

With the Lucas pre-focus type bulb fitted in these lamps, the filament is correctly positioned during manufacture in relation to the focal point of the reflector. No further focusing is necessary.

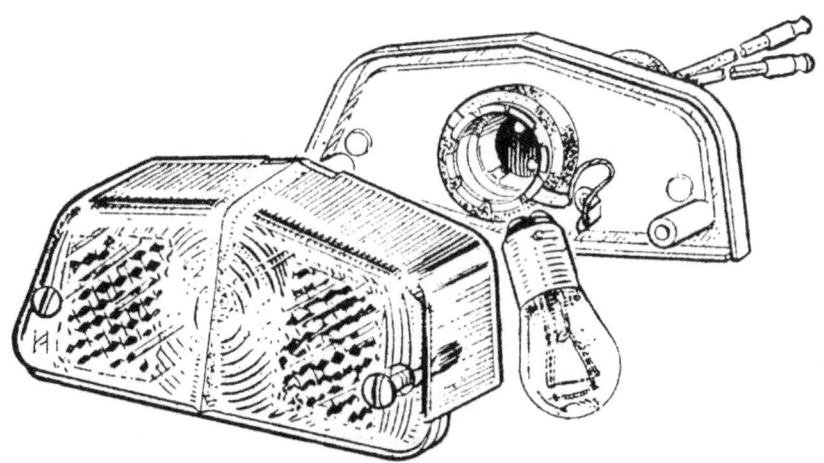

Fig. 59. Stop-Tail Lamp Model 564 incorporating Reflex Reflectors.

PARKING LIGHT

The parking light is simply pushed into the main light unit and is fitted with a 6 volt 3 watt Lucas No. 988 bulb, for all markets.

REAR LAMP

Access to rear light bulbs is gained by removing the two moulded cover retaining screws. The correct replacement for the stop tail lamp is Lucas No. 384 6 volt 6/18 watt bulb. This bulb has offset securing pins to prevent incorrect insertion into the bulb holder and to ensure that the higher wattage filament is illuminated when the brake pedal is depressed. In the event of failure of the 6 watt filament do not change the cables over to obtain rear lighting from the 18 watt filament as the heat generated will probably burn the plastic lens.

NACELLE TOP UNIT

REMOVAL (Dynamo Equipped Models)

Battery. Disconnect the battery positive lead.

Steering Damper. Unscrew and remove.

Headlamp. Unscrew the retaining screw at the top of the headlamp retaining ring and ease the headlamp away from the ring, pulling from the top. Disconnect the earth wire (black) from the bulb holder frame, and the two headlight leads (black) at the snap connectors.

Retaining Ring. Remove by unscrewing the two small screws at the sides of the ring.

Motifs. Unscrew the four screws and two nuts securing the motifs and remove.

Rear Nacelle Retaining Screws. Remove the two small screws and nuts holding the rear of the top unit to the fork covers, being careful not to lose the nuts.

Five Point Connector. Disconnect all leads at the connector. If the top unit only is being removed, leave the connector in position on the stanchion. If however, it is intended to remove the fork assembly, remove the connector from the stanchion and disconnect the leads so that the connector remains with the top unit.

Speedometer. Unscrew the speedometer drive cable at the head.

Removing Headlamp and Nacelle

Horn. Disconnect both leads.

Dipswitch Lead to Light Switch. Disconnect at the light switch (No. 2 position).

Assembly. Re-assemble in the reverse manner.

REMOVAL (A.C. Equipped Models)

Dismantle as for T100 & T110 to "Rear Nacelle Retaining Screws" and proceed as follows:—

Lighting and Ignition Switch. Unscrew the small grub screw at the side of the plastic switch lever and pull the lever away from the switch. Unscrew the brass nut around the switch body, remove the name disc and push the switch through into the nacelle.

Horn. Disconnect the black lead from the horn terminal.

Speedometer. Unscrew the speedometer drive cable at the head and detach the speedometer light.

Ammeter. Disconnect the brown leads at the ammeter: one from the L.H. terminal and two from the R.H. terminal.

NOTE

If it is intended to remove the top unit only, it is unnecessary to proceed any further. If the forks are to be removed however, it will be necessary to disconnect the blue lead from the dipper switch to switch position number 3 and also the red and black pilot light lead. Both these leads are fitted with snap connectors.

Assembly. Re-assemble in the reverse manner.

BATTERY

Topping Up

During charging, water is lost by gassing and evaporation and this must be replaced to maintain the battery in a healthy condition. Once a month or more often in warm climates, the level of the electrolyte in the cells of the battery must be examined; if necessary, distilled water must be added to bring the electrolyte just level with the top of the separators.

Never use a naked light when examining the condition of the cells, as there is a danger of igniting the gas coming from the active materials.

The MLZ 7E battery with the translucent casing must not be filled to the top of the separators. The battery must be lifted and distilled water added up to the line moulded in the casing.

Battery Maintenance

Checking the Condition of the Battery

Occasionally check the condition of the battery by taking measurements of the specific gravity of the electrolyte in each of the cells. A small volume hydrometer is required for this purpose—this instrument resembles a syringe containing a graduated float which indicates the specific gravity of the acid in the cell from which the sample has been taken.

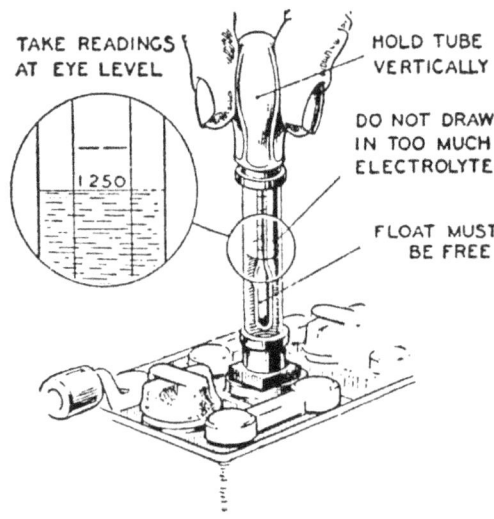

Fig. 60. TAKING HYDROMETER READINGS.

Measurements should not be taken immediately after the cells have been "topped-up" as the electrolyte will not be thoroughly mixed.

The space between each separator is not wide enough to permit the nozzle of a hydrometer to be inserted. Before taking a sample, tilt the battery to bring sufficient electrolyte above the separators.

Specific gravity readings and their indications are as follows:—

    1.280-1.300 ... ... Cell fully charged.
    About 1.210 ... ... Cell about half discharged.
    Below 1.150 ... ... Cell fully discharged.

The reading for each of the cells should be approximately the same.

If one cell gives a value very different from the rest, it may be that acid has spilled or has leaked from that particular cell, or there may be a short circuit between the plates. In this case the battery should be examined by a Lucas Service Depot or Agent.

Battery Maintenance

Never leave the battery in a discharged condition. If the motorcycle is to be out of use for any length of time have the battery fully charged and every fortnight, give it a short refreshing charge to prevent any tendency for the plates to become permanently sulphated.

Detachable Cable Connectors

When connecting the battery, unscrew the knurled nut and withdraw the collet or cone shaped insert, noting that it is not interchangeable with the collet in the other terminal. Bare the end of the cable for about one inch and thread one bared end through the knurled nut and collet. Bend back the cable strands over the narrow end of the collet and insert the collet and cable into the terminal block. Secure the connection by tightening the knurled nut.

Battery Earth

The A.C. Lighting-Ignition Unit and dynamo unit have been designed for positive (+ve) earth systems. If the battery connections are reversed the equipment will be damaged.

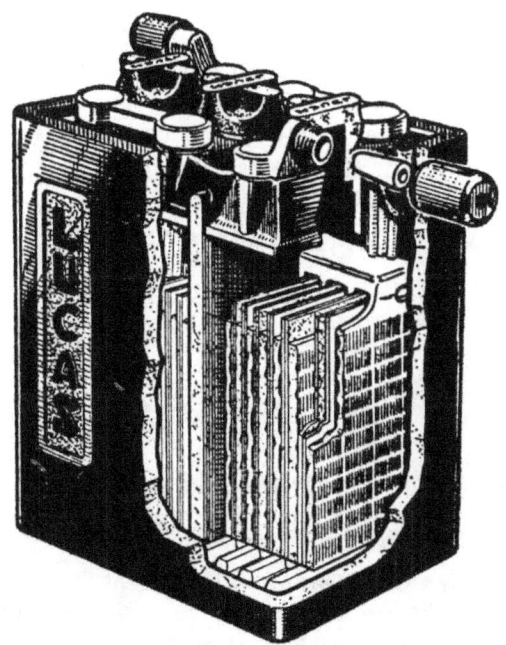

Battery model PU7E/9, showing correct-acid-level device and detachable cable connectors.

Fig. 61. BATTERY MODEL PU7E/9.

ELECTRIC HORNS

These horns, before being passed out of the Works, are adjusted to give their best performance, and will give a long period of service without any attention.

Electric Horn

If the horn becomes uncertain in its action, giving only a choking sound, or does not vibrate, it does not follow that the horn has broken down. First ascertain that the trouble is not due to some outside source, e.g. a discharged battery, a loose connection, or short circuit in the wiring of the horn. In particular, ascertain that the horn push bracket is in good electrical contact with the handlebars.

It is also possible that the performance of a horn may be upset by its mounting becoming loose.

Adjustment
The following adjustment will not alter the tone of the horn. It will take up any wear of the moving parts which, if not corrected, may result in loss of power and roughness of note.

Accurate adjustment requires the use of a 0-10 amp. D.C. ammeter—the maximum permissible current consumption being 6 amperes at 6 volts—but the owner rider, who may not possess one of these instruments can carry out the following procedure if the horn note is considered to have deteriorated:—

> Operate the horn push and turn the adjustment screw anti-clockwise until the horn just fails to sound. Release the horn push and turn the adjustment screw clockwise for six notches i.e. a quarter of a turn, when the original performance should be restored. If further adjustment is necessary, turn the screw one notch at a time.
>
> If the original performance cannot be restored by adjustment do not attempt to dismantle the horn, but return it to a Lucas Service Depot for examination.

SPARKING PLUGS

The sparking plug is of great importance in satisfactory engine performance and every care should be taken to fit the correct type when replacements are necessary.

There is little to be gained by experimenting with different types of plugs as the type fitted to standard equipment, are best suited to your particular engine. (See Technical Data for your Machine). Sparking plugs required for racing purposes are much "harder" and advice on such matters should be obtained from the manufacturers. The correct gap setting of the sparking plug is 0.020 in. (0.50 mm.). Do not guess this distance but use a feeler gauge. When re-setting, bend the side electrode only. Never bend the centre electrode as this may split the insulator tip.

The alloy head models are fitted with long reach plugs. If either plug indicates tightness when removing, pour a little penetrating oil around the base of the plug and allow it to seep around the threads. By doing this the plug will be more easily removed and the cylinder head plug threads will not be damaged. Smear the threads with graphite grease before replacing.

Sparking Plug

When the sparking plug is removed for examination, the insulator will show one of the following conditions:—

ASH WHITE. This is a sign that the plug is over-heating. Usual cause is the mixture strength too weak (a common cause being a faulty carburetter to manifold or manifold to cylinder head joint washer) or the ignition too far retarded.

DULL BLACK. This indicates that the plug is running too cold or, in other words the insulator is insufficiently hot to burn off the carbon. This is caused by too rich a mixture or the engine left running with a generous slow running setting (pilot air adjusting screw).

LIGHT BROWN. This shows that the mixture strength is correct and the engine is running at the right temperature.

Before re-fitting the plugs, make sure that the copper washers are not defective in any way. If they have become worn and flattened, fit new ones to ensure that a gastight joint is obtained.

When installing plugs, first screw the plugs down by hand as far as possible, then use spanner for tightening only. Always use a tubular box spanner to avoid possible fracture to the insulator, but do not under any circumstances use a movable wrench. Paint splashes, accumulation of grime dust etc., on the top half of the insulator are often responsible for poor plug performance. Plugs should be wiped frequently with a clean rag.

To save petrol and prevent difficult starting, plugs should be cleaned and tested at regular intervals, and it is suggested that this service be performed at your garage on a special "Air Blast" service unit. Plugs which are allowed to remain oily and dirty with corroded electrodes will seriously impair the efficient running of the motor and waste precious petrol.

To obtain maximum efficiency from the engine and also to maintain good petrol consumption which the motorcycle has when new, plugs should be changed at regular intervals as old plugs are wasteful and cause poor and sluggish running. We recommend inspection, cleaning and testing every 3,000 miles (5,000 kms.), and it will be found economical to replace with new ones annually.

Toolkit

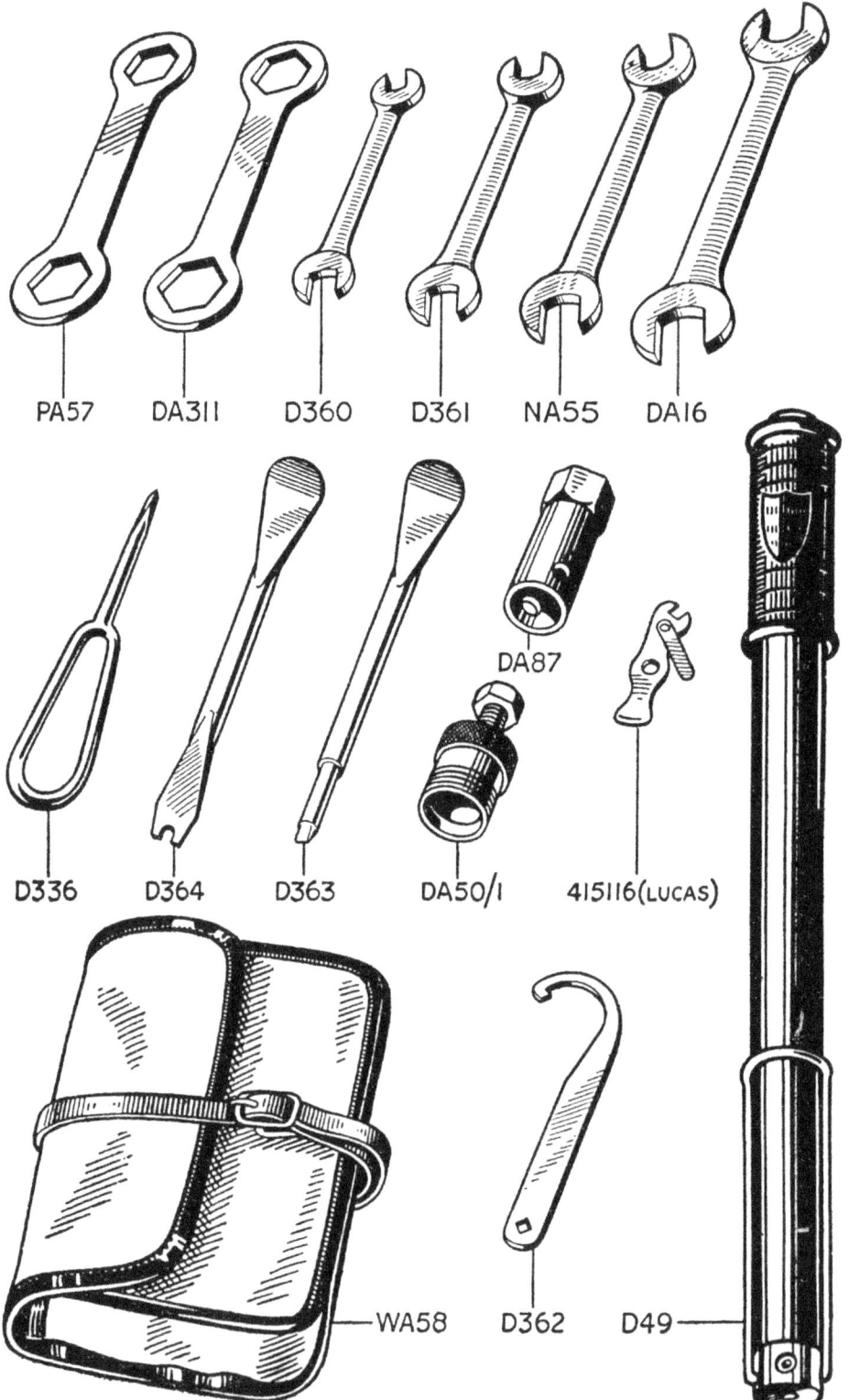

Fig. 62. TOOLKIT.

TOOLKIT

Part No.	Description.	Purpose.
D.360	Spanner, open ended $\frac{1}{8}$ in. × $\frac{5}{32}$ in. Whit.	General
D.361	Spanner, open-ended $\frac{3}{16}$ in. × $\frac{1}{4}$ in. Whit.	,,
NA.55	Spanner, open-ended $\frac{1}{4}$ in. × $\frac{5}{16}$ in. Whit.	,,
DA.16	Spanner, open-ended $\frac{3}{8}$ in. × $\frac{7}{16}$ in. Whit.	,,
PA.57	Spanner, closed $\frac{1}{2}$ in. × $\frac{9}{16}$ in. Whit.	Wheel nuts
D.311	Spanner, closed $\frac{5}{8}$ in. × $\frac{11}{16}$ in. Whit.	Wheel nuts
D.362	'C' Spanner and Tappet Key	Suspension units
D.87	Spanner, box	Sparking plugs
D.336	Screwdriver, Phillips head	General
D.363	Tyre lever—screwdriver	,,
D.364	Tyre lever—clutch key	Clutch adjustment
DA.50/1	Extractor	Clutch hub
415116	Spanner	Contact breaker points
WA.58	Tool roll	
D.49	Tyre inflator (15$\frac{1}{4}$ in. long)	
D.296	Tyre inflator (12 in. long)	

TECHNICAL DATA 1956-59

MODEL	5T	6T	T100	T110 & TR6	TR5	T120
ENGINE. Bore & Stroke mm.	63 × 80	71 × 82	63 × 80	71 × 82	63 × 80	71 × 82
Capacity—c.c.	498	649	498	649	498	649
Compression Ratio	7 : 1	7 : 1	8 : 1	8 : 1	8 : 1	8.5 : 1
Power Output-b.h.p.@r.p.m.	27 at 6,300	34 at 6,300	32 at 6,500	40 at 6,500	33 at 6,500	46 at 6,500
Tappet Clearance—in.	0.010	0.010	0.010	0.002 In. 0.004 Ex.	0.002 In. 0.004 Ex.	0.002 In. 0.004 Ex.
Valve Timing in Degrees with 0.020 in. (0.50 mm.) tappet clearance for checking	$26\frac{1}{2}$ $69\frac{1}{2}$ $61\frac{1}{2}$ $35\frac{1}{2}$	$26\frac{1}{2}$ $69\frac{1}{2}$ $61\frac{1}{2}$ $35\frac{1}{2}$	$26\frac{1}{2}$ $69\frac{1}{2}$ $61\frac{1}{2}$ $35\frac{1}{2}$	27 48 48 27	27 48 48 27	34 55 48 27
IGNITION. Type	Coil	Coil	Magneto	Magneto	Magneto	Magneto
Contact Gap—in.	0.014-016	0.014-016	0.012	0.012	0.012	0.012
Timing (fully advanced)	Ret'd. $\frac{1}{32}$ in.	Ret'd. $\frac{1}{32}$ in.	$\frac{3}{8}$ in.	$\frac{23}{64}$ in.	$\frac{15}{32}$ in.	$\frac{7}{16}$ in.
SPARKING PLUG Champion, K.L.G., Lodge	L.7, F.80, H.14	L.7, F.80, H.14	N.4, FE.100, HLN	N.4, FE.100, HLN	N.4, FE.100, HLN	N.4, FE.100, HLN
Plug Gap—in.	.020	.020	.020	.020	.020	.020
CAPACITY. Petrol (galls.)	4	4	4	T110 4; TR6 3	3	4
Oil—pints	5	5	5	5	5	5
Gearbox—pints	$\frac{2}{3}$	$\frac{2}{3}$	$\frac{2}{3}$	$\frac{2}{3}$	$\frac{2}{3}$	$\frac{2}{3}$
Primary Chaincase—pints	$\frac{1}{4}$	$\frac{1}{4}$	$\frac{1}{4}$	$\frac{1}{4}$	$\frac{1}{4}$	$\frac{1}{4}$
Fork Leg—pints	$\frac{1}{6}$	$\frac{1}{6}$	$\frac{1}{6}$	$\frac{1}{6}$	$\frac{1}{6}$	$\frac{1}{6}$

MODEL	5T	6T	T100	T110 & TR6	TR5	T120
CARBURETTER. Type	376	S.U. MC2	376	376	376	376 (2)
Main Jet	200	0.090 in.	220	250	220	240
Needle Jet	.1065	—	.1065	.1065	.1065	.1065
Needle Type	C	M9	C	C	C	C
Needle Position	3rd	—	3rd	3rd	3rd	3rd
Throttle Valve	376/3½	—	376/3½	376/3½	376/3½	376/3½
Pilot Jet	30	—	25	25	25	25
GEAR RATIOS. Top	5.0	4.57	5.0	4.57	5.24	4.57
3rd	5.95	5.45	5.95	5.45	6.24	5.45
2nd	8.45	7.75	8.45	7.75	8.85	7.75
Bottom	12.20	11.20	12.20	11.20	12.80	11.20
ENGINE SPROCKETS Solo	22	24	22	24	21	24
Sidecar	19	21	19	21	—	—
CHAIN LENGTH Primary ½ in. × .305 in.	70	70	70	70	70	70
Rear ⅝ in. × ⅜ in.	100	101	100	101	100	101
TYRE SIZE. Front	3.25 × 19	3.25 × 19	3.25 × 19	3.25 × 19	3.25 × 19	3.25 × 19
Rear	3.50 × 19	3.50 × 19	3.50 × 19	T110 3.50×19 TR6 4.00×18	4.00 × 18	3.50 × 19
BRAKE SIZE. Front—in.	7	7	8	8	7	8
Rear—in.	7	7	7	7	7	7

TECHNICAL DATA 1960

MODEL	6T	T110	TR6	T120
ENGINE. Bore and Stroke—mm.	71 × 82	71 × 82	71 × 82	71 × 82
Capacity—c.c.	649	649	649	649
Compression Ratio	7 : 1	8 : 1	8 : 1	8.5 : 1
Power Output—b.h.p. at r.p.m.	34 at 6,300	40 at 6,500	40 at 6,500	46 at 6,500
Tappet Clearance—in.	0.010	0.002 In. 0.004 Ex.	0.002 In. 0.004 Ex.	0.002 In. 0.004 Ex.
Valve Timing, in Degrees, with 0.020 in. (0.50 mm.) tappet clearance for checking	26½ 69½ 61½ 35½	27 48 48 27	27 48 48 27	34 55 48 27
IGNITION. Type	Coil	Magneto	Magneto	Magneto
Contact Gap—in.	0.014-0.016	0.012	0.012	0.012
Timing (fully advanced)	Ret'd. $\tfrac{1}{32}$ in.	$\tfrac{23}{64}$ in.	$\tfrac{23}{64}$ in.	$\tfrac{7}{16}$ in.
SPARKING PLUG. Champion, K.L.G., Lodge	L7, F.80, H14	N.4, FE.100, HLN	N.4, FE.100, HLN	N.4, FE.100, HLN
Plug Gap—in.	0.020	0.020	0.020	0.020
CAPACITY. Petrol (galls.)	4	4	3	4
Oil—pints	5	5	5	5
Gearbox—pints	$\tfrac{2}{3}$	$\tfrac{2}{3}$	$\tfrac{2}{3}$	$\tfrac{2}{3}$
Primary Chaincase—pints	$\tfrac{1}{4}$	$\tfrac{1}{4}$	$\tfrac{1}{4}$	$\tfrac{1}{4}$
Fork Leg—pints	$\tfrac{1}{4}$	$\tfrac{1}{4}$	$\tfrac{1}{4}$	$\tfrac{1}{4}$

MODEL	6T	T110	TR6	T120
CARBURETTER. Type	376	376	376	376 (2)
Main Jet	270	250	250	240
Needle Jet	.1065	.1065	.1065	.1065
Needle Type	C	C	C	C
Needle Position	3rd	3rd	3rd	3rd
Throttle Valve	376/3½	376/3½	376/3½	376/3½
Pilot Jet	25	25	25	25
GEAR RATIOS. Top	4.46	4.46	4.66	4.66
3rd	5.30	5.30	5.55	5.55
2nd	7.55	7.55	7.88	7.88
Bottom	10.9	10.9	11.38	11.38
ENGINE SPROCKET. Solo	23	23	22	22
Sidecar	20	20	—	—
CHAIN LENGTH. Primary ½in. × 305 in.	70	70	70	70
Rear ⅝ in. × ⅜ in.	99	99	99	99
TYRE SIZE. Front	3.25 × 18	3.25 × 18	3.25 × 19	3.25 × 19
Rear	3.50 × 18	3.50 × 18	4.00 × 18	3.50 × 19
BRAKE SIZE. Front—in.	7	8	8	8
Rear—in.	7	7	7	7

RECOMMENDED LUBRICANTS

UNITED KINGDOM

UNIT	REGENT	MOBIL	B.P.	CASTROL	ESSO	SHELL
Engine—Summer Winter	Havoline SAE.30 Havoline SAE.20W	Mobiloil A Mobiloil Arctic	Energol SAE.30 Energol SAE.20	Castrol XL Castrolite	Esso Extra Motor Oil 20W/30	Shell X-100 30 Shell X-100 20-20W
Gearbox	Havoline SAE.50	Mobiloil D	Energol SAE.50	Castrol Grand Prix	Esso Extra Motor Oil 40/50	Shell X-100 50
Primary Chaincase	Havoline SAE.20W	Mobiloil Arctic	Energol SAE.20	Castrolite	Esso Extra Motor Oil 20W/30	Shell X-100 20-20W
Telescopic Fork—Summer Winter	Havoline SAE.30 Havoline SAE.20W	Mobiloil A Mobiloil Arctic	Energol SAE.30 Energol SAE.20	Castrol XL Castrolite	Esso Extra Motor Oil 20W/30	Shell X-100 30 Shell X-100 20-20W
Wheel Bearings **Swinging Fork**	Marfak Multipurpose 2	Mobilgrease M.P.	Energrease L2	Castrolease L.M.	Multipurpose Grease H	Shell Retinax A
Easing Rusted Parts	Graphited Penetrating Oil	Mobil Spring Oil	Energol Penetrating Oil	Castrol Penetrating Oil	Esso Penetrating Oil	Shell Donax P

RECOMMENDED LUBRICANTS

OVERSEAS

UNIT	CALTEX	MOBIL	B.P.	CASTROL	ESSO	SHELL
Engine—Above 90°F. ... 32°—90°F. ... Below 32°F. ...	Caltex SAE.40 Caltex SAE.30 Caltex SAE.20W	Mobiloil AF Mobiloil A Mobiloil Arctic	Energol SAE.40 Energol SAE.30 Energol SAE.20W	Castrol XXL Castrol XL Castrolite	Esso Extra Motor Oil 20W/40	Shell X-100 40 Shell X-100 30 Shell X-100 20-20W
Gearbox	Caltex SAE.50	Mobiloil D	Energol SAE.50	Castrol Grand Prix	Esso Extra Motor Oil 50	Shell X-100 50
Primary Chaincase ...	Caltex SAE.20W	Mobiloil Arctic	Energol SAE.20W	Castrolite	Esso Extra Motor Oil 20W/40	Shell X-100 20-20W
Telescopic Fork ... Above 90°F. ... 60°—90°F. ... Below 60°F. ...	Caltex SAE.50 Caltex SAE.30 Caltex SAE.20W	Mobiloil D Mobiloil A Mobiloil Arctic	Energol SAE.50 Energol SAE.30 Energol SAE.20	Castrol Grand Prix Castrol XL Castrolite	Esso Extra Motor Oil 20W/40	Shell X-100 50 Shell X-100 30 Shell X-100 20-20W
Wheel Bearings, Swinging Forks, Steering Races	Marfak Multipurpose 2	Mobilgrease M.P.	Energrease L2	Castrolease L.M.	Multipurpose Grease H	Shell Retinax A
Easing Rusted Parts ...	Caltex Penetrating Oil	Mobil Spring Oil	Energol Penetrating Oil	Castrol Penetrating Oil	Esso Penetrating Oil	Shell Donax P

ENGINE REVOLUTIONS PER MINUTE

M.P.H.	4.4	4.57	4.78	5.0	5.24	5.5	5.7	5.8	6.0	6.25	6.5	6.9	7.06	7.14	7.5	8.0	8.85	9.8	10.6	11.58	12.2	13.9	14.3	15.25	16.0	17.8	18.85
20	1144	1188	1244	1300	1364	1428	1480	1508	1560	1624	1688	1796	1836	1856	1948	2080	2300	2548	2756	3012	3172	3612	3720	3964	4160	4628	4900
25	1430	1485	1555	1625	1705	1785	1850	1885	1950	2030	2110	2245	2295	2320	2435	2600	2875	3185	3445	3765	3965	4515	4650	4955	5200	5785	6125
30	1716	1782	1866	1950	2046	2142	2220	2262	2340	2436	2532	2694	2754	2784	2922	3120	3450	3822	4134	4518	4758	5418	5580	5946	6240	6942	—
35	2002	2079	2177	2275	2387	2499	2590	2639	2730	2842	2954	3143	3213	3248	3409	3640	4025	4459	4823	5271	5551	6321	6510	6937	—	—	—
40	2288	2376	2488	2600	2728	2856	2960	3016	3120	3248	3376	3592	3672	3712	3896	4160	4600	5096	5512	6024	6344	7137					
45	2574	2673	2799	2925	3069	3213	3330	3393	3510	3654	3798	4041	4131	4176	4383	4680	5175	5733	6201	6777							
50	2860	2970	3110	3250	3410	3570	3700	3770	3900	4060	4220	4490	4590	4640	4870	5200	5750	6370	6890								
55	3146	3267	3421	3575	3751	3927	4070	4147	4290	4466	4642	4939	5049	5104	5357	5720	6325	7007									
60	3432	3564	3732	3900	4092	4284	4440	4524	4680	4872	5064	5388	5508	5568	5844	6240	6900										
70	4004	4158	4354	4550	4774	4998	5180	5278	5460	5684	5908	6286	6426	6496	6818	7280											
80	4576	4752	4976	5200	5456	5712	5920	6032	6240	6496	6752	7184	7344	7424													
90	5148	5346	5598	5850	6138	6426	6660	6786	7020	7308																	
100	5720	5940	6220	6500	6820	7140	7400	7540																			
110	6292	6534	6842	7150	7502	7854																					

NOTE.—Engine R-P-M are calculated in conjunction with 3.50 × 19 Rear tyre equipment—780 R-P-Mile—and will deviate slightly from above figures for models not so equipped.
4.00 × 18 Rear Tyre 785 R-P-Mile. 3.50 × 18 Rear Tyre 803 R-P-Mile. 4.00 × 19 Rear Tyre 756 R-P-Mile.

GEAR RATIOS WITH 46T WHEEL SPROCKET
FOR 43T SPROCKET SEE PAGE 192

GEARS	STANDARD RATIO				WIDE RATIO				CLOSE RATIO			
Engine Sprocket	Top	3rd	2nd	1st	Top	3rd	2nd	1st	Top	3rd	2nd	1st
17	6.46	7.7	10.94	15.8	6.46	9.22	14.30	18.85	6.46	7.06	8.42	11.00
18	6.10	7.28	10.32	14.9	6.10	8.70	13.50	17.80	6.10	6.66	7.95	10.40
19	5.80	6.9	9.8	14.15	5.80	8.25	12.80	16.85	5.80	6.32	7.54	9.84
20	5.50	6.55	9.3	13.4	5.50	7.84	12.18	16.0	5.50	6.00	7.15	9.35
21	5.24	6.24	8.85	12.8	5.24	7.46	11.58	15.25	5.24	5.72	6.81	8.90
22	5.00	5.95	8.45	12.2	5.00	7.13	11.05	14.55	5.00	5.45	6.50	8.50
23	4.78	5.69	8.09	11.69	4.78	6.82	10.60	13.90	4.78	5.23	6.23	8.12
24	4.57	5.45	7.75	11.2	4.57	6.54	10.14	13.35	4.57	5.00	5.96	7.78
25	4.40	5.24	7.45	10.75	4.40	6.26	9.73	12.80	4.40	4.80	5.73	7.46
Gearbox Reduction	1.0	1.19	1.69	2.44	1.00	1.425	2.21	2.915	1.00	1.09	1.30	1.695

Lubrication Chart

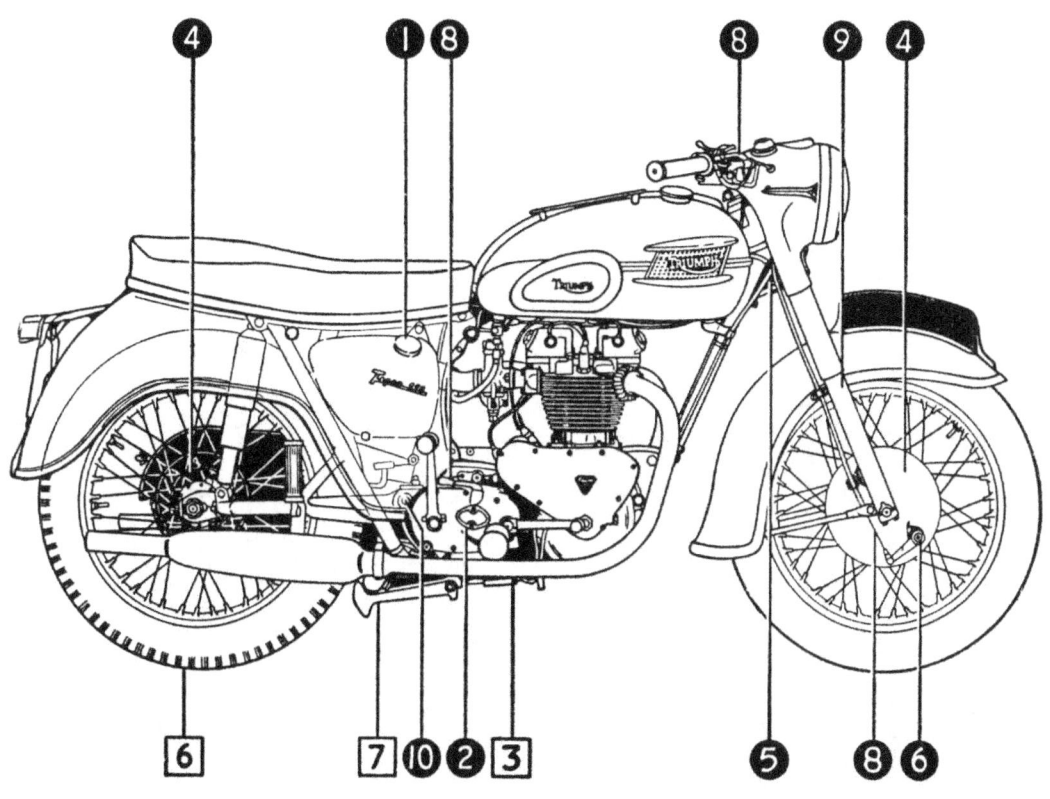

Fig. 63. LUBRICATION CHART.

No.	Part	S.A.E.	No.	Part	S.A.E.
1	Engine Oil Tank	20 or 30	7	Footbrake Pedal Spindle	Grease
2	Gearbox	50	8	Exposed Cables	20
3	Primary Chaincase	20	9	Fork (Hydraulic)	20
4	Wheel Hubs	Grease	10	Swinging Fork Spindle	Grease
5	Steering Head	Grease		OIL-CAN LUBRICATION All Brake Rod Joints and Pins	
6	Brake Cam Spindle	Grease			

FAULT FINDING

The following paragraphs have been drawn up to enable the rider to diagnose trouble which may arise during normal service. For each failure, the faults and antidotes are arranged in order or probability. In each case the rider should always look for the obvious, such as no petrol, oil, controls incorrectly set, cut-out wire shorting, and, before searching for an "A.C." ignition fault, always check over all electrical connections and clean and tighten if necessary; then follow with the process of elimination.

ENGINE WILL NOT START

Lack of Fuel	Tank empty, obstruction in Petrol Pipes or Tank Filters choked.
Excessive Flooding	Dirt under Float Needle Seating (See Page 142).
Oiled up or fouled, Sparking Plug ...	Remove, clean off carbon and wash in petrol. Allow to dry.
Engine Valve stuck open	See Page 35 for Valve Removal.
Exhaust Valve seatings burned ...	See Page 35 for Valve Removal.
Magneto Cut-out shorting	Disconnect Terminal at Magneto and check spark at Plug.
No Spark at Plugs (Coil ignition) ...	See Page 165.
Contact Points dirty	Clean with Carborundum Stone, wash with Petrol and re-gap.
Incorrect Contact Point Gap ...	Re-gap to 0.012 in.-0.015 in. (Magneto) 0.014 in.-0.016 in. (Coil) (0.3-0.4 mm.) ,, (0.36-0.40 mm.) ,,
Contact Breaker Arm Sticking ...	Remove Arm and clean Pivot with fine emery, grease lightly and replace Arm. Check gap.
H.T. Collector shorting to body ...	Remove Pick-ups and thoroughly clean; replace if cracked or damaged.
Condensation on Sparking Plugs	Remove Plugs and heat up.

FAULT FINDING

ENGINE STOPS

No Petrol or Fuel obstruction ...	Check Fuel in Tank. Supply at Carburetter if no supply. Remove Pipes and Tank Filters if necessary.
Choked Main Jet	See Page 142.
Water on H.T. Leads, Pick-ups or Sparking Plug	Dry Ignition System.
Water in Float Chamber	Remove Carburetter and clean out.
Vent Hole in Petrol Tank Filler Cap choked ...	Clean out Vent Hole.
Battery lead off (Coil)	Re-connect.

ENGINE MISFIRES

Defective or oiled Sparking Plug ...	Clean and test Plugs.
Water fouling Main Jet	Clean Carburetter.
Incorrect Contact Breaker Gap ...	Check and adjust to 0.012 in.-0.015 in. (Magneto) 0.014 in.-0.016 in. (Coil) (0.30-0.40 mm.) ,, ,, (0.36-0.40 mm.) ,,
Contact Points burned and arcing ...	Remove Points and true with a Carborundum Stone. Replace and re-gap; change Condenser if trouble persists. This fault can be caused by continuous running in the "EMG" position (Coil).
Weak or broken Valve Spring ...	See Page 35 for Replacement.
Partial obstruction of Petrol Supply ...	Clean out Carburetter and check Petrol supply at Carburetter end.
Slow Running Orifice choked ...	See Page 142.
H.T. Cable perished and shorting to frame ...	Replace H.T. Cable.
Sparking Plug insulation cracked ...	Replace Sparking Plug.
Condenser failing	See Page 165.
H.T. Cable on Coil faulty (Coil Ignition)	Replace.

FAULT FINDING

LOSS OF POWER

Faulty Sparking Plugs	Change.
Incorrect Tappet adjustment	See Page 34.
Lack of Lubrication	See that Oil Indicator Button is working (See Page 26). Check Supply in Oil Tank.
Weak or broken Valve Spring	Remove Cylinder Head (See Page 35).
Sticky Valve	Remove Cylinder Head (See Page 35).
Valves not seating	See Page 35.
Broken or gummed up Piston Ring	See Page 35.
Brakes binding	Place Machine on the Stands and re-adjust Brakes.
Engine requires Decarbonising	See Page 35.
Head Gasket blowing	Change Gasket.
Air Filter choked	Remove, wash in Petrol, re-oil and replace (See Page 144).
Dirty Carburetter	Remove and Clean.

ENGINE OVERHEATS

Lack of Lubrication	Check supply of Oil, see that the Indicator Button is operating when the engine is running; if not, refer to Page 26. Ensure that the correct Oil is used.
Faulty Sparking Plugs	Can cause pre-ignition; change and test.
Engine requires Decarbonising	See Page 35.
Ignition Timing too late	Check Timing (See Pages 73 and 74).
Exhaust Valve burned, or pitted Valve Seats	See Page 35.
Silencer choked	Remove and clean in a solution of caustic soda.
Piston Ring worn or seized in Piston Groove	Dismantle Engine, See Page 35.
Weak Mixture	Partly choked Jet, worn Throttle Slide, check by closing Air Lever.

ILLUSTRATION INDEX

Fig.		Page
1	Control layout	14
2	Petrol tap positions	19
3	Engine lubrication diagram	24
4	Oil pump	25
5	Oil pressure release valve	26
6	Crankcase assembly	32
7	Crankshaft assembly	32
8	Adjusting the tappets	34
9	Engine in vice	40
10	Camwheel removal and replacement (Tool Z.89)	41
11	Removing the camwheel	42
12	Removing the crankshaft pinion with Tool Z.121	43
13	Assembling the tappet block	46
14	Taper faced piston ring position	48
15	One-piece crankshaft showing oil tube	53
16	To assemble the two-piece crankshaft	54
17	To fit the connecting rods	55
18	Replacing the camwheel	57
19	Position of timing pinion in relation to camwheels and crankshaft pinion	58
20	Timing diagrams	59
21	Fitting the cylinder barrel	60
22	Magneto in timing position	67
23	Distributor in timing position	69
24	Slickshift gearchange mechanism	73
25	Gearbox (component parts)	74
26	Kickstarter return spring and spindle	78
27	Gearbox casing in vice	81
28	Clutch and shock absorber	85
29	Removal of clutch nuts	86
30	Use of clutch extractor	88
31	Replacing shock absorber rubbers	90
32	Gearbox in position	93
33	Chains	94
34	Chain rivet extractor	95
35	To test the adjustment of the steering head races	97
36	Telescopic fork (current type)	98
37	To align the front fork	104
38	Telescopic fork (earlier pattern)	108
39	Adjusting the brakes	114
40	Front wheel with full width hub	116
41	Front wheel (earlier TR6, T100 and T110)	118
42	Replacing floating brake shoes	120
43	Rear wheel	122
44	Quickly detachable rear wheel	128
45	Illustration showing the position of the valve if the tyre has crept round on the rim	132
46	Girling hydraulic suspension unit	135
47	Twistgrip	137

ILLUSTRATION INDEX

Fig.		Page
48	Amal monobloc carburetter	141
49	Air filter	143
50	S.U. carburetter (component parts)	146
51	S.U. carburetter (diagram)	148
52	Wiring diagram (models with dynamo)	154
53	Primary chaincase cover removed to show rotor and stator	158
54	Wiring diagram (5T & 6T)	159
55	Alternator (Model RM.14)	160
56	Wiring diagram (later T110, TR6 & T120)	161
57	Distributor Model DK X2A	162
58	Distributor Model 18 D2	163
59	Stop tail lamp model 564 incorporating reflex reflectors	167
60	Taking hydrometer readings	170
61	Battery model PU7E/9	171
62	Toolkit	174
63	Lubrication Chart	183

INDEX OF CONTENTS

		Page
A.	A/C lighting and ignition equipment	157
	Adjusting the brakes	114
	Adjusting the steering head races	96
	Air filter	143
	Aligning the front fork	103
	Alternator	160
	Assembling and installing the front fork	102
	Assembling the brake drum and sprocket assembly (Q.D. rear wheel)	129
	Assembling the clutch	90
	Assembling the engine	56
	Assembling the fork pressure tube	111
	Assembling the front brake anchor plate	119
	Assembling the front wheel	119
	Assembling the gearbox	80
	Assembling the Q.D. rear wheel	130
	Assembling the rear brake anchor plate	125
	Assembling the rear brake anchor plate (Q.D. rear wheel)	127
	Assembling the rear wheel	125
B.	Battery	169
C.	Carburetter (Amal Monobloc)	140
	Carburetter (S.U.)	145
	Chain alterations and repairs	94
	Chain maintenance	93
	Chain rivet extractor	95
	Chains	92
	Changing the fork springs	105
	Changing the oil	28
	Charts (engine revolutions and gear ratio)	182
	Clutch and shock absorber unit	84
	Coil	164
	Controls	15
D.	Decarbonising	35
	Dismantling, preparation and assembly of the engine units	44
	Dismantling, preparation and assembly of fork units	101
	Dismantling, preparation and assembly of gearbox units	77
	Dismantling the anchor plate assembly (Q.D. rear wheel)	127
	Dismantling the brake drum assembly (Q.D. rear wheel)	127
	Dismantling the clutch	84
	Dismantling the engine	40
	Dismantling the fork pressure tube assembly	110
	Dismantling the front brake anchor plate	115
	Dismantling the front wheel	115
	Dismantling the gearbox	76
	Dismantling the Q.D. rear wheel	126
	Dismantling the rear brake anchor plate	124

INDEX OF CONTENTS

		Page
	Dismantling the rear wheel	123
	Distributor	162
	Dynamo	153
E.	Electrical equipment	153
	Engine (description)	31
	Exhaust camshaft timing	64
F.	Fault finding (A/C ignition)	165
	Fault finding (General)	184-186
	Fitting a sidecar	139
	Fitting the front wheel to the fork	119
	Fitting the Q.D. rear wheel to the frame	130
	Fitting the rear wheel to the frame	126
	Frame	134
	Front wheel	115
G.	Gearbox (with Slickshift)	71
	Girling suspension units	134
H.	Headlamp and top nacelle unit	168
	Horns	171
I.	Ignition timing (coil)	68
	Ignition timing (magneto)	67
	Inlet camshaft timing	65
	Inspection and replacement of worn parts (front wheel)	117
	Inspection and replacement of worn parts (Q.D. rear wheel)	127
	Inspection and replacement of worn parts (rear wheel)	124
	Installing the engine	62
	Installing the gearbox	82
L.	Lamps	166
	Lubrication system	23
M.	Magneto	155
O.	Oil pump	25
	Oil release valve and indicator	26
P.	Petrol tank mounting	37 & 144
	Petrol tap adjustment	138
	Primary chain adjustment	92
	Proprietary fittings (addresses)	5
R.	Racing ignition timing	66
	Racing valve timing	64

INDEX OF CONTENTS

	Page
Rear chain adjustment	92
Rear wheel (quickly detachable)	126
Rear wheel	121
Recommended lubricants	180-181
Removing the brake drum and sprocket (Q.D. rear wheel)	126
Removing the engine from the frame	39
Removing the front fork from the frame	100
Removing the front wheel from the forks	115
Removing the gearbox from the frame	76
Removing the Q.D. rear wheel from the frame	126
Removing the rear wheel from the frame	121
Replacing the brake drum and sprocket in the frame (Q.D. rear wheel)	129
Routine maintenance	29
Running-in	21

S.
Service arrangements	4
Slickshift gearchange	71
Sparking plugs	172
Speedometer drive	92
Starting the engine (Amal)	18
Starting the engine (S.U.)	20
Swinging fork	134

T.
Tachometer drive	92
Taking over the machine	18
Tappet adjustment	34
Technical data	6-13, 176-179
Telescopic forks	96-113
Timing the engine	64
Toolkit	174
Twistgrip control	137
Tyres	131

V.
Valve timing record table	66

W.
Wheels	114
Wiring diagrams	154, 159 & 161

GEAR RATIOS (USING 18T G/BOX SPROCKET 43T REAR WHEEL SPROCKET)

GEARS	STANDARD RATIO				WIDE RATIO				CLOSE RATIO			
Engine Sprocket	Top	3rd	2nd	1st	Top	3rd	2nd	1st	Top	3rd	2nd	1st
17	6.02	7.18	10.18	14.78	6.02	8.62	13.35	17.6	6.02	6.60	7.87	10.30
18	5.71	6.78	9.60	13.92	5.71	8.12	12.60	16.65	5.71	6.24	7.44	9.70
19	5.40	6.42	9.13	13.2	5.40	7.71	11.97	15.75	5.40	5.90	7.05	9.20
20	5.12	6.1	8.65	12.50	5.12	7.32	11.38	14.95	5.12	5.60	6.68	8.75
21	4.89	5.82	8.25	11.98	4.89	6.97	10.81	14.22	4.89	5.35	6.36	8.32
22	4.66	5.55	7.88	11.38	4.66	6.66	10.32	13.6	4.66	5.10	6.07	7.94
23	4.46	5.31	7.55	10.9	4.46	6.38	9.90	13.00	4.46	4.88	5.82	7.60
24	4.28	5.10	7.21	10.5	4.28	6.10	9.50	12.45	4.28	4.66	5.56	7.26
25	4.10	4.90	6.92	10.0	4.10	5.85	9.10	11.95	4.10	4.48	5.35	6.98
Gearbox Reduction	1.00	1.19	1.69	2.44	1.0	1.425	2.21	2.915	1.00	1.09	1.30	1.695

SEE PAGE 182 FOR ENGINE R.P.M. CHART.

VELOCEPRESS MANUALS – MOTORCYCLE BY MAKE

AJS 1932-1948 SINGLES & TWINS 250cc THRU 1000cc (BOOK OF)
AJS 1945-1960 SINGLES 350cc & 500cc MODELS 16 & 18 (BOOK OF)
AJS 1955-1965 SINGLES 350cc & 500cc (BOOK OF)
AJS 1957-1966 FACTORY WSM - ALL SINGLES & TWINS
ARIEL UP TO 1932 (BOOK OF)
ARIEL 1932-1939 PREWAR MODELS (BOOK OF)
ARIEL 1933-1951 (WORKSHOP MANUAL)
ARIEL 1939-1960 4 STROKE SINGLES (BOOK OF)
ARIEL 1958-1964 LEADER & ARROW FACTORY WSM & PARTS LIST
ARIEL 1958-1964 LEADER & ARROW (BOOK OF)
BMW R26 R27 (1956-1967) FACTORY WORKSHOP MANUAL
BMW R50 R50S R60 R69S (1955-1969) FACTORY WORKSHOP MANUAL
BRIDGESTONE 90 SERIES FACTORY WSM & PARTS CATALOGUE
BRIDGESTONE 175 SERIES FACTORY WSM & PARTS CATALOGUE
BRIDGESTONE 350 SERIES FACTORY WSM & PARTS CATALOGUES
BSA SERVICE SHEETS MASTER CATALOGUE ALL MODELS 1945-1967
BSA BANTAM D1 TO D7 1948-1966 FACTORY SERVICE SHEETS MANUAL
BSA BANTAM ALL MODELS FROM 1948 ONWARDS (BOOK OF)
BSA BANTAM D14 FACTORY SERVICE MANUAL
BSA DANDY FACTORY WORKSHOP MANUAL (COMPILATION)
BSA SINGLES & V-TWINS UP TO 1926 inc. 1927 SUPPLEMENT (BOOK OF)
BSA SINGLES & V-TWINS UP TO 1930 (BOOK OF)
BSA SINGLES & V-TWINS UP TO 1935 (BOOK OF)
BSA SINGLES & V-TWINS 1936-1939 (BOOK OF)
BSA C10, C11 & C12 1945-1958 FACTORY SERVICE SHEETS MANUAL
BSA OHV & SV SINGLES 250-600cc 1945-1959 (BOOK OF)
BSA C15 & B40 1958-1967 FACTORY SERVICE SHEETS MANUAL
BSA OHV & SV SINGLES 250cc (ONLY) 1954-1970 (BOOK OF)
BSA B31, B32, B33 & B34 1945-60 FACTORY SERVICE SHEETS MANUAL
BSA OHV SINGLES 350 & 500cc 1955-1967 (BOOK OF)
BSA M20, M21 & M33 1945-1963 FACTORY SERVICE SHEETS MANUAL
BSA TWINS A7 & A10 1948-1962 FACTORY SERVICE SHEETS MANUAL
BSA TWINS A7 & A10 1948-1962 (BOOK OF)
BSA TWINS A50 & A65 1962-1965 FACTORY WORKSHOP MANUAL
BSA TWINS A50 & A65 1962-1969 (SECOND BOOK OF)
DOUGLAS 1929-1939 PREWAR ALL MODELS (BOOK OF)
DOUGLAS 1948-1957 POSTWAR ALL MODELS FACTORY SHOP MANUAL
DUCATI 160cc, 250cc & 350cc OHC MODELS FACTORY SHOP MANUAL
HONDA 50cc ALL MODELS UP TO 1970 INC MONKEY & TRAIL (BOOK OF)
HONDA 90cc ALL MODELS UP TO 1966 (BOOK OF)
HONDA TWINS & SINGLES 50cc THRU 305cc 1960-1966 (BOOK OF)
HONDA TWINS ALL MODELS 125cc THRU 450cc UP TO 1968 (BOOK OF)
HONDA C100 50cc SUPER CUB O.H.C. 1959-1962 FACTORY WSM
HONDA C110 50cc SPORT CUB O.H.C. 1960-1962 FACTORY WSM
HONDA 50-65-70-90cc O.H.C. SINGLES 1959-1983 FACTORY WSM
HONDA 100-125cc SINGLES CB/CD/CL/SL/TL 1970-1984 FACTORY WSM
HONDA 125-150cc TWINS C/CS/CB/CA 1959-1966 FACTORY WSM
HONDA 125-160-175-200cc TWINS 1965-1978 WORKSHOP MANUAL
HONDA 250-305cc TWINS C/CS/CB 1961-1968 FACTORY WSM
HOHDA 250-350cc TWINS CB/CL/SL 1968-1973 FACTORY WSM
HONDA 250-360cc TWINS CB/CL/CJ 1974-1977 FACTORY WSM
HONDA 350F & 400F 4-CYLINDER 1972-1977 FACTORY WSM
HONDA 450cc TWINS CB/CL 1965-1974 K0 TO K7 WORKSHOP MANUAL
HONDA 500cc & 550cc 4-CYL 1971-1978 FACTORY WORKSHOP MANUAL
HONDA 750cc SHOC 4-CYL 1969-1978 K0~K8 WORKSHOP MANUAL
INDIAN PONYBIKE, BOY RACER & PAPOOSE ILL PARTS LIST & SALES LIT
J.A.P. ENGINES 1927-1952 & MOTORCYCLES 1934-1952 (BOOK OF)
MATCHLESS 1931-1939 ALL MODELS 250cc THRU 990cc (BOOK OF)
MATCHLESS 1945-1956 350 & 500cc SINGLES (BOOK OF)
MATCHLESS 1955-1966 350 & 500cc SINGLES (BOOK OF)
MATCHLESS 1957-1966 FACTORY WSM - ALL SINGLES & TWINS
NEW IMPERIAL ALL SV & OHV FROM 1935 ONWARDS (BOOK OF)
NORTON 1932-1939 PREWAR MODELS (BOOK OF)
NORTON 1932-1947 (BOOK OF)
NORTON 1938-1956 (BOOK OF)
NORTON 1945-1963 MODELS 16H, Big4, ES2, 19 & 50 WSM'S & PARTS
NORTON 1955-1963 MODELS 19, 50 & ES2 (BOOK OF)
NORTON 1948-1970 DOMINATOR TWINS FACTORY WSM'S & PARTS
NORTON 1955-1965 DOMINATOR TWINS (BOOK OF)
NORTON 1960-1970 TWIN CYLINDER FACTORY WORKSHOP MANUAL
NORTON 1970-1975 COMMANDO 850 & 750cc FACTORY WSM
NORTON 1975-1978 MK 3 COMMANDO 850 cc FACTORY WSM
PANTHER 1932-1958 LIGHTWEIGHT MODELS 250 & 350cc (BOOK OF)
PANTHER 1938-1966 HEAVYWEIGHT MODELS 600 & 650cc (BOOK OF)
RALEIGH MOTORCYCLES 1919-1933 (BOOK OF)
ROYAL ENFIELD 1934-1946 SINGLES & V TWINS (BOOK OF)
ROYAL ENFIELD 1937-1953 SINGLES & V TWINS (BOOK OF)
ROYAL ENFIELD 1946-1962 SINGLES (BOOK OF)
ROYAL ENFIELD 1952-1963 700cc TWINS FACTORY WORKSHOP MANUAL
ROYAL ENFIELD 1958-1966 250cc & 350cc SINGLES (SECOND BOOK OF)
ROYAL ENFIELD 1962-1970 INTERCEPTOR WSM'S & PARTS (Compilation)
RUDGE 1933-1939 (BOOK OF)
SACHS 1968-1975 100cc & 125cc ENGINES WSM & M/CYCLE PARTS LIST
SUNBEAM 1928-1939 (BOOK OF)
SUNBEAM 1946-1957 S7 & S8 (BOOK OF)
SUZUKI 50cc & 80cc UP TO 1966 (BOOK OF)
SUZUKI T10 1963-1967 FACTORY WORKSHOP MANUAL
SUZUKI T20 & T200 1965-1969 FACTORY WORKSHOP MANUAL
SUZUKI TWINS 1962 ONWARDS 125-500cc WORKSHOP MANUAL
TRIUMPH 1935-1949 SINGLES & TWINS (BOOK OF)
TRIUMPH 1937-1951 SINGLES & TWINS WORKSHOP MANUAL
TRIUMPH 1945-1955 PRE-UNIT 350cc, 500cc & 650cc TWINS WSM No.11
TRIUMPH 1945-1959 TWINS (BOOK OF)
TRIUMPH 1956-1969 TWINS (BOOK OF)
TRIUMPH 1957-1963 UNIT CONSTRUCTION 350-500cc WSM No.4
TRIUMPH 1963-1974 UNIT CONSTRUCTION 350-500cc FACTORY WSM
TRIUMPH 1956-1962 PRE-UNIT 500cc & 650cc TWINS WSM No.17
TRIUMPH 1963-1970 UNIT CONSTRUCTION 650cc FACTORY WSM
TRIUMPH 1968-1974 TRIDENT T150 & T150V FACTORY WSM
VELOCETTE 1925-1970 ALL SINGLES & TWINS (BOOK OF)
VELOCETTE 1933-1952 MOV-MAC-MSS RIGID FRAME FACTORY WSM
VELOCETTE 1954-1971 MSS-VENOM-THRUXTON-VIPER FACTORY WSM
VILLIERS ENGINE UP TO 1959 INC. 3 WHEELERS (BOOK OF)
VILLIERS ENGINE UP TO 1969 (BOOK OF)
VINCENT 1935-1955 (WORKSHOP MANUAL)
YAMAHA 1961-1967 YA5 & YA6 (WORKSHOP MANUAL & ILL PARTS LIST)
YAMAHA 1971-1972 JT1& JT2 (WORKSHOP MANUAL & ILL PARTS LIST)

VELOCEPRESS TECHNICAL BOOKS – MOTORCYCLE

1930'S BRITISH MOTORCYCLE CARBS & ELEC COMPONENTS (BOOK OF)
1930'S BRITISH MOTORCYCLE ENGINES (OVERHAUL & MAINTENANCE)
1930'S BRITISH MOTORCYCLE GEARBOXES & CLUTCHES (BOOK OF)
CATALOG OF BRITISH MOTORCYCLES (1951 MODELS)
LUCAS ELECTRONICS BRITISH M/CYCLES REPAIR & PARTS (1950-1977)
MOTORCYCLE ENGINEERING (P.E. Irving)
MOTORCYCLE ROAD TESTS 1949-1953 (Motor Cycle Magazine UK)
SPEED AND HOW TO OBTAIN IT (Motor Cycle Magazine UK)
TUNING FOR SPEED (P.E. Irving)
WIPAC (COMBO) MANUAL NUMBER 3 + M/CYCLE & SCOOTER MANUAL

VELOCEPRESS MANUALS – SCOOTERS BY MAKE

BSA SUNBEAM SCOOTER WORKSHOP MANUAL 1959-1965
BSA SUNBEAM SCOOTER 1959-1965 (BOOK OF)
LAMBRETTA 1947-1957 ALL 125 & 150cc MODELS (BOOK OF)
LAMBRETTA 1957-1970 LI & TV MODELS (SECOND BOOK OF)
NSU PRIMA 1956-1964 ALL MODELS (BOOK OF)
TRIUMPH TIGRESS SCOOTER WORKSHOP MANUAL 1959-1965
TRIUMPH TIGRESS SCOOTER (BOOK OF)
VESPA 1951-1961 (BOOK OF)
VESPA 1955-1963 125 & 150cc & GS MODELS (SECOND BOOK OF)
VESPA 1955-1968 GS & SS (BOOK OF)
VESPA 1963-1972 90, 125 & 150cc (THIRD BOOK OF)

VELOCEPRESS MANUALS – MOPEDS & MOTORIZED BICYCLES

CYCLEMOTOR (BOOK OF)
NSU QUICKLY 1953-1963 ALL MODELS (BOOK OF)
PUCH MAXI N & S MAINTENANCE & REPAIR (3 MANUAL COMPILATION)
RALEIGH MOPEDS 1960-1969 (BOOK OF)

VELOCEPRESS MANUALS - THREE WHEELER'S

BOND MINICAR THREE WHEELER 1948-1967 (BOOK OF)
BMW ISETTA FACTORY WORKSHOP MANUAL
BSA THREE WHEELER (BOOK OF)
RELIANT REGAL THREE WHEELER 1952-1973 (BOOK OF)
VINTAGE MORGAN THREE WHEELER (BOOK OF)

VELOCEPRESS MANUALS – AUTOMOBILE BY MAKE

ALFA ROMEO GIULIA WORKSHOP MANUAL 1300 TO 2000cc 1962-1975
ALFA ROMEO GIULIA TECH MANUAL CARBURETED CARS FROM 1962
ALFA ROMEO GIULIA TECH MANUAL FUEL INJECTED CARS FROM 1969
ALFA ROMEO GIULIETTA & GIULIA 750 & 101 SERIES 1955-1965 WSM
AUSTIN-HEALEY SPRITE & MG MIDGET WORKSHOP MANUAL 1958-1971
BMW 600 LIMOUSINE FACTORY WORKSHOP MANUAL
BMW 600 LIMOUSINE OWNERS HAND BOOK & SERVICE MANUAL
BMW 2000 & 2002 1966-1976 WORKSHOP MANUAL
CORVAIR 1960-1969 WORKSHOP MANUAL
CORVETTE V8 1955-1962 WORKSHOP MANUAL
FERRARI HANDBOOK ROAD & RACE CARS (SERVICE/SPECS) 1948-1958
FERRARI 250/GT SERVICE & MAINTENANCE MANUAL 1956-1965
FIAT 500 FACTORY WORKSHOP MANUAL 1957-1973
FIAT 600, 600D & MULTIPLA FACTORY WORKSHOP MANUAL 1955-1969
JAGUAR E-TYPE 3.8 & 4.2 SERIES 1 & 2 WORKSHOP MANUAL
JAGUAR MK 7, 8, 9 & XK120, 140, 150 WORKSHOP MANUAL 1948-1961
METROPOLITAN FACTORY WORKSHOP MANUAL
MGA & MGB OWNERS HANDBOOK & WORKSHOP MANUAL
MG MIDGET TC, TD, TF & TF1500 WORKSHOP MANUAL
PORSCHE 356 1948-1965 WORKSHOP MANUAL
PORSCHE 911 2.0, 2.2, 2.4 LITRE 1964-1973 WORKSHOP MANUAL
PORSCHE 911 2.7, 3.0, 3.2 LITRE 1973-1989 WORKSHOP MANUAL
PORSCHE 912 WORKSHOP MANUAL
PORSCHE 914 & 914/6 1.7, 1.8, 2.0 LITRE 1970-1976 WSM
TRIUMPH TR2, TR3, TR4 1953-1965 WORKSHOP MANUAL
VOLKSWAGEN TRANSPORTER, TRUCKS & WAGONS 1950-1979 WSM
VOLVO 1944-1968 ALL MODELS WORKSHOP MANUAL

VELOCEPRESS TECHNICAL BOOKS - AUTOMOBILE

HOW TO BUILD A FIBERGLASS CAR
HOW TO BUILD A RACING CAR
HOW TO RESTORE THE MODEL 'A' FORD
MASERATI OWNER'S HANDBOOK
PERFORMANCE TUNING THE SUNBEAM TIGER
SOUPING THE VOLKSWAGEN
SOLEX CARBURETORS (EMPHASIS ON UK & EU AUTOMOBILES)
SU CARBURETORS (EMPHASIS ON UK AUTOMOBILES)
WEBER CARBURETORS (EMPHASIS ON ALFA & FIAT)

VELOCEPRESS BOOKS & GUIDES - AUTOMOBILE

COMPLETE CATALOG OF JAPANESE MOTOR VEHICLES
FERRARI 308 SERIES BUYER'S AND OWNER'S GUIDE
FERRARI BROCHURES AND SALES LITERATURE 1968-1989
FERRARI SERIAL NUMBERS PART I - ODD NUMBERS TO 21399
FERRARI SERIAL NUMBERS PART II - EVEN NUMBERS TO 1050
HENRY'S FABULOUS MODEL "A" FORD
MASERATI BROCHURES AND SALES LITERATURE

VELOCEPRESS BOOKS – RACING

CARRERA PANAMERICANA - MEXICAN ROAD RACE (BOOK OF)
DIALED IN - THE JAN OPPERMAN STORY
VEDA ORR'S NEW REVISED HOT ROD PICTORIAL

www.VelocePress.com

Please check our website:

www.VelocePress.com

for a complete up-to-date list of available titles

www.ingramcontent.com/pod-product-compliance
Lightning Source LLC
Chambersburg PA
CBHW081420230426
43668CB00016B/2296